Praise fo___
The Secret Curren___

"Funny, insightful, and brutally honest, this book is *Sex and the City* meets the *Wall Street Journal*, with a sprinkle of Dostoevsky. Hilary Black has inspired stellar writers to wax poetic (and at times, hilariously pathetic) on the last taboo: money. Juicy, smart, dramatic, and insightful—an addictive read."

—Beth Kobliner, author of
Get a Financial Life: Personal Finance in Your Twenties and Thirties

"In Hilary Black's compelling new anthology, a number of prominent female writers (including Julia Glass, Laurie Abraham, and Joni Evans) spill the beans about money in their own lives."

—*Time* magazine

"Unstintingly—even shockingly—candid, the writers in *The Secret Currency of Love* describe how their feelings about finances shaped or contributed to good and bad marriages, abuse, divorces, breakups, crushes, or even avoidance of relationships. This exceptionally honest and poignant collection deserves a place on the bookshelves of women of all ages, backgrounds, income, net-worth levels, and walks of life."

—*Publishers Weekly* (starred review and Pick of the Week)

"The most interesting anthology I've seen in years. I read it with fascination, to the very last page."

—Cathi Hanauer, novelist and editor of *The Bitch in the House*

"All the bases are covered here, from the hard lessons women learn (and impart) to the inextricability of romance and cold hard cash."

—*Elle*

"Reading this mesmerizing collection of personal stories was like sneaking a peek at someone else's diary. Deeply honest and scandalously revealing, *The Secret Currency of Love* offers a mirror into our own complicated feelings about money and relationships—and every woman who reads it will see herself in its pages. You won't be able to put it down!"

—Liz Lange, Founder, Liz Lange Maternity

About the Editor

HILARY BLACK has spent her career as an editor in both books and magazines. She has held positions at Random House, HarperCollins, Simon & Schuster, *More* magazine (where she was a founding editor), and *Tango* magazine (where she was editor-in-chief). She lives in New York City.

The SECRET CURRENCY of LOVE

The Unabashed Truth About Women, Money, and Relationships

An anthology of personal essays edited by

Hilary Black

HARPER

NEW YORK · LONDON · TORONTO · SYDNEY

HARPER

A hardcover edition of this book was published in 2009 by William Morrow, an imprint of HarperCollins Publishers.

FIRST HARPER PAPERBACK PUBLISHED 2010.

Designed by Susan Walsh

Library of Congress Cataloging-in-Publication Data is available upon request.

ISBN 978-0-06-156097-2 (pbk.)

10 11 12 13 14   OV/RRD   10 9 8 7 6 5 4 3 2 1

For Matthew
the best and the last

CONTENTS

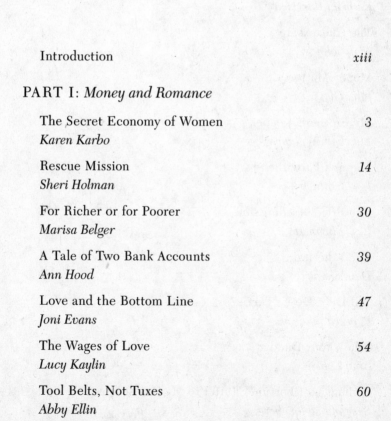

PART III: *Money and Self*

So you think that money is the root of all evil. Have you ever asked what is the root of all money?

—Ayn Rand, *Atlas Shrugged*

INTRODUCTION

It's just as easy to marry a rich man as a poor man. Or so the saying goes.

A few years ago, I decided to end a relationship that—at least according to this standard—should have been a no-brainer. Handsome, unpretentious, and independently wealthy, Ted was, on the face of it, the perfect boyfriend. I'd grown up in the suburbs of Washington, D.C., glued to *Masterpiece Theater* and the novels of F. Scott Fitzgerald. Here, it seemed, was the modern equivalent of the dashing heroes I'd idolized during my girlhood.

But as the months passed, I began to realize that Ted's Gatsby-esque aura could not compensate for our basic differences. Though we never argued, I often felt as if our conversations were taking place on parallel planes. We weren't interested in the same things; we didn't share similar views about important issues. In short, we just didn't connect—and no amount of money was going to bridge that gap.

As my interest in Ted waned, so did my girlish fantasy of being swept away by Prince Charming. Nevertheless, an awful lot of people seemed to think I should marry him as soon as possible. After all, they reasoned, I would be a modern-day Cinderella, swept out of my workaday toil to a life of unparalleled privilege. "This is a man who can take care of you *for life!*" one friend said. "You've hit the jackpot—literally," said another.

I was surprised that these women—educated, intelligent, and self-supporting—would harbor such archaic opinions. But perhaps I shouldn't have been. Society may have come a long way since Jane Austen's time, when a woman's entire future depended on landing a husband with a reliable income. But despite the enlightened attitudes of the past few decades about financial independence and gender equality in the workplace, the notion of finding a wealthy Prince Charming still lingers. In fact, according to the latest data, the majority of American women still rate a prospective mate by the size of his bank account. A recent poll conducted by Prince & Associates, a Connecticut-based wealth research firm, reported that two-thirds of its female respondents were "very" or "extremely" willing to marry for money. Asked how much a potential spouse would need in order to qualify as money-marriage material, women in their twenties said $2.5 million; the going rate fell to $1.1 million for women in their thirties and rose again to $2.2 million for women in their forties.

I made a different choice. Unable to overcome my doubts about our long-term compatibility, I broke up with Ted. But despite the relative ease of our parting, my experience was deeply affecting. How often, I wondered, does greed—or even simple pragmatism—win out over emotion? Why is it that some people are able to rely on love to overcome financial hardship, while others are not? How does money inform the decisions we make, and to what extent does it underwrite the values we keep? In short, what happens when love and money collide?

The answers can be found in these pages. When asked, the most interesting women I know had astonishing confessions to make—

not only about the role of money in their romantic lives but about its impact on their relationships with parents, children, siblings, friends, and ultimately with themselves. In these essays, they reveal what money has brought to their most private affairs, and what it has taken away. In so doing, they expose the complex ways in which personal finance has shaped their experiences, their philosophies, and their most important life decisions.

In many ways, money remains a taboo subject in American culture. Most women would rather discuss their sex lives than their income (let alone their husband's income). But as I soon discovered, underneath that surface reticence is a roiling, largely secret stew of powerful emotions. Some of the stories in this collection are illuminating. Others are shocking. Still others are poignant. All are fascinating.

When I first began approaching women to write for this book, I was surprised by the visceral response to the subject at hand. The mere mention of money and relationships unleashed an array of stories that I might have deemed implausible had they not come directly from the source. In many cases, my queries elicited intense emotion; one writer actually became choked up and had to call me back before she could continue. And some of the stories I unearthed proved to be too dangerous to publish—like the finished piece by another writer who withdrew it because she felt it would end a friendship.

For some of the contributors here, exploring the highly charged intersection of love and money meant discovering some painful truths about themselves. Abby Ellin, a lifelong feminist, admits her long-veiled hope that the man she marries will ultimately support her. Bliss Broyard discloses the jealousy and ambivalence she's felt in the presence of wealthier friends. Julia Glass, the major breadwinner in her family, reveals herself to be a financial naïf, hapless as both an earner and a spender. And Laurie Abraham confesses that when it comes to personal finance, ignorance is bliss.

For other contributors, family relationships are at the forefront of their most urgent money issues. Dani Shapiro tries to make sense of why she was cut out of her mother's will; Amy Sohn deconstructs the impact of her father's frugality during her childhood. Elizabeth Williams wrestles with her brother's financial dependence on her. And Lori Gottlieb comes to grips with the price—financial and otherwise—of having a child on her own.

Perhaps least surprisingly, money is front and center as contributors explore the inner workings of their romantic relationships. Sheri Holman explains how she fell in love with a homeless drug addict. Joni Evans reveals the drama—and trauma—of divorcing an extremely wealthy (and sadly vindictive) man. Karen Karbo ruminates on how she has come to be the primary breadwinner in her most serious romantic relationships. And Ann Hood examines why she and her husband of almost two decades have decided to keep their financial affairs completely separate.

We are, I believe, fascinated by other people's financial issues because we all want to know the same things: *Is she like me? Is her life better? Worse? Does she have more than I do? Is what I have enough?* In this regard, these essays offer a peek through the keyhole of a door that is often locked tight. (In certain instances, it should be observed, names have been changed to protect privacy.)

As you'll see, the women who chose to share their lives in this anthology are witty, fiercely intelligent, and startlingly candid. They are poor and rich, single and married, savers and spenders, corporate and freelance. I hope the profound insight in their stories will illuminate the murky intersection of money and relationships—and spark a healthy debate about how the two affect and transform each other. Some of the pieces here are regretful; others are ambivalent; many are triumphant. But there is one constant: for all of us, money is about much more than loans and interest rates. It is about hope and shame, envy and security, fear and joy. It is as personal as it is nuanced. Money is, in the end, the secret currency of love. I hope that these stories will help to unveil that secret.

—Hilary Black

The
SECRET
CURRENCY
of
LOVE

PART I

Money and Romance

The Secret Economy
of Women

Karen Karbo

Robbie Schulman was my first boyfriend. From our relationship you will be able to extrapolate, tea leaf–like, how my romantic life would play out over the next forty years.

It was kindergarten. Robbie and I lived in the same glittery stucco apartment building in Sherman Oaks, California. We were deeply attached. We did everything together. We sat on the school bus together, swam together in the kidney bean–shaped pool after school, and drew elaborate, block-long hopscotch patterns on the sidewalk. He was my pal and my beloved.

He also was my business partner, and this is where things fell apart. It was my first lesson in keeping my money separate from my love. For Christmas that year, I had received a toy ironing board and iron. Rather than setting about ironing doll clothes, I hatched a moneymaking scheme that involved ironing tissues. Why I thought this was a terrific idea remains a mystery, but I was convinced that people in our apartment building would pay three cents for a piece of tissue that had its folds ironed flat like a piece of phyllo dough.

Robbie agreed because Robbie was agreeable. He'd play Ken to my Barbie, Paul to my John (*A Hard Day's Night* had just been released), and even Marco Polo with only two people. I pilfered a box of my mother's Kleenex from the linen closet, and we were in business. Robbie's contribution was to watch me iron and to carry the ironed tissues, balanced across his tanned boy's forearms, as we went from door to door. We sold them all, not because anyone on earth needs an ironed tissue, but because we were both enchanting and ridiculous and our product cost three cents. Some people even gave us a nickel.

The big breakup occurred when Robbie wanted a fifty-fifty split. In that a five-year-old can be incredulous, I was. The entire enterprise had been my idea, from my toy iron to my chatty sales pitch. The tissue had come from beneath the bathroom sink in my house. Aside from Robbie's role as bearer of the ironed tissues, he'd done nothing but gone along. Nothing. *He* was incredulous that he wasn't entitled to 50 percent of the profits. We tussled. I hit him with the iron. He cried. His mother called my mother, and that was the end of both our business partnership and our romance.

In the aftermath of the failed ironed-tissue enterprise, my mother did the proper motherly thing and gave me a lecture about not using my toy iron to settle a dispute. She did not, however, applaud me for sticking up for my rights, for she was a firm believer in the secret economy of women. Without a college education, she'd still had enough smarts to land my father, a cultured, well-educated man who made a solid upper-middle-class living. (There's an amazing picture of the two of them walking down the aisle after their vows. She's winking at someone in the pews—a wink that says, "Look at what I landed!")

My mother believed that men were born to make the money and women were born to be pretty and pleasing, like one of those feathery, sparkling fly-fishing lures. Once you caught the man, you were installed in a nice house, where you vacuumed on Monday, dusted on Tuesday, shopped for groceries on Wednesday, and shared a beer with a girlfriend by the pool on sunny afternoons. It was the husband's job to make and save the money, and the wife's job to spend his money in such a way that he never could figure out where it was going. The wife was also responsible for putting dinner on the table every night— which, since I've been dealing with the dinner issue every night for decades (it should be added to death and taxes as another thing in life that can't be avoided), strikes me as a monumental feat of constancy and creativity.

My mother died when I was seventeen, and so I never had the opportunity to shoot my mouth off when I was twenty-two or so, telling her in a hurtful and uncharitable manner that she had wasted her life, that a wife needed to be more than an ornament, a house gnome, and a consumer, that her system of landing a breadwinner and then exploiting his hard labor kind of basically sucked, that it was antediluvian and poor modeling (for me) and just plain old boring, and how could she stand to live such a life?

Of course now, decades later, after spending my adult life as the primary breadwinner in most, if not all, of my relationships, I've changed my tune. I think my mother was pretty brilliant. She leveraged what she had to work with, and at the end of the day isn't that the wisest thing for all of us to do?

I didn't set out to be the breadwinner. In high school I never gave it a thought, and in college I assumed, as do most girls, that one day a guy would come along and I would marry him and, well, he'd take care of it. This is one of the fundamental unsung ways in which men differ from women. Growing up, boys assume they're going to make the money (or at least *half* the money) if and when they get married. Rare is the boy who imagines that marriage will spell a free economic ride and nurtures his incredible hotness to that end.

While I couldn't imagine being my mother, vacuuming on Monday, dusting on Tuesday, and waiting around, always, for my father and me to come home so she could wait on us, neither did I see myself as a high-powered high-earner—a lawyer, doctor, advertising executive, whatever. I switched majors from journalism to physical therapy to film. I got good grades, which was something I knew how to do, but beyond that . . . well, there was no beyond that.

It's of note that I was never a girl who dated around. I've never placed my dainty index finger against my comely chin and wondered, in an Austenian fashion, whether I should choose this suitor or that suitor. I was never a romantic ditherer. I liked someone, and either he liked me or he didn't. If he did, we would go on to become inseparable, until there was a horrific breakup in which we would both shriek and sob and engage in a little stalking and, years later, wind up good friends.

In film school, I had a short, strange romance with a French guy. Guillaume drove a beat-up sports car he called La Poubelle—the garbage can—and wore a lot of Paco Rabanne. He liked silk shirts. Unlike a lot of other film students, in their black T-shirts and holey jeans, he seemed very manlike. Guillaume had impeccable manners and paid for everything everywhere we went. I don't think I opened my purse in his presence once during the time we dated. It was exciting and romantic. Even though I didn't come close to loving him, I was happy. Then came finals and my mother's secret economy reasserted itself.

One night Guillaume stopped over at my apartment at 11:00 P.M. and caught me in a pair of red, paint-stained sweatpants, my hair in a scrunchie. He was appalled and refused to come in with me looking that way. I argued that *he* dropped in on *me* without any advance warning. He felt that since we were in a relationship, I should always look my best in the event that he did drop in, as if I was a babe-on-call, ready at all hours to be seductive and kittenish. Yeah, I'll get right on that. Adieu, Guillaume.

I met my first husband on the heels of my breakup with the ridiculous Guillaume. James's student films were hilarious. He was droll, liked to talk and read, liked to travel. We lived together for an embarrassing number of years before we married and had our daughter.

In the early years we were financial idiots, putting film stock on our credit cards to shoot the documentaries we were coproducing and living on Top Ramen. I was not the de facto alpha breadwinner, but I had the steady job, at a nonprofit film arts center. James freelanced as a sound editor on features.

It didn't start out as a terrible arrangement. But James wanted to direct, and he started to turn down sound editing work. This left me making not just the steady money, but *all* the money. His big break was around the corner. His big break was always just around the corner.

By the time the marriage ended, I'd published two books and had begun writing for magazines. It wasn't a reliable living, but it wasn't a bad one either. As long as I kept my overhead low, I could make it work, and did. I often wonder, if I had been dependent on James financially, would I have walked out so easily? That question brings up another that can only be posed uneasily: is it better for marriage if one party (usually the woman) feels financially trapped?

It's not just a problem from my mother's era. Several years ago, a friend of mine decided she'd had enough of her arts administrator job (working for a nonprofit being its own circle of hell). With the support of her husband, who worked somewhat unhappily as an anesthesiologist, she quit her job with the idea of taking a year off to "really decide what she wanted to do." The year slid into two, then three. She walked her dogs a lot, attended daily yoga classes, read the novels on whatever list Oprah had going on at the time. Then her life became a third-rate show on basic cable: she discovered her anesthesiologist husband was having an affair with a nurse, and worse, when she confronted him, he said he wasn't going to stop seeing her.

My friend was devastated. She knew she had to end the marriage, but couldn't bring herself to file for divorce. I imagined she was afraid to be alone, that she would miss her husband's companionship (they seemed to have had a good marriage), their tennis games and road bike adventures and obsession with 24. "There's always Match.com," I said, trying to console her.

She snorted. "It's not that. I don't have a job, and I don't think I could get a job that would pay enough."

Enough to live in the way she'd become accustomed to, she meant. This was years ago. They are still married.

My second marriage was an enormous disaster of Springer-esque proportions. The short-form answer as to what went wrong was that the more money I made, the less inclined my husband felt to contribute. It didn't start out that way. I didn't size him up and think, *There's a guy who, with a little encouragement, can become a dead-beat of dazzling proportions who stops getting dressed in the morning and thinks selling enchanted weapons on* World of Warcraft *is the same as being employed!*

The Cuddle Bum (as I've pseudonymously come to call him) had a good job when I met him, working in construction. I realize that most men who toil in that field might not call it a good job. There's a lot of getting up before dawn, working until after dark, sore muscles, and the always-present risk of accidentally shooting yourself in the head with a nail gun, but I was impressed. This man seemed to have a basic work ethic. He grasped the homely importance of bringing home a regular paycheck. He did not want to direct. I'd hoped that now the CB would be the steady wage earner and I would be able to write without the burden of having to support our suddenly largish family of three children—my daughter and his daughter and son from previous marriages.

The first year we were together the Cuddle Bum quit his job on a whim. I was in L.A. for several weeks researching a book, and he thought it would be fun and romantic to simply show up one day. Surprise! To have said "What in the hell have you done?" would have been unsexy and unfun. I would have morphed into a shrew-wife with her hair in curlers, standing on the front porch wielding a rolling pin. Instead, I said nothing.

There was, of course, something else going on. The Cuddle Bum hated his job—and who could blame him? He wanted to get into another field, perhaps one that required his going back and finishing his bachelor's degree. He'd made a unilateral decision to spring into unemployment, promising to find "something else," which he only did after I left him (driving a truck delivering French bread to local restaurants).

In the meantime, together, we decided the Cuddle Bum would be the househusband. My role as breadwinner was thus made official. The Cuddle Bum's idea of his role involved pouring a bowl of cereal for each child before school, playing video games for ten hours, and then allowing himself to be hounded into making dinner at six. For almost a year, I told him that this wasn't working for me, that if he wasn't going to care for the entire household the way a wife would (vacuum on Mondays, dust on Tuesdays . . .), then he needed to go back to work. Much of the time I expressed this wish to the back of his head as he worked at slaying orcs, sirens, and two-headed ogres.

When we divorced, he wanted alimony, child support, and the house—the house that was my house, purchased with my money, in my name. During one of our last conversations, I wept with incomprehension. He wanted my *house*? What happened to movie separations, where the husband packed a bag and moved into a sad hotel, leaving his wife (whom he supported) in the house? The Cuddle Bum said that if I insisted on leaving him, he had no choice but to play hardball. No *choice*? Where was my toy iron when I needed it?

(For the record, the Cuddle Bum got shit. I stepped up my freelancing work and got a better lawyer. Don't talk to *me* about hardball.)

Years ago, I sat next to Jackie Onassis at a literary event at the Kennedy Library in Boston. We got to talking—or rather she talked and I sat in breathless awe—and she said the piece of advice she always gave young women was "never marry, never mix your money." There was another young woman listening in, and I could see her expression harden in disapproval. But I understood exactly what Jackie meant.

For those of us predetermined to be the breadwinners, it's more fun to date a man than to marry him. We understand that the more people there are living under our roof, the more it costs us, I am appalled by how unromantic this sounds, but there you have it. The breadwinner will *always* be worrying about replacing the clutch in her car, or paying her life insurance premiums, or, if she's a homeowner, covering all the uninteresting expenditures that go with *that*. (New gutters for the roof, anyone?) So it's a huge amount of fun to go to dinner, movie, and dessert and walk away at the end of the evening without having plucked that smokin' debit card out of our wallets *once*. I'm sure Jackie was talking about something completely different, about the trials of being married to very wealthy men. But I took her point.

And this time around I've taken her advice. Jim (yes, another one) and I have lived together for six years and are happy—defined as we laugh a lot; have good, regular sex; and never call names when we argue. He's a computer consultant who pays his own way and buys me the occasional unexpected present. Once, walking the streets of Manhattan on a summer day, I admired a fountain pen in the window of a shop that sold only fountain pens; while I was waiting at the corner for the light to change, he ducked in and bought it for me. I swooned.

The day Jim and I moved in together, I gave him a formal accounting of how much our monthly nut would be; he would pay for himself, and I would pay for my daughter and me. Since then, he's written me a check for his portion on the fifteenth of every month. Sometimes he buys the groceries, and sometimes I buy the groceries. But he always pays for both of us when we go to the movies and spends lavishly on buttered popcorn and Milk Duds. I am always touched by this.

As well as this works for us, I am often reminded that I am a freak among women. Not long ago, at my daughter's annual school auction, Jim and I sat at a table with six other couples. Since the fourth grade, our girls had been on the basketball team together, and now they were in eighth grade, on the verge of graduating.

We gaily tossed down the wine, and when the auction began, the women at the table led the bidding on the Adirondack chairs hand-painted by the second-grade class and the mosaic-topped patio table assembled by the sixth-grade class. The men at the table joked and complained loudly about what this was costing them. The gender lines were well drawn: the women were profligate, and the men fake-worried. But I spied a few of the guys out of the corner of my eye. Their mouths were thin lines. They were obliged to feign fake worry, but they understood too well how much all this dumb crap really cost. (Yes, I know, it was for the school, anything for the good of our children, blah blah blah.)

Still. Two thousand dollars is a lot for a black-and-white photograph of an empty bike rack.

I realized the night of the auction that I'd evolved into the female breadwinning equivalent of Tom Smith, the not-fit-for-human-companionship trainer from *Seabiscuit*. Smith was so used to dealing with horses that human beings and their habits struck him as mysterious and impenetrable. I felt similarly with those mothers of my daughter's classmates.

As I do when certain friends share stories about going on shopping sprees and hiding their purchases from their husbands, or buying a handbag half with cash and half on credit so their husbands will think it cost half as much as it really did, or launching a campaign to wear their husbands down on the matter of a new kitchen remodel, or spending Christmas in Rome. I listen to them, fascinated. I find them both ridiculous and lucky. For their part, they think I'm far more well off than I am, because if I want something I simply go out and buy it.

For I have never gone through all this rigmarole. If I had to, I don't think I'd know how to go about buttering up a man. It sounds freeing,

and it is—but I also feel as if I missed out on some fundamental rela-
tional intrigue. It's like I've been a tourist in a country where the shopkeepers expect you to bargain, but I've just gone ahead and dumbly
paid full price, depriving us both of the simple pleasure of haggling.

I have no doubt figuring out how to get stuff out of men would
just be a change of misery. But that said, I believe I would love to be
a pampered princess. My definition of "pampered princess" is amaz-
ingly specific: if you are able to splurge on a pair of $600 sandals
without wondering whether this will bite into the money you've set
aside for the property taxes, you qualify.

I especially would like to be one of those women who show up
every year around Christmastime in jewelry commercials, the ones
who are sitting before the fire sipping a cup of tea, a cashmere throw
over their knees. Suddenly, their beloved swoops in from out of frame
with a velvet-covered box, bearing some hideous pendant that nevertheless cost real money. I envy this woman, because she is so taken
with her beloved's generosity. She never, ever says, "Honey, why did
you buy me this piece of crap when you know I need a new crown on
that back molar?" I would love to be the woman who can forget—if
only for the time it takes to buy a tube of $250 eye cream—that the
money I'm spending is money I made by the proverbial sweat of my
own brow. And if I splurge for the eye cream, I will have to put off
paying the electricity bill for a week, something I am loath to do.

I suppose that what I am rather ridiculously pining for is the
luxury of having someone else pick up the slack. It has always been
a girl's prerogative, hasn't it? To choose to either make money or not,
as her spirit and biological clock move her? And if she chooses to
make money, she can just as easily choose not to make it. But being
responsible for making all the money all the time means being forever
prevented from engaging in the magical thinking that money matters
less than love and romance.

Maybe I've got it all wrong. Maybe women like my mother, who
chose to throw in their lot with men who make all the money, understand very well the degree to which practical reality sometimes

trumps love. Throughout history the armies of wives who've had to put up with horrible husbands or risk penury are legion; they may have mastered the secret economy, but it turns out to be no easier to negotiate than the real economy. My experience has taught me that you are either the one thinking up the ironed-tissue scheme or the one carrying the tissues. I'm sure it's more complicated than that, but I'm too busy earning a living to sort it all out.

Rescue Mission

Sheri Holman

Every night the neon cross from St. Vincent's House flashed outside my bedroom window:

GET RIGHT WITH GOD/SIN WILL FIND YOU OUT
GET RIGHT WITH GOD/SIN WILL FIND YOU OUT

I had chosen my first apartment, deep in the heart of Hell's Kitchen, for the romance of this cross and its urgent command. It was 1988 and I was twenty-two years old, newly arrived in New York City with a single suitcase heavy with books, a respectable theatrical résumé earned at a small Virginia college, and $800 to start my new life.

My roommates were two other actresses, one from Tennessee and another from Leningrad. Our furniture consisted of a futon on the floor and three stacks of phone-book-thick manuscripts I was paid $5 a piece by a disreputable literary agent to read and reject. We covered the stacks with a blanket and used it for a sofa. In the refrigerator was a bottle of sweet champagne, some contraband Soviet caviar, and a box of Pop-Tarts. I was artistically and ironically impoverished, using a metal bust of Lenin for a candlestick holder and letting recession-plagued New York serve as the backdrop to the unfolding movie of my life.

Angie from Tennessee lasted a month. She moved in with her rich boyfriend, leaving only Katya and me. Beautiful, exotic Katya was soon being courted by two actors who would go on to become quite famous. But I was the true artist of the bunch. You could tell by the way I eschewed the nice, earnest boys who asked me out, choosing instead to sit alone, hunched over my journal on the fire escape. You could also tell by how doggedly I went to auditions where I was rejected, only to return home to reject would-be novelists. My notions of love and art weren't tainted by the social or professional marketplace; they were taken whole-cloth from my major influences at the time: Kathe Kollwitz, the existentialist philosophers, and most especially Dostoyevsky, the patron saint of all those in late adolescence. I began with *The Brothers Karamazov* and was soon on to *Crime and Punishment,* where I wept over the prostitute Sonya who followed her lover to the gulag. Love according to the Russian master meant laying aside the self and living completely for others; the truly extraordinary person would love those whom no one else could love, expecting nothing in return. Alone at night during those first months in New York City, swinging between self-doubt and great anticipation, I lay on my back watching the red shadow of the cross pulse on my bedroom ceiling. The one thing I had to believe, that would justify my having come here, was that I too was extraordinary.

Each morning, as the cross faded out with the sunrise, a line of men formed below my window. They were not the long-suffering poor of the books I'd been reading, but a wholly different order of wretched. They were the newly minted "homeless," and they used the term with a sort of tentative pride. (A businessman on his way to work would shout, *Get a job, you bums,* and someone on line would call back: *We're not bums anymore! We're homeless!*). They were other things too, new to me, new to the late 1980s—victims of HIV/AIDS and crack cocaine. I'd sit on the fire escape and watch them gather for their free breakfast: the shoeless men with their thick yellow toenails, the wasted, toothless grandfathers with ashy and ulcerated legs, the fat child-man with Coke-bottle glasses who wore green trash bags lashed to his body but left his flaccid belly raw to the weather. Watching them felt like a presumption, but the only thing worse, it seemed to me, would be to look away and pretend they didn't exist. And so each morning I watched the line form with the same incredulous fascination I'd watched a parade of elephants lumber down Ninth Avenue, driven to Madison Square Garden for the opening of the circus.

Soon, I realized this herd of black and brown bodies had its own de facto barker. A young man in his late twenties stood out as one of the few white faces, clean and dressed in jeans and a vintage bowling shirt. He seemed to be running things, directing the men inside to breakfast and the morning sermon, laughing and joking with them. He was tall and lean with wild blue eyes and a head of cherubic blond ringlets. After breakfast, he'd lead an elderly blind priest and his Seeing Eye dog out for their morning stroll, as gentle and solicitous as he'd previously been brash. Each afternoon, he was always the first down the brownstone steps to help unload the City Harvest truck that pulled up with donations of expensive restaurant food. When he wasn't manically bustling around, giving orders and teasing, he sat on the stoop in the thin early-spring sunshine and read books about theology and smoked. I couldn't figure him out. He looked as out of place as I felt, but instead of sitting by and watching, he was doing something, he was making a difference. Young and passionate and lonely, I swiftly converted every strong emotion into the currency of sex, and soon I found myself obsessively thinking about kissing him.

In memory, it was months before we spoke, but looking back over my journal of the period, I see it was a matter of weeks. Home alone one night, having finished the bottle of sweet champagne and seeing him talking with another man in a pool of lamplight, I seized a bouquet of roses one of the soon-to-be famous actor boyfriends had presented my roommate and tossed them, stem after stem, from the balcony of the fire escape. They fell scattershot in and out of shadow between the two men, who looked up, wondering. Moments later my buzzer rang.

I raced to the door. To my dismay, it was the other one, an ebony Senegalese man with hepatitis yellow eyes. For the first time I realized how foolish I'd been, inviting strange men into my apartment.

"Hello, pretty lady," he said, presenting me with my roses. "You dropped these."

"No," I said. "They were for you. And your friend. Did he leave?"

"Ah, Patrick," he said, looking me up and down. "He's gone in for curfew."

"Curfew?" I asked.

"Ten o'clock. They lock the doors."

"Even for the people who work there?" I asked.

The Other One laughed low and deep. "Patrick doesn't work there," he said. "He lives there, just like everybody else."

Had I been in a different place in life, this story might have ended here. The man I fantasized about lived in a homeless shelter. But if anything, the knowledge only deepened my curiosity. He was young and white and obviously educated, and my life experience had taught me those three things gave a person options. Like me, then, he must have chosen to be where he was. But why?

Days went by. I continued to watch Patrick, and now I saw that he also watched me. Outside, standing with a group of men, he would catch my eye whenever I left the house and smile. I heard one of his companions grumble, "How come she only ever says hi to you?"

Not long after the night of the roses, I spent the day in a good, old-fashioned barn-raising, building temporary bungalows for homeless families on the Lower East Side. Coming home tired with my cheap Chinese dinner, I found myself locked out of my apartment. I sank down on the stoop to eat and wait for Katya to get home, when suddenly I saw Patrick walking toward me. He wore a big nervous grin and fidgeted with kidlike energy. I smiled broadly, wondering if he had any idea how intently he'd been speculated upon.

He stood with his hands in his pockets and kept a certain distance, which I interpreted as respect for our differing stations. "At last we meet," he said.

As I was to learn about nearly everything he said, he managed to pack a universe of paradoxical emotion into that little phrase. It seemed to me there was acknowledgment and hope and wry humor and irony, there was self-effacement and shyness and the hint of a dare. His smile was both challenging and strangely vulnerable, and there was nothing more compelling to me back then than that specific combination. I introduced myself and told him I'd lost my keys.

"You're in luck," he said. "It's seven o'clock. You can join me for evening service." Then his face erupted into a devilish grin, and he shook his hands above his head like Al Jolson singing "Mammy."

"I'm a foooooooool for Jesus!"

That was the first time I stepped into the basement of St. Vincent's House and took my place as Wendy among the Lost Boys. It was a dank, carpeted, rec room of a place, with folding metal chairs for pews, a pulpit, a microphone, and an electric keyboard. I was the only woman in a room full of men, and all eyes turned as Patrick led me to the front and sat me in the chair next to him. He whispered to me throughout the service, interrupting himself to belt out the chorus of a hymn. He told me that, after years of searching, he'd finally found where he belonged. He had accepted Jesus Christ as his personal savior. He was a skeptical optimist, he said, and I was hyperconscious of his leg pressed against my leg. When the sermon was over, he walked me home to my stoop next door, touched my hand, and said good night. I felt in my coat pocket and discovered my keys had been there all along.

After that, every night at seven, I joined him for service. I could count on two hands the number of times I'd been to church in my life, but this felt like something different, something more authentic than my mother's dressy Episcopal chapel or my father's pedestrian Methodist wooden box. Sin had found these men out, and they were here to get right with God. I began to learn the words to the hymns myself, and soon the music director, a hulking man named Big James, who had penned the fifties hit "Jimmy Mac, When Are You Comin' Back," handed me the microphone and asked me to sing a solo. I hesitated. I was here for Patrick, not God, I knew in my heart. But Patrick was beaming at me with tears streaming down his face, and so I took up the microphone and sang a haunting melody, "El Shaddai."

Manuscripts waiting to be rejected piled up, and I skipped auditions in favor of spending my mornings in St. Vincent's kitchen, flipping pancakes for the men I used to watch snaking down the block. Now they knew me by name as I brewed coffee and set out cups of syrup. (I learned early on that crack addicts craved sweets so badly that they would steal the bottles if we left them out.) The blind priest patted me on the head and offered to pay for me to take Bible classes at the local seminary; I accepted so that I might spend more time with Patrick. He was working on rebuilding the wall in the back garden, and I helped him move bricks and haul buckets of water to mix with mortar. It felt good to be out of my head, to work with my body in the service of others. We passed each other by the spigot in the shade, and at a moment when my hands were full and my shoulders ached, he kissed me. We were lovers the next day.

Patrick and I shared our stories during sunny, languorous afternoons of lovemaking while the rest of New York was working. My parents had divorced when I was thirteen but knew I wanted to come to New York to seek my fortune. He was one of four children from a nice, middle-class family. About the time my parents divorced, his moved to a larger town, where he had trouble keeping friends and began experimenting with drugs. He wanted to be a music promoter and had come to New York on business with $8,000 of his partner's money. Over the course of a long weekend, locked in a hotel on the Upper West Side, he'd smoked it all in crack. Every penny. He was too ashamed and afraid to go home, so he'd ended up at St. Vincent's

House. First he found God. Now he'd found me, and everything would be different. To prove it, he bought me a ring. *I don't have much now,* he said, with that wide-mouthed, jittery grin. *But here's a promise of things to come.* It was a paste ring from a bubble gum machine, and I laughed at how silly and sweet he was. Then we fell back into bed.

Patrick brought me little gifts all the time. It didn't matter that they were free or unearned; it was, as my mother had always told me, the thought that counted. He brought me uneaten delicacies from Manhattan's best restaurants courtesy of City Harvest: chocolate-covered strawberries, poached salmon, olive and currant bread. He picked through the mountains of donated clothes and came out with minidresses, go-go boots, and once, an entire wardrobe with the Macy's price tags still on (the last shopping spree of a manic-depressive woman who had thrown herself out of her apartment window).

We had been lovers for a month when Patrick asked me for something in return: a key to my apartment. He wanted to be able to take a shower when I wasn't there, he said; I couldn't know how humiliating it was to live in a house full of men with no privacy. Over the weeks, he'd complained about the other residents in what I perceived as a singularly un-Christian way, but I'd seen no motion toward his looking for a job and leaving. I hesitated again. I still had a roommate, though she was rarely home. He was a recovering drug addict I'd known for a month. But there was something even more troubling about his proposal. I felt I was becoming a sort of currency, inflating his worth among the men at St. Vincent's House. He had something they didn't have: A woman. A key. I saw it when we went to church in the evenings, the way he snaked his arm around me possessively and bristled when the other men spoke to me. Yet, if I loved him as I told myself I did—in Dostoyevsky's extraordinary way—it shouldn't matter. I would be capable of the sort of love that opened itself to risk, because that vulnerability, that totality, lay at the heart of true love. Patrick was asking me for the gift of faith, extending what we professed each night in the basement chapel. He became impatient when I didn't answer right away.

"I can't," I said at last.

"You're a fucking selfish cunt!" he hurled at me and left my apartment, slamming the door.

I didn't see Patrick for several days, and during that time I slowly became frantic by all I'd left undone during the month we'd lost ourselves in each other. I needed to pay my rent, I had no money for groceries. I took the train to the Upper East Side to visit my employer, the disreputable literary agent, dragging a suitcase full of manuscripts. It was getting harder and harder for me to read them to the end, knowing the futility with which I was doing so. Nevertheless, I swapped out my rejected manuscripts for new, rejectable ones, took my fee and the $20 he gave me for cab fare, and lugged my suitcase back onto the subway.

Coming home that afternoon, turning onto Fifty-first Street, I saw three men sitting outside, passing a joint between them. It was Patrick and two other residents of St. Vincent's House. I passed them without comment. When I tearfully dragged my suitcase upstairs, my Russian roommate was home. *Go scream at him,* she ordered me when I told her what I'd seen. *Go hit him, if you need to, but don't just sit here feeling sorry for yourself.*

I flew back onto the street like an avenging angel. I wanted to tell Patrick what a weak, pathetic liar he was, how justified I'd been in not letting him into my house. But what came out was much closer to the truth. I fell on my knees in the middle of a busy Hell's Kitchen sidewalk and sobbed like I'd never sobbed before. *I love you,* I said. *You are killing yourself. I don't want you to die.*

It was clear to me that Patrick needed to be away from bad influences. If he was ever to get clean, he needed someone who believed in him more than he believed in himself, who knew he was capable of change. I gave up my apartment, and we moved to a tenement around the corner, leaving the neon cross behind.

Recommitted and on our own, Patrick and I were determined to live like a normal couple out in the wider world. More than anything, I wanted to show him that I wasn't ashamed of who he was. *Come home with me,* I said. *I want you to meet my mother.* Two train tickets to Virginia were a big expenditure, and we were both nervous about the trip. As our departure date approached, I focused on, of all things, his hair—his dreadlocks, as he called them, though his head more closely resembled the matted coat of an unbrushed dog after a week in the woods. It was the external symbol of all the things I knew my mother would most disapprove of, and it was a testament to how well Patrick wanted the visit to go that he endured my combing it out for hours. He lay with his head in my lap while I gripped the roots carefully, teasing out each blond knot. When I was done, his hair was a broken, frizzed wedge standing out from his head. We both looked at it in horror, before I reached for a ponytail holder and pulled it back.

I have pictures of that trip—the only one we ever took together—of the two of us posing for a friend's camera, our heads together, each wearing our own sad and distracted smile. We tried hard, but Patrick talked too much, and I said little at all. I crept downstairs one morning as Patrick slept to find my mother sitting at the kitchen table with her face in her hands. I had always been a child difficult to direct, and I'm sure she felt she'd finally lost me. She told me later that she worried I'd be murdered in my bed.

Back in New York, spending every day and night together, it soon became clear to me that Patrick was not well. I had convinced myself that an $8,000 crack binge had been an aberration, not the symptom of something darker. But as the months passed, I could no longer fool myself. Patrick's behavior grew increasingly erratic. There was no more talk of God; Jesus had been yet another place for him to lose himself, and our relationship had become the next wild rush. He would shimmy around the apartment to blaring house music, full of wild plans for a business we could start. Vintage clothing! He had great taste, I could work the counter, yes! We'd make a fortune in vintage clothing! Any question I put to him resulted in profound irritation: I was always putting him down, I didn't want him to succeed. These manic episodes would peak in pitched, ugly battles, and then he'd crash, sleeping for days at a time, or waking only to stare dully at the television.

Why are you selling yourself so short? my friends would ask, as if I were making a terrible business deal. *What's in this for you?* I always had an answer. Companionship. He had no life of his own, and so he was always there when I wanted him. Sex. It was plentiful and exciting, and did I mention plentiful? I told myself I'd be paying the same rent if I lived alone, I'd be buying the same groceries, working the same job. I prided myself on my independence, on needing nothing from anyone. But in truth, it was much safer for me to focus on all the things I could live without and to call that strength, rather than to face all the things I desired that I might not get. It was easier to go out and save someone else.

One afternoon I began to understand how differently we viewed our situation as we were walking up Fifth Avenue, past the named fortress apartment buildings with their liveried doormen.

"I'm going to live in one of those," Patrick said.

"If I wanted to be living in one of those, I'd be making very different choices right now," I replied, laughing.

"You can't be happy living like this. The way you are now."

"Of course I am," I replied. "I have you. What more could I want?"

It was the first time I glimpsed what I would only come to understand years later. Patrick was horrified that I wanted nothing for myself—and frankly, he didn't believe me. For him, the fact that I was content living in a dingy apartment with a penniless man with no prospects showed how little I valued myself. No, I wanted to tell him. It's only because I am so special that I can contemplate a life with you. I can divorce money from its alter ego, worth, and see past the trappings of possessions to something more valuable. To want an apartment like that would require a lifestyle and a partner to go with it, which clearly would mean leaving *you*. Couldn't he appreciate that I was paying him the highest compliment of all by loving him in spite of himself? But he looked at me like I was the crazy one. *This is all about you*, he said. *It's always all about you.*

S ix months into our relationship, with Patrick not working and me struggling to support us both, I ran out of money. I'm sure my parents would have lent me some if I had asked them, but I had chosen life with a drug addict, and asking for money would have been an admission of defeat. We gave up all luxuries: movies, dinners out, birth control pills. My appendix had burst when I was eighteen, and the doctors told me I might have difficulty conceiving. Now, desperate, I reached for those words as if they were their own prophylactic, with the inevitable results. I told Patrick I was pregnant as we were walking through Central Park; his face lit up, and he whooped and began wildly planning our future. We would leave New York and live with his parents and get on the dole and raise our family. I stared at him in dismay. Like the key to my apartment, at a moment when he asked for faith, I had none to give him. I'm going to get an abortion, I said. Would you like to be there?

September 9, 1989, is the date I wrote in my battered yellow journal. Just that. With no elaboration.

That night Patrick slept beside me, snoring, and I hated him with such a fury I thought I would grab the pillow from beneath his head and smother him. I had thought to pull him up, and instead he dragged me down. We were the blind leading the blind, each living in a world of reckless denial, helpless to help each other or ourselves. I couldn't stand to be in the same room with him anymore, and so I climbed to the roof of our building, where, not long before, we'd watched Hurricane Hugo blow in through the city. I walked to the cornice of the five-story building and sat down with my legs dangling over the edge. From that height I could see over the West Side to the dark ribbon of the Hudson River and the lights of New Jersey. Behind me, the St. Vincent's cross still flashed black and red: Sin Will. Get Right.

I leaned forward, gently rocking. Even at this lowest moment, I was still aware of the picture it made—a young girl in a white nightgown, backlit by a cross, the city spread out before her. I hated that I couldn't turn it off, that I couldn't stop living my life in the third person. I was not a character in a play or a Russian novel, and I could no longer watch the story of my life unfold, pretending my actions had no consequences. When I had handed over my life to a higher power, be it God or Love, it was with the implicit understanding that surrender meant I would be taken care of. But who was there to take care of me? I was a smart and talented girl, yet I had no money, no meaningful work, no happy relationship. And worst of all, I had failed at sainthood, unable to shake that nagging, gnawing bit of self that just couldn't believe, that couldn't make the leap. Here I sat, not even able to commit suicide, but waiting to fall, as if my Death, like my Life, would be just one more thing that Happened to Me. *If only someone cared,* I thought, full of self-pity and self-loathing for what I'd just done. Anyone. If only in this whole rotten, tired world one good deed would shine through, I could find the strength to get up and keep struggling.

Then, like the voice of God, I heard behind me: *Miss, will you step away from the edge?*

I turned and saw two police officers standing by the door to the stairway. Someone had seen me on the roof and called 911, they said. I stared at them in amazement. The first police officer said, *You weren't going to jump, were you, miss?* And I answered, babbling: *You know, Jean-Paul Sartre wrote that when a man stands at the edge of a cliff, he is not worried that he might fall but that he might jump.* And the second police officer said: *Don't talk that way, miss, or we'll have to take you to Bellevue.*

I cast my eyes over the dark windows of Ninth Avenue, wondering who had been watching me as I had watched Patrick and the men of St. Vincent's House from my fire escape months before. The officers were waiting for me on the rickety linoleum steps of the tenement building. I stood up stiffly and walked to where they held the door. On the second-floor landing, Patrick was awake and anxious. *What's going on?* he asked. *Nothing,* I said. *Let's go back to bed.*

That night on the roof was the great Cosmic Wake-Up Slap I needed. From that moment on, I stopped living completely for Patrick. I had begun to realize the profound narcissism that had allowed me to believe my love might rescue another human being, but now I felt trapped. I had a man living in my house whom I alternately loved and hated. I began insisting on more from him. I couldn't support us both anymore, I told him; he had to find a job or he had to move out. Patrick got a job as a bike messenger and lost it, got a job as a painter and lost it. It was then that I lost the last vestige of my naïveté about addiction. When he was financially dependent on me, right down to his cigarette money, he stayed clean. When we were always together, he couldn't get out to score. I had strangled his habit with sanctions and blockade. But once he had his own money, he started spending it again on crack. He swore he wasn't getting high, he didn't come home because he was painting a movie theater and had to do it at night because they showed films during the day. It became easier to believe the lies than to endure the violent fights. Coming home from my soulless temp job to find him searching the sofa cushions for coins or going through my old coat pockets, I'd scream: *I got you out of St. Vincent's House, you've got to take responsibility for yourself.* Or more often: *I can't take this anymore. Pay your share of the rent or get out!* Our fights escalated, but no matter what I said or did, he wouldn't leave. I couldn't live with him—but neither could I stand to be responsible for sending him back to the mission, or worse, onto the street. I'd storm away in tears and prowl the city half the night, feeling suffocated and panicked. Then I'd come home to find him asleep, want ads circled in the newspaper, and feel guilty for being so hard on him. He was struggling with what I was beginning to realize was profound manic depression.

That helpless inner struggle, waged through relapse after relapse, was the most painful thing to witness and was what kept me from walking out. Patrick had developed the habit of fishing every pay phone slot in the hopes someone had rigged it. One night, outside of an Indian restaurant on Sixth Street, he hit the jackpot. He wiggled a spot deep inside the coin return and quarters poured out like a slot machine. Over $10 in all overflowed his cupped palms. He stood for a long time, and I waited for him to make up some excuse for where he needed to go, what he needed to do. But he didn't. Instead, he took me by the hand, led me into the restaurant, and bought me dinner.

Not long afterward, we found an ad on the back page of the *Village Voice,* looking for participants in the first human trials of Prozac. Patrick's drug taking went legit, and for the first time since I'd known him, the wild mood swings leveled out. His odd jobs lasted longer, and he began contributing to rent. Feeling less responsible for him, I thought more seriously about myself and what I wanted. I got my temp agency to switch me to a publishing house and signed up for classes at St. Mark's Poetry Project. Patrick would meet me after class on Saturday mornings, and we would walk to Chinatown and eat dumplings and buy little griddle cakes, twenty for a dollar. We spent one idyllic afternoon, a day of truce and normalcy, wandering like any happy couple through its narrow, brightly decorated back alleys. On lower Mott Street, we stumbled upon an arcade famous for its Dancing Chicken, a plump white hen behind a piece of Plexiglas that shuffled over an electrified spinning plate. Next to her was another chicken that played tic-tac-toe. I fed a few of our precious quarters into the slot while Patrick stood behind me, calling out strategy. I was laughing so hard I made all the wrong choices. I lost to the chicken. *You didn't even force a draw,* he said, suddenly sober. *You lost. To a chicken.*

The Prozac trial ended, and without insurance or money for pills, we were back to where we started.

We lived this way for three years.
    I could have found a more permanent job, married Patrick, and gotten him benefits. But I knew I wouldn't be reading to the end of this particular story. Though I loved him, I had no real faith in him; he knew it and hated my condescension. Toward the end, when the fights had become incessant and increasingly violent, Patrick got a friend to wire him a bus ticket to California. Within a few weeks he was begging me to wire him one home. I agreed, but stepping over the homeless people at Port Authority to pick him up at 3:00 A.M., I realized how happy I'd been when he was gone. He moved back into my house, but we stopped having sex or pretending we were a couple. It was a relief for us both.

The difference between help and rescue is sometimes difficult to see. But for me, it had become about the difference between duty and illusion. It was necessary as a decent, loving human to get involved. The night I sat on the roof, when I was at my most desperate, a complete stranger had seen I was in trouble and stretched out a hand in help. I took it. But no matter how far I stretched for Patrick, because of his illness, because of my own moral superiority, he was never able to step away from the edge. I finally reached a point where stretching any further would have done nothing more than take me down with him. Dostoyevsky's love was irrational, excessive, fictional love. The only person I could save was myself.

I said good-bye to Patrick in a small hotel back in Hell's Kitchen. Somehow along the way, despite him or because of him, I had begun writing seriously—first poetry and later, a try at my first novel. An instructor who had been especially encouraging told me he had spent several years in Greece, where it was very cheap to live. I decided to take what I'd saved working at the publishing house and move there to finish my first book. I told myself I was going to save money, but really I was moving to escape Patrick. He would never go, and I knew by now I would never have the strength to make him. So there was nothing to do but leave myself. I don't remember how he reacted when I told him I was going—and ironically, as with so many other big events in my life, I have no written record of it. What I do remember is saying good-bye to him in the cramped room he'd rented after I gave up our apartment. I had no idea how he was getting the money to pay for it, and I didn't ask. His birthday was a week before I left. It was a schizophrenic late April day, unable to decide if it was spring or winter. I brought him a slice of cake on a paper plate, and he invited me into the rat's nest of donated clothes he'd been collecting for the vintage shop he still vowed to open one day. We cleared a space on his narrow bed and shared the piece of cake, taking turns with the fork.

That day we made small talk and laughed, a little ruefully, because the room he'd taken was directly across the street from St. Vincent's House. He had a perfect view of that cross, still flashing, even in the daylight, as insistent and oblivious as ever. I was almost twenty-five years old. He had just turned thirty-one. I stood up and kissed him softly good-bye, more of a sister than a lover. Sometime while I was gone, diligently writing my first novel that was to be, poetically enough, rejected, Patrick moved away. For years after, as I wrote my first—published—novel, my second, my third, got married, had kids, he would phone me randomly, in and out of rehab. Then he stopped. From time to time, I run his name through search engines, wandering the Internet as we used to wander the back alleys of Chinatown. I don't even know what I want to say. Thank you? I'm sorry? You taught me the value of a human life? I search but I never find him. Then I stop.

For Richer or for Poorer

Marisa Belger

For the first few months of my relationship with Paul we never thought about money. I mean, what use would it be when we had everything we needed already? His spacious studio apartment—on the wrong side of the edge of pretty Venice Beach—had a comfortable queen-sized bed (where we spent most of our time), a shower with plenty of hot water, and a fluffy gray carpet that begged to be rolled upon. When we got hungry, we slipped on our flip-flops and strolled past a gay bathhouse to the little Thai restaurant with the mesmerizing fish tank and the best noodle stir-fry in town ($6.95), or we ordered mango lassis and greasy samosas ($10) from the grungy Indian joint across the street. But mostly we stayed inside, in bed, eating easy, inexpensive foods that will forever be sexy: chicken breasts broiled with mozzarella and basil, green salads strewn with edible flowers from the farmers' market, big hunks of chocolate.

When not at home, we could be found cruising in his 1998 beige pickup truck—complete with crew cab, functioning CD player, and room for two surfboards. Here we'd belt out Bruce Springsteen ballads and wiggle in our seats to old hip-hop songs. Paul never flinched when I put my hot feet on the cool dashboard. And I thought it was sexy when he steered with his knees as he put sugar in his coffee. We stopped only for milkshakes or gas, and when we did he paid, but sometimes I did too.

Between the truck and the queen-sized bed was Paul—always Paul. I fell hard for his blue eyes, firecracker sense of humor, and rowdy Irish family. I loved that he played the guitar, was the first to grab the mic during karaoke, and had as many childhood friends as I did. I was sure that I was the only woman dating a guy who could dance like James Brown, who closed every call to his mother *and* brothers with a sincere "I love you," and who could mesmerize both babies and dogs with his playful antics. When I left him for a week during our courtship to visit a friend in Hawaii, he read me a love letter he had written, over the phone, too impatient to wait for my return. It's blurry now, but it had something to do with knights and wild horses and whisking me off to a castle in the forest. Money? What money?

Paul and I met in early September, covered in dust and sequins at the Burning Man festival in the Nevada desert. Founded by a small collaborative of northern California free spirits in the mid-eighties, the event blossomed into a massive—over forty thousand people at last count—experiment in radical self-expression and large-scale art that's held each year on a dried-out lakebed outside of Reno. Glowing from the rush of colors and costumes and the burn of the midday sun, I'm sure that we bumped into each other precisely because we weren't looking.

I know now that I'd made the journey from New York to the middle of nowhere in hopes of finding an antidote to the empty, unfulfilling relationship I had been spinning in for the past year. My time with Jack was self-imposed torture. A handsome, charismatic reporter who lived in Los Angeles, he kept me in limbo—avoiding the emotional commitment I craved, but unmotivated to end what we had. I was unhappy, but stuck—afraid to ask for more and afraid to leave with nothing. For months I had been searching for the strength to break things off, and as I packed for my Nevada adventure, I secretly hoped that I would find it while dancing in the desert with thousands of strangers. I also hoped that I would find my self-respect, my recently departed creativity, and a renewed appreciation for life. Love was the last thing I was looking for.

So when Paul and I crossed paths at one of the festival's many impromptu parties and found that we laughed at the same jokes, grew up in the same section of New Jersey, and had birthdays exactly six months apart, romance did not ensue for us—not yet. It was clear that we had some kind of connection—enough to exchange numbers—but neither of us was pressed to discover what kind.

By fate or luck or chance, a week later I was scheduled to fly to Los Angeles, where Paul was then living, to break up with Jack in person (or as I liked to say, "tie up some loose ends"). I tied those ends—messy, painful, sad—and was soon sharing spicy tuna rolls with Paul in tiny Japanese restaurants on the west side of the city. We also drank beers on the beach, went for long rides on Highway 1, and made out like teenagers who expected their parents to walk in at any second. Paul could do the snake (a coveted break-dancing move from the eighties), as well as a spot-on Woody Allen imitation and would chase me around with a bloodthirsty look while wearing vampire fangs from the Halloween before. He made me laugh until I ached.

When the bill came, we either went Dutch, he'd toss his credit card on the table, or I'd hand over mine. And through the foggy haze of brand-new love-lust, I couldn't help but notice a few key facts about Paul's finances: (1) he wasn't a rich man—rich men don't live in neighborhoods where hourly motels outnumber residential buildings; (2) his work in sales for a popular sports drink company rendered him gainfully employed albeit minimally compensated; and (3) after a loose attempt at breaking into acting, he had no long-term professional goals. This information did little to dissuade me from professing my love or encouraging him to break his lease, drive cross-country, and move into my studio in Manhattan.

I owned that studio, purchased with the help of my mother and stepfather. Comfortably upper-middle-class, they had given me a plush suburban childhood complete with yearly vacations, a car at seventeen, and both bachelor's and master's degrees with no lingering loans. Though down to earth, they are the kind of people who can comfortably navigate a wine list, recognize obscure French cheeses, and communicate with taxi drivers in many of the world's big cities. They introduced me to foreign movies and five-star dining, and they encouraged me to write and travel. And though I imagined they fantasized about a future son-in-law with a Dr. or Esq. connected to his name, they were entirely accepting of every guy I brought home.

When I met Paul, I had already lived in France and the Netherlands, vacationed regularly in Mexico and the Caribbean, and toured far-off locales like South Africa and Korea. I had a favorite neighborhood in Rome and a favorite street in Paris. I had sunned on almost all of the Greek islands—Ionian and Cyclades—and welcomed the year 2000 by skinny-dipping in the crystalline ocean of the Big Island of Hawaii.

I was educated and articulate, with a geeky love of books. I'd keep a tally of the words my friends mispronounced, correcting them gently, "It's actually "EPHEM-er-al" not "eph-EM-er-al." If a potential date misspelled "you're" as "your" in a flirty e-mail, I was decidedly less interested.

When I met Paul, he had been out of the country exactly once. He went to college at a local school in New Jersey and worked each summer repairing roofs or installing stainless-steel kitchen appliances. He had a handful of books, mostly plays from when he was pursuing acting, and was a terrible student with an ADD-like inability to focus on a text or write a paper. He took his first job when he was six—sweeping up a family friend's butcher shop—and many more followed. Some involved manual labor, others were sales or marketing. All were short-lived.

Later I would wonder if Paul didn't miss having money because it was never there in the first place. His mother, divorced in her thirties, struggled to raise three kids while maintaining the overhead on their rambling, unfinished house. His grandparents, who lived down the street, often stepped in with a necessary hot meal. Paul was eligible for his school's free lunch. He called himself poor.

But he wasn't lonely. His family was big—huge actually. Every gathering included a long list of aunts, uncles, cousins, and family friends who had a palpable love and affection for each other. My parents were warm, but I had never seen people enjoy each other like Paul's clan did. There were no reserved giggles like the ones that took place at my Thanksgiving table, but whooping guffaws. And whether it was a funeral or a wedding, music was everywhere. Guitars and fiddles and harmonicas were pulled from their cases (shaker eggs for the musically impaired), and songs were sung. People got drunk and danced on tables. A current of loyalty and dedication swept through this crowd where first cousins were best friends and spouses were sucked into the fold and instantly made family. Suddenly I found myself with thirty new people who would do anything for me.

Paul asked me to marry him one year to the day after we met, and I didn't hesitate, saying, *yes, yes, yes, I would be honored and humbled to share my life with you.* Our wedding would be ten months later at a sprawling inn by the Hudson River in upstate New York. My parents would pay for the lavish affair—all we had to do was show up.

I knew couples who had allowed their finances to infiltrate their union, like an evil ménage à trois. But that wasn't the way it was with us. Even newly engaged, money continued to have almost no influence on our relationship. I attributed some of it to what I believed were my exceptionally reasonable needs. I prided myself on being low-maintenance, a truly modern woman. As long as I had the flexibility to go out to dinner once in a while—at an average establishment, nothing fancy—and to buy the occasional treat, like a pair of boots or a plane ticket to visit a girlfriend in L.A., I considered myself lucky. So, when Paul lost his job three days before our wedding, I barely winced. We'd just charge our honeymoon on the credit cards that I'd recently cleared, and we'd pay them off when he was back on track. No problem.

In the beginning, adapting to our shrunken income was fun. Really.

I'd make us big bowls of pasta with garlicky tomato sauce and remind Paul that this was what peasants ate in Italy. We'd drink cheap wine and snuggle up on the couch, laughing because kissing was free. It was romantic. Really. In bed, before falling asleep, we'd softly sing the famous lyric from that cheesy seventies folk song: "Even though we ain't got money, I'm so in love with you, honey." And we'd mean it.

But then things changed. I'll never know if something inside of me shifted or if it was the revealing of a truth that was already there, but as Paul moved into month two of his search for work, I was suddenly and clearly *not* okay. As a freelance writer, I barely supported myself. Sustaining the two of us left me crumpled on the floor at the end of each month, surrounded by bills that were impossible to pay. I tried to brush it off—to be cool, Zen, removed, relaxed. I told myself that there were people out there who never paid their Con Ed bill on time and still went on to lead happy, fulfilling lives. But the tears still streamed down my face as I sent American Express my last penny and ticked off the days until my next paycheck.

Paul was sorry and ashamed that we were in this position. He took part-time work and stepped up his job hunt, but nothing stuck. Meanwhile, I was trapped in a vortex of worry, often close to despair. I didn't recognize the pushy, nervous person that I had become. When I watched Paul as he brushed his teeth or made our bed in the morning, it seemed as if I had allowed a stranger into my life.

There was a time—I was sure of it—when I was in touch with what *really* matters (love, if you're wondering). I could have sworn that I wasn't superficial or materialistic or needy. And Paul was destined to be my ultimate partner, the one man who could match me in strength and ambition and potential. There was no way that he was lost and insecure and confused. But he was. And so was I.

I missed the bright, charismatic man who had once made me laugh so hard that I almost choked on my iced tea. Where was the guy who could talk to anyone, from lumberjack to astrophysicist, the one who humbled me with his innate understanding of world history and politics? My rudimentary knowledge of psychology (which I gleaned, like most people, from *Oprah* and some free therapy sessions during college), told me that Paul's struggle as a child had conditioned him to be comfortable with lacking, that he was okay with not having enough. And I wondered if having a familial safety net was what allowed me to take risks and aim high.

Love couldn't save us now. When Paul pulled me close, I had visions of a future filled with late charges and coupon snipping, and I became distant and cold. I was supposed to marry a man who could easily fill in the financial holes that would inevitably arise as I pursued writing. I pictured myself working at a comfortable pace, taking only the assignments that excited me and outlining the book I'd one day write. And when we had our first baby, of course I would stop working, for at least a good few months. This was how it was supposed to be. This was the plan.

At first I was sad. Then resentful. Then angry. I was angrier than I had ever been in my life. When I saw the defeated look in Paul's eyes, I would make some clumsy attempts to be understanding and supportive. But I couldn't get past the fact that I had plans and he was demolishing them. I was furious at myself for marrying this man without seriously considering his current financial status and money-making potential—furious that I had married for love. I resented my touchy-feely tendency to spend more time in the realm of the emotional than the practical. So I yelled. I threw things. I slammed doors and stomped away.

Five months into marriage, I'd find myself rehearsing the speech I'd eventually give to my parents: *I know you spent a significant chunk of your retirement savings on our wedding, and I admit that I used to make fun of celebrities who divorce before a year. But I just can't do it. I'm sorry. I'm sorry.*

Eight months into marriage, after a particularly awful fight—the walls of our apartment still vibrating from the screaming—I curled on our bed after Paul stormed out and stared through the window, past the New York City skyline to the blue-gray sky above. I saw myself packing a bag and running away. I'd go somewhere exotic, perhaps Vietnam or

Malaysia—somewhere thousands and thousands of miles from my wilt-ing marriage and empty wallet. Maybe Australia. Maybe South Africa.

My heart began to calm as I mentally planned this trip, making a list of what to pack—sunscreen, mosquito repellent, jeans for cool evenings. Then I saw myself buying the ticket. I may have been brave enough to walk away from my marriage, to disappoint my family, and to shock my friends. But the balance in my checking account left no room for international airfare. I was trapped and the claustrophobia was paralyzing.

I lay there in the dark room gasping, my breath tight and shallow. And just as I was absolutely sure that I was headed toward a full-blown panic attack, I found a crack in the thick layer of anxiety that had sur-rounded me. Through this crack streamed a clear beam of light. I had the books, I knew how this went: *Conversations with God, The Celes-tine Prophecy, The Four Agreements.* They were given to me by one of my many pseudospiritual aunts at Christmas, and I poked fun at their clunky syntax and heavy-handed messages. But if tonight was my moment to receive a nugget of wisdom from a higher power, I was all ears. I held my breath, closed my eyes, and braced myself for what I hoped would be some sort of transcendental message, a celestial piece of wisdom that would keep us out of couples therapy and far away from divorce court. I waited for the strumming of a distant harp or a flutter of pixie dust, but what I received was decidedly less heavenly. "It's your fault too," said the voice inside my head, sounding not unlike a cranky grandmother. "And don't you forget it."

When it comes to prayer, I'm not the most experienced. But I spent the next fifteen minutes actively praying that Paul would choose to come home that night instead of leaving me forever. (He did. At 2:00 A.M. Tipsy and remorseful.) I needed him to come back because my crotchety fairy godmother was right—it was my fault too. What I needed to do was abundantly clear: stop criticizing Paul for what he wasn't and focus on what I was—whiny, critical, demanding . . . and able-bodied and capable of contributing to our marriage. It was as easy as it sounds.

A lifelong freelancer, I left my free-agent ways behind and accepted a full-time job as an editor. The security of a steady paycheck and health benefits triggered a spark of love for my new husband that I had been convinced I'd never feel again. Instead of slogging off to work, resentful of my role as primary breadwinner, I wore the title proudly. And looking for even more ways to pad our finances, I suggested that we trade our tiny, expensive Manhattan apartment for a cheaper option in Brooklyn.

Employment must be contagious because Paul soon followed my new job with a job of his own, working with kids and schools. Each day, he woke up motivated and inspired. Now fortified with dual incomes, we began to believe that our marriage might stand a chance. I wondered if this surge of optimism was a result of my recent attitude adjustment—or if it was nothing more than the desire to be different from our parents. His were divorced before he was in the third grade; mine were out of each other's lives before I could speak in full sentences. After more than twenty-five years apart, his mother and father still refuse to be in the same room; my parents don't have to worry about bumping into each other because my dad hasn't spoken to us in years. In our early days of dating, Paul and I used to joke that the statistics were stacked firmly against us—that a child of divorce is destined to be a terrible spouse, and that two children of divorce, well, they shouldn't even bother. Maybe things began to get better simply because we bothered.

If that cranky grandmother who'd caught me planning my escape had chanced to look down upon Paul and me on the night of our first anniversary, she'd have found a gainfully employed couple squished into the folds of a dingy white love seat in a not-too-small living room in Brooklyn—cheek smashed against cheek, legs wrapped around legs, happily married for good.

A Tale of Two Bank Accounts

Ann Hood

My parents married very young—my mother at nineteen and my father at twenty-one. As an enlisted man in the navy, my father did not make very much money. Instead of a diamond engagement ring, he gave my mother a set of American Tourister luggage. They were going places, literally.

In their first ten years of marriage, my parents lived in Naples, Italy; Annapolis, Maryland; and Washington, D.C. By the time they settled in Rhode Island, my brother and I were in elementary school. My mother went back to work, as a tax auditor for the IRS, where my father worked in management. Although we were not rich, we were a two-car family before most people we knew. We took family vacations in the summer and ate out at restaurants.

My parents' philosophy was to enjoy what you have today and let tomorrow take care of itself. Although our lifestyle was not lavish, we never did without anything. My brother and I each got a car when we turned eighteen. Our college was paid for. And even into adulthood, when times got tough, we knew our parents would help us out financially.

I see now that that my parents' financial ease was derived from their shared attitude about money. They had a joint checking account, and both deposited their paychecks into it. If my mother wanted new shoes or a new sofa, she simply wrote a check for them, no questions asked. If my father wanted to go out with the guys on a Friday night for steaks and martinis, no problem. They both worked hard, and they both enjoyed living well. It did not occur to me that couples did it any other way. So it's interesting to consider that in my own marriage my husband and I keep our finances completely separate.

For most of my dating life, the guy paid for dinners and movies. I managed my own money—first as a flight attendant after college, and later as a sometimes struggling, sometimes successful, writer. With this income, I found myself able to buy a co-op in Manhattan, try new restaurants, and occasionally splurge on a taxi instead of the subway. I loved having financial independence and cringed when married friends described hiding pairs of new shoes from their husbands or sneaking out to upscale bars. My husband, I imagined, would be my equal, someone who spent money the same way I did, on the same kinds of things.

Luke was my first real adult relationship. An actor who worked nights as a bartender at a trendy bar, he made huge tips—and after he paid the rent, he spoiled me with tulips and Converse sneakers, dinner at my favorite Mexican restaurant and sexy lingerie. I did the same for him, finding the obscure music he liked and buying nice wine for the meals I liked to cook. Some months we were both broke and happily stayed at home watching old Tarzan movies on television, eating pasta, and kissing.

Sadly, Luke's acting career stalled, and I was too immature to see him through the tough emotional times. At a book party shortly after our relationship ended, I met Douglas, a man with a successful job in advertising. I was attracted to many things about him. He was older than I, and his career was more stable. I liked how smart he was, and how sociable. Luke was shy; we didn't go to many parties or go out with friends very often. Douglas was the complete opposite: always inviting people to join us, often hitting two or three events in one night. Part of that was his job, but he also liked going out. And so his stinginess came as a surprise to me. He had a good job, a big savings account, and family money as well. When we dated, we went to the ballet and to Sammy's Romanian Restaurant, where a veal chop cost over $30; we went to Broadway shows whenever one opened that we wanted to see; we went on ski vacations to Utah and Colorado and Idaho.

And I paid exactly half. Of everything.

Early on, at a fancy Italian restaurant near his office, Douglas quickly did some calculating when the bill arrived. He told me my share, making sure to mention that I owed more because I'd had three glasses of wine and he'd had only two. "Oh," I said, shocked. I paid up. That night, as we played Boggle and laughed together, I struggled to reconcile what mattered more in a relationship. How many men out there loved playing Ghost on long car trips, watching Preston Sturges movies, and having picnics on the living room floor? And didn't these valuable qualities offset my new boyfriend's frugality?

But when Douglas and I moved in together a year after we met, the question wasn't so easily answered. If I'd had one of those terrible months when my writing barely covered the bills, he wrote down what we had spent in a little notebook and then asked me for my half when I got my next check. "Cheap with money, cheap with love," my mother said. She was right. Douglas had a complicated and often volatile relationship with his parents, and he'd had few serious relationships with women. Hesitant to commit, he'd lived alone his entire adult life, and admitted his inability to be open with a partner. From my parents to previous romantic relationships, I was accustomed to people who loved eagerly and without bounds. Douglas couldn't do that. He wanted to; I could see that in the way he awkwardly tried to be open and intimate. But he was smart and funny, and I saw his inability to be generous in love and in money as a sign that he was wounded. And although I was not someone who liked to save people,

I thought my own openness and generosity would show him a new way, a better way.

My parents disapproved of our decision to move in together. "He's too stingy," my father said. When they came to visit our spacious apartment in a beautiful brownstone, I took down and hid the list he kept on the wall:

Milk: $2.39
Eggs: $1.89
Wine: $12.00
Ann owes me: $8.14

The list grew whenever Douglas ran an errand or picked up take-out food. When I paid, the total was crossed out. Eventually, that tally became sad evidence of a relationship that got nickel-and-dimed to death. We would argue over the choice of words we used, the details of an event, where to go for dinner. In short, we became *that* couple, the ones who make everyone around them feel uncomfortable while they bicker over whether some trivial thing happened at nine or nine-thirty, or who said what and when. That stinginess crept into every part of our lives, it seemed.

In the end we didn't break up over money directly. But when I told people we had split, I often heard myself using this story as an example of why: Once, sick in bed with a high fever and the flu, I asked Douglas if he would go to the drugstore and get me cough medicine. Not only did he make me wait for hours while he did some work in his study, but he asked me for the money as soon as he got back. (No halvsies this time; the Robitussin was all mine!) I remember looking at him through my feverish eyes, his hand outstretched, the receipt laid out on the pillow beside me, and knowing that it was over. The emphasis on money became symbolic of something deeply wrong in this relationship. Just as a lack of money had brought Luke and me closer, stinginess had finally torn Douglas and me apart. I could not stay with a man who could not share his heart fully. Douglas couldn't share anything, except his wit and intelligence. Ultimately, that wasn't enough for me.

Douglas left me with a parting financial shot: a few years earlier, when we had made some investments together, he had made a mathematical error. Now we owed the brokerage company money—a lot of money. I was presented with an equation that showed that since I had made three times the amount of money he had that year, I should pay three times the amount owed. I was disgusted and angry, but not surprised. Easier to just do it and be rid of him, I decided. So I sold my car, cashed in my savings, wrote out a check, and found myself completely broke.

Why did I spend so much time with a man who never once helped me financially or shared his own financial success? To this day, the answer is difficult to discern. I was not desperate for love or marriage or babies. In fact, while I was with Douglas, I often missed the private pleasures of living alone. Had I left him earlier, I would have come out of the relationship financially more solid than I did by staying. Yet I stayed. And to this day that fact embarrasses me. Embarrasses me and colors my financial situation with Lorne, my husband of sixteen years.

A few months after Douglas moved out, I went to give a talk at my alma mater. A handsome guy seemed to appear everywhere I went. At the pretalk dinner he smiled at me from across the dining room; he sat in the front row during my presentation; and finally, he cornered me in the coatroom as I left the reception. "Stop!" he said. "I have to get to know you!" As it turned out, we had met years earlier in high school, circled each other in college, and still had friends in common. When he asked me to go with him for a glass of wine, I readily agreed.

That night I learned that Lorne's last marriage was a traditional one in which he was the breadwinner. His wife stayed home, even before they had their daughter. When they got divorced, he ended up in debt after years of child support payments and splitting assets. His ex-wife went on one last shopping spree before the divorce was finalized; he was stuck with credit card bills from Dress Barn and Payless Shoes, in addition to all the debt they had incurred during their marriage. In a way, there was something almost exciting in coming together as a couple bumping against forty and starting completely clean. Lorne's ex-wife had taken their furniture, their dishes, everything they'd acquired as a couple. Here we both sat, reasonably successful, without anything to show for it. Except our willingness to fall in love.

Which we did. Madly. And so fast that we jumped in without discussing the nuts and bolts of marriage. When we finally got around to finances, I couldn't believe how different we were. Lorne brought spreadsheets and budgets. His priorities for big-budget expenditures were things like exercise equipment and new windows; mine were weekends in Paris and more Fiestaware. It wasn't long before our money differences were thrown into sharp relief.

Soon after we first got married, Lorne presented me with a household budget. I saw that he had earmarked only $5 for family Christmas presents; my own family tended to use Christmas as a time for extravagance. Expenditures like going to the movies and out to dinner didn't even appear—they were luxury items to him and necessities to me. With such different priorities, keeping money separate made more sense to me than fighting over plasma TVs or meals at the new bistro. And so, in all our years together, we have never shared our money. No joint checking account. No Christmas clubs or IRAs or CDs. We struggled separately through tough financial times and used windfalls for our own private pleasures.

Did I slide into this setup as a reaction to my last relationship? Did I fear that exposing my finances would lead to scrutiny, accusations, and worry? With Douglas, I practically flaunted a new dress or computer. They meant that I was doing well, no thanks to him. But with Lorne, I often hid those things. Brought up to wear frugality like a badge of honor, he seemed to judge me poorly if a purchase was, in his opinion, a splurge. He never said that; I just felt it.

In time, Lorne and I both pulled ourselves out of the financial holes our previous relationships had helped us to dig. After four years of renting, we were able to buy our own house, send our son to a private school, and get premium cable. Since I was only working part-time to be home with our kids, Lorne took on the lion's share of costs. Somehow we fell into a rhythm of who paid for what: I covered all the household expenses, kids' lessons and clothes, groceries, and small repairs. He paid for the mortgage and various insurances and tuitions.

I can't say that I always feel comfortable with this arrangement. As a writer, I have had some very lean years and have even gone into debt to pay for my share of our life together. And although I entered into this agreement with my eyes wide open, I sometimes find myself hiding my new pair of shoes so he won't call me a spendthrift—and resenting the trendy gadgets he buys.

Two summers ago, Lorne spent many thousands of dollars traveling to Russia to climb a mountain. He was gone three weeks, visiting Moscow and Amsterdam during the trip. He was thrilled. I was . . . ambivalent. The thing is, I *wanted* him to climb mountains. I *wanted* him to indulge in the things that make him happy. But I also regarded that trip with resentment. After all, I was still taking part-time teaching jobs and too many writing assignments just to make my end of things meet. Sure, Lorne had worked and made enough money to support such a trip. But the inequity was all too clear to me.

And that inequity cut both ways. Of course, I realized that Lorne frowned on some of my expenditures too: tickets to Broadway plays, last-minute upgrades on flights. My reasoning for these luxuries was that I wanted to reward myself for my hard work. These quiet resentments, this push and pull of money—how to get it, how to spend it, how to share it—grew more tense over time.

But last year everything changed. My novel *The Knitting Circle* had been published eight months previously. Since that time, excited e-mails kept arriving. The book had made bestseller lists; it went into a second printing, then a third, and on into its sixth printing. I had received royalty payments before, usually modest ones. And so the day the check for this book slid through my mail slot I carried it around unopened for hours. I didn't know the amount—even though for months I had been doing the math to guess at what it might be. But I knew this one would be the biggest yet.

Finally, I took a breath and opened the envelope. I had to keep counting the digits to be sure I was reading the amount correctly. After several times, I was certain: I was holding the biggest check I'd ever earned.

Some women in this situation would run to the phone and call their husband. In fact, probably most women would. But my hesitation in opening it in the first place had a lot to do with not calling my husband. I studied the check one more time, picked up the phone, and called my mother to share my good news.

When I deposited that check in the bank, I paid off all of my debt—incurred not for frivolous things but to keep up my share of the household payments (even during the three hard financial years I'd had a while back). My credit card balance is finally zero. I still have enough money to do the things I've wanted to do for a long time—renovate the kitchen, replace worn chairs, reupholster the sofa. I opened a real savings account for the first time since I've been married. I can, at last, sigh with relief.

With those burdens lifted, I am taking a harder look at the way my husband and I live our financial lives. My parents were more like-minded than we are; their financial intertwining was smooth. Ours will take more patience, more negotiating—and yes, even some arguing—before we ever open a joint checking account. Negotiating expenditures, creating a united financial vision—all of it terrifies me. But twenty years after I first saw Douglas's list of household expenses, split carefully in half, I think I may be ready to move toward a more integrated financial future. Nobody really owes anybody half when you're married. At least, they shouldn't. So I will take a deep breath, open my bank account statements, and try to do it right this time.

Love and the Bottom Line

Joni Evans

Mine was a highly public divorce. We were a high-profile couple, as we worked together in the same field: book publishing in its most gossiped-about days. It was the early eighties, and the business of books—authors, deals, agents—were beginning to land on the front pages of newspapers.

My husband was the head of one of the most successful publishing companies in the country, instilling fear and excitement into the industry with his take-no-prisoners style. He was rich, powerful—and worse, he was my boss. He was in his midfifties, secure in his seven-figure salary, multistock options, and multiyear contract (which included access to company jets, a car and driver, a corporate chef, and a corporate penthouse apartment).

I had access to these perks as long as I had access to my husband. But at forty-five, I was no trophy wife. I had worked my way up from a junior position as "manuscript girl" at a magazine to—fifteen years later—an associate publisher of my husband's book company. I too was a well-paid, ambitious executive with a strong track record, earning a handsome salary with some stock options of my own. Indeed, I felt privileged to enjoy the use of our company's corporate jet, the car and driver, the apartment, and all the other perks that came with my husband's title.

I never really thought about the money. I only thought about the love. We had both left our previous marriages not long after our first meeting—although neither of us dared to admit (at least, I didn't to myself) that our divorces were inevitable in the face of our attraction to one another. I thought only about the man: fearless, powerful, fun, and smart, though increasingly possessive of me. I thought his stormy, obsessive, and erratic personality was exciting. I thought our marriage would last forever.

Less than ten years into it, we despised each other.

I assumed, at first, we'd just shake hands and go our separate ways. I was playing the Good Girl, the role I always played with this man. We were still good colleagues. (He had graduated, deservedly, to the most senior position in the parent company, and I had graduated, also deservedly, to publisher of the book division.) With record profits, I was willing to believe I could keep my job of fourteen years and keep our split separate. He too saw no reason to break up our office alliance.

The first anxiety I felt about money was when I sought a new place to live. The single asset the two of us had bought and owned together before we were married was a fourteen-room Normandy-style country home on seventy-five acres. In the 1970s real estate crash, we had paid $400,000 for it, though it was a known white elephant. Since I earned less than 20 percent of what my husband did, I struggled to keep up with our payments. But I wanted to help realize our dream, which was to make the house our Tara and turn it into a showplace. (And indeed we did: the house is currently on the market for $28 million. Literally.)

When we first purchased the property, I had naively insisted upon an agreement that simply stated I could get my money back if the two of us ever broke up—something I never thought would happen. I had neglected to ask for interest and appreciation, and the repayment schedule extended over three years. The terms were so unfair that I asked for an accelerated payment of what I had contributed to the property. Mr. Husband laughed at me. These were the terms I had asked for, he said. When I tested the agreement legally, I was turned down. I was a sophisticated publisher used to contracts. I had counsel at the time. An agreement is an agreement. So be it.

But what about our ten years of marriage? We had no preexisting agreement there. What about the union that had me working as hard for his career enhancement as my own? And vice versa. What about the partnership? What about the fact that my total work ethic was devoted to his company, my total home effort was devoted to his house, and my total family commitment was devoted to his children? In the 1990s, very few professional women "fought" for financial settlements at the end of a marriage. The draconian divorce laws of New York State had traditionally favored the husband. And in those heady postfeminist times, it was considered unseemly for a woman who made an independent salary to ask for money of any kind from her soon-to-be ex-husband.

In the eighties, a new divorce law known as "equitable distribution" had become the subject of much speculation. Some interpreted it to mean the courts were beginning to see marriage as a fifty-fifty partnership, regardless of who earned what percentage of the household money. I brought this up to Mr. Husband, and he laughed again: not one red cent. He insisted that equitable distribution did not apply to women with careers such as mine. Especially women with six-figure salaries, no children between us, and only a ten-year marriage.

One day I had a brainstorm. I called Gloria Steinem, whom I knew slightly and admired enormously, to ask about my husband's theory. She said clearly: if you followed Mr. Husband's argument— that women who were successful financially would not be entitled to equitable distribution—it would follow that no woman contemplating marriage would ever choose to work. If she did, it would endanger her forever should she ever get divorced. Of course. Mr. Husband's logic was totally illogical.

I tried to have a friend who was a lawyer talk with him. The word back was that I deserved nothing; I was the one who had chosen to leave. Our country house would become his, and our city apartment (owned by the company) would become his. The good life we had experienced together came from him. My success in business came from him. He was the one who gave me the opportunities. He promoted me. I was nothing without him.

When it was clear that I could no longer stay at our company, Mr. Husband asked my colleagues to testify against me in court. He had already cut off all our joint charge cards and privileges at the bank. I was prohibited from visiting my two dogs. (Well, I was permitted one visit—albeit at the bottom of our driveway—a few days before one of them died of a terminal illness.) My stepchildren severed all ties. You get the picture.

Have I forgotten to mention that in the meantime I was forced to walk away from fourteen years of my professional life and find a new path in my career? Most of my ex-authors who might have wanted to follow me to my new position were tied into their contracts and could not follow. Many of my old colleagues were forbidden or refused to talk to me. Our social friends either dropped me willingly or were frightened of Mr. Husband's wrath. A smear campaign against me seemed to be everywhere. I was demanding millions of dollars of alimony or invading the children's special trust funds. I would hear of the parties I wasn't invited to. I found myself reading about the weddings of couples who had been my traveling companions for a decade. Good friends looked away. It was war.

But there was some good news. The equitable distribution laws of New York State had taken hold, and women were beginning to avail themselves of their new rights. In the not-so-distant past, God forbid a woman committed adultery: she could lose everything, since husbands who committed adultery had no financial penalties. But under equitable distribution, the divorcing couple were viewed as equal partners. Now divorce lawyers were interested in representing the wife who, in previous decades, was usually left with three teenage daughters and little to no money. (Alimony maybe—but generally not enough to cover house payments. So the woman in question usually ended up selling the house, while her husband continued to earn more and more and lived happily ever after with his new "trophy" wife.) I found the best lawyer in the business, Robert Stephan Cohen—and miraculously, he took my case.

My mother and my sister became my army. They came with me to court. They stayed up all night poring over depositions and transcripts. They loaned me practically all their money when mine ran out. They took my calls in the middle of the night when I couldn't sleep. They went out and bought me clothes when the demands of my new job gave me no time to do anything else. They told me over and over that it didn't matter about the press, about the job, about the money. It mattered that I was free, and that justice be done. My lawyer and his team were the best in the world. They became my extended family. I would win. Hold on.

Now I know I told you I was married for ten years. What I haven't told you was that I was divorcing for the next seven. *Seven!* Five years in battle, and then two more for two appeals—the last an attempt to be tried by the highest court in the state. It was among the longest, most bitter divorces in the State of New York, and it received a substantial amount of press. Two or three times the judge tried to broker an out-of-court settlement. But Mr. Husband had made it clear that he was giving me nothing. Discovery (the process of finding out what his assets were) took more than two years since he refused to cooperate and would not turn over his true net worth. Not only was divorce court a terrifying experience, but it was expensive. I was served with papers on my way to work in front of colleagues. Mr. Husband hit me with motions and subpoenas on a weekly basis. About taxes. About phone bills from three years before.

Court. What I remember most was how dirty and cold the courtrooms were. The bathrooms were icy. There were almost no benches in the hallways, so people waiting to be called had to pace up and down the dingy corridors. Reporters could show up and take notes, and you didn't know if they were for you or against you.

Mr. Husband would arrive, smirking, with his battery of lawyers—sometimes four at a time—all carrying briefcases the size of steamer trunks. He had a battery of expert witnesses and a collection of ever more high-powered people from our industry. Colleagues would appear to testify as to my competence, incompetence, exorbitant salary, or underpaid compensation. It was a dizzying, humiliating experience.

When Mr. Husband claimed I didn't know how to cook, old thumbed cookbooks were produced as counterevidence. When Mr. Husband claimed all I did was work, passports with stamps proving exotic holidays were produced. When Mr. Husband claimed I stopped having sex with him a year before, there was no rebuttal. Ugh. The press wrote down every juicy detail.

Almost seven years after our divorce proceedings had begun, I was sitting at the airport in Pittsburgh, where I had been on business. While I was waiting for my flight, I could have sworn I heard the name "Joni Evans" broadcast over the loudspeaker. Now, I had never been paged in an airport before, much less anywhere else. But the name was mine. I heard it over and over, and my heart started to pound. Surely something terrible had happened. My mother, near eighty, could have had a stroke. My sister could have been in an accident. I ran for the phone.

I can still remember the light in the room where I took that call: flickering, fluorescent, as if to say, "Pay attention. Pay attention." I was alone. I couldn't recognize the voice on the other end of the line at first, though I knew it was familiar. Someone I liked. Someone who knew me.

"Joni. You won."

What?

"The judge just ruled. You won the divorce. You are entitled to half of his money, half of his stock options, half of everything he has. And you are to receive all of it within thirty days." The number, the now-recognizable voice of my beloved divorce lawyer assured me, would exceed my costs twice over.

———

I sat down in the Pittsburgh airport and missed my plane. I sat there, taking deep breaths and feeling my heart beat out of my chest. I had won. It was a victory. Mr. Husband was wrong. He was wrong about equitable distribution, and just about everything else. Justice had come.

At fifty years of age, I had started all over. I had bought new television sets, had made an entire new set of friends, and had not slept through the night for months. I had endured reading articles carrying lies about me too personal and embarrassing to digest. I had called my sainted mother at four in the morning in terror; my sister and brother-in-law had talked me down every month or two. I visited a psychiatrist for the first time. (As it turned out, she was too afraid to keep me as a patient and asked me to leave because, since my husband was her publisher, she didn't want her book to be endangered.) *I had won.*

It was delicious. It was spectacular. But the sweetest news of all was knowing that all those times my husband had said I owed everything to him—that I was no one without him—was bull. I had waged this war. I had won this war. I had finally succeeded on my own, and no one ever again was going to make me doubt myself. And no one ever has.

The Wages of Love

Lucy Kaylin

I met Kimball during the go-go eighties, a time of gaudy ego and reckless consumption, of stockbroker as rock star. In New York City, how common it was to see bands of those raucous, self-satisfied money men in their striped power ties pouring out of bars after yet another world-beating bell-ringer of a day downtown.

Occasionally, I got caught up in it—we all did—dancing with boys in suits at cavernous fantasia clubs, choking down martinis. But at heart, none of that was really me. The daughter of arty-farty, self-deprecating lefties, I knew I was little more than a tourist of the decade.

Kimball, whom I'd repeatedly glimpsed on campus during graduate school and finally met years later at a book party, was much more my type. Apart from his good looks (lean, with coat hanger shoulders, a fetchingly craggy face, eyebrows that looked like they'd been woven from horsehair), he had deep knowledge about esoteric things like bookbinding, marine fossils, and Beat poetry; for our first date, he took me to see the Gutenberg Bible at the Morgan Library. He wore cool thrift-store suit jackets over sweaters with zippers; down the road, he calligraphed me love notes on handmade paper. Unlike the overstuffed, red-faced financial dudes who wore their ambitions so garishly, Kimball had mystique.

What he didn't have, however, was bank. Armed with that license to print money, a master's degree in library science, he worked as a rare book expert at one of the big auction houses. I loved and admired him for the expertise, the connoisseurship it took to do that job—for the sheer righteousness of turning his obsession with books into a career. But, as the eighties became the nineties and the tech stock boom threatened to turn everyone around us into millionaires, Kimball's defiantly boho worldview was, for me, losing some of its allure. While friends were buying condos, we were pooling our change for the $12 Mexican entrée.

Problem was, I loved him. I loved his quiet obsessions, his chic reserve, his utter devotion to me. Amid the breast-beating vulgarians chasing a buck, I prized his singular uncheesiness and his appetite for quirk, however unremunerative. I loved the way he hunched over his loopy little art projects, making woodcuts and collages and inscrutable tableaux from bits of foil and newsprint—the way he'd dip his pen nib in an inkwell and scratch out a couplet. For my birthday one especially penniless year, he painted phrases on T-shirts, one of which read "I love your chestnut eyes"—stacking the last four words in such a way that they spelled my first name vertically.

And yet . . . I wasn't so unaffected—so uninfected—by the times that I didn't crave some piece of the pretty good life. I'd grown crass enough to want to live like an adult someday, with chairs and couches I hadn't hauled in from the sidewalk; I hoped to graduate, eventually, from a futon to a bed. Working long hours as an assistant at a magazine, treating my apartment like a walk-in closet, eating popcorn for dinner (topped with grated parmesan if I was feeling flush)—I indulged in the archaic, sexist fantasy of a guy swooping in one day and taking me away from all that.

But was Kimball, with whom I'd been involved at this point for a couple of years, the guy to do it? The son of a self-made father of four who compulsively switched off lights around the house and ground out a living by repossessing the TVs, couches, and cars of folks who couldn't pay their bills, Kimball had no stomach for hardball—no appetite for the aggressive pursuit of a buck. Instead, he rid himself of the dirty stuff the moment he got his hands on some, compulsively picking up the bar tab when out with friends—even second- and third-tier friends—never mind that the tab might constitute a full quarter of his salary. Kimball was the sort of guy who'd sooner gouge out his own eyeballs with a fork than publicly split a check and figure out the tax. And he found the unseemly settling up one is expected to do each month with utility and credit card companies to be such an unremitting buzz-kill that he tended those relationships haphazardly.

Of course, I brought fiscal baggage of my own to the relationship, having grown up modestly in a quaint little town in Connecticut. My father was that very cool thing, a writer—originally of pulp fiction and later of the would-be great American novel. Sadly, a publishing contract for the latter never materialized; my father literally went decades without making a nickel. To be fair, this turn in his career took place after my sister and I had already left for college, so it's not as if we suffered (my father had a day job at a publishing company while we were growing up; my mother was a social worker). But the concomitant deferral of dreams would become a source of constant, low-grade stress in the family. Although I revered him totally and grew up valuing the unmercenary, cultured pursuit, I also feared it; I knew how that kind of rarefied idealism could betray you. For better or worse, so much hinges on one's ability to earn—especially if one is a man. When it came to Kimball, I wasn't eager to take on the disappointments, limitations, and, yes, failings of yet another purist.

As such, over the course of the next few years, our relationship was dizzyingly on and off. During breakups that typically lasted a month or two, I'd set about dating a woolly array of seemingly more marriageable guys—the suit-wearing VPs and financial analysts who crowed about their investments over dinner and thwapped down the plastic as nonchalantly as if shooing a fly. Some actually owned cars— can you imagine? Virtually all wore clothes they'd bought new—pinstripes and cotton that reeked equally of dry-cleaning chemicals and prosperity.

But try as I might, I couldn't break free of Kimball, as circumstances repeatedly threw us into each other's path. One night I was at a restaurant on a date with someone else when he walked in, alone. And I was so pole-axed by the sight of him that the date banter quickly dwindled to monosyllables. Soon after, Kimball and I actually left together, with the bemused blessing of the guy I'd come in with. Even he could see we were meant to be together.

About six years into our checkered relationship, Kimball conquered his fear of convention and institutions long enough to actually propose marriage to me. The reception, I like to think, was quintessential us—spirited and classy in spite of itself, thanks to things money can't buy, like a sky full of stars and fireflies lighting a dance floor ringed by ancient hemlocks. In that carefree, generous, soul-expanding idyll, who could have known we were about to embark on the year of living stingily—in every sense?

It was my doing. Yes, I'd surrendered to my love for this man, but that didn't mean I couldn't reform him, couldn't fix him. So desperate was I to protect us—me—from the sort of financial lassitude I'd feared would be our undoing, I chased down every penny that came and went from our home. With the stealth of someone who thinks she's being cheated on, I snuck peeks at Kimball's bank and credit card statements and grilled him about them later. *Did you pay it? How much? When does the late fee kick in? Have you communicated with your creditors? Call the good folks at Amex and tell them what's up.* When a limited edition print or a book with a hand-tooled binding showed up—not some midlife crisis-y electronics or a Bugatti, mind you—I questioned Kimball on how much it cost. *Can we afford this?* Having thrown my lot in with his, I made it my mission to put his financial affairs in order and transform him into a fit life partner.

Our first wedding anniversary arrived in June. We celebrated with an uncharacteristically pricey dinner downtown at an haute celeb-haunt. Feeling giddy about the more or less good year we'd had, I raised my glass of champagne to him, expressed my love, and proposed a bit of a parlor game: let's each say what our big hopes and desires are for our marriage in the year to come.

Me first: head cocked, starry-eyed, yet somehow still . . . *corrective* in tone, I suggested something about communicating more fully and anticipating each other's needs. We clinked glasses and took a sip on that, amid the posh clatter of A-listers nibbling miso cod.

Then came Kimball's turn.

He squared his shoulders and looked right at me—not his style, really. "My hope for this year is that you will get off my back about money," he said, lowering the champagne glass—his blue eyes turning stormy. "My hope is that you will stop hounding me about my credit cards and what I spend. Because if you don't, we're not going to make it. I'm serious about this."

Kimball leaned back in his chair, without breaking eye contact. "I'm thirty-nine years old; I've been taking care of myself for a long time. And maybe I'm not perfect with money, but I'm not irresponsible. I've always had a roof over my head and everything I've needed. I'm fine. And you can love me or not—that's your choice. But you have to stop trying to change me, because it's not going to work."

It was a classic come-to-Jesus moment—the most dire of my life. I hadn't had them often, accustomed as I was to spackling over tensions with chitchat and rhetoric; there is very little I cannot rationalize, and it simply isn't like me to be rendered speechless. But tonight was different. I felt the space between us growing, as if the table itself were pushing us apart; I saw Kimball hardening—saw the hairline cracks in his typically loving facade. I saw the damage I had done. Although he is not the type to issue threats, the message was clear. I saw in that moment that I stood to lose everything.

"Okay," I said—nothing more. We clinked glasses.

In the dozen years since, amazing things have happened. Once it sunk in that acceptance, trust, and faith are the real mortar of a marriage, I eased up considerably on the nudging and the judging—even rolling with the occasional overdraft notice, the sort of thing that used to send me into a white-hot, hand-wringing, garment-rending freak-out. For his part, Kimball actually developed an interest in finance. Not only did he start making decent money as an art adviser and appraiser, having parlayed his bone-deep passion into a wildly marketable skill, but he even began gravitating to the stock pages and making appointments with be-suited investment advisers with names like Mike. Unbelievably, Kimball is now in charge of our financial affairs—he's our liaison with the tax guy, our point person on estate matters—and doing a darn good job of it. We're fine. We own a three-bedroom co-op in Manhattan, for god's sake. The wolves simply aren't at the door.

Did he take all of this on for me? Maybe, in part—I can be a pest, but never a monster, and I know he wanted things between us to work out. But we also had a baby on the way, and it's amazing how the mere idea of that can transform a person.

Most important, with me off his back, Kimball could grow and change on his own, as opposed to being clipped and pruned and tortured into some unnatural shape. I shouldn't have been so surprised that this was all it would take; some years earlier, after much haranguing and cajoling on my part to get him to give up cigarettes, he quit cold turkey—while out of town for a few weeks on business, alone and away from me.

Not that he'll be donning tweed and nestling into a club chair anytime soon. I count on Kimball, now the fit and happy father of two, for his defiantly offbeat take on what it means to be the man of the house—whether he's papier-mâché-ing cereal boxes in the kitchen with the kids, reading them some elliptical, transcendental verse by way of a bedtime story, or defending my son's right not to get a haircut. Kimball is a great provider in the deepest sense of the word. As for the lesson in real love he taught me, I'll always be in his debt.

Tool Belts, Not Tuxes

Abby Ellin

Time: seven o'clock on a Tuesday evening. Place: a windowed room in the NASDAQ building, high above Times Square. I am there to celebrate the one-year anniversary of *Fast Money*, a manly man gabfest on CNBC. The party is overflowing with testosterone: wagonloads of über-mensches with fancy watches and sparkling teeth. I make small talk with some of them, but frankly, the conversation is not that compelling. Oh, they're perfectly nice, good-looking, and accomplished. But they just don't charge my batteries.

After an hour I leave. And then—wouldn't you know it—one of the sexiest guys in the place is waiting for the elevator. He's wearing a white dress shirt, a black bow tie, and black slacks, but also sports an earring and a goatee. He's awfully cute for a trader dude—edgy and out there—and I'm pleased. I usually don't go for these business types. But maybe, finally, the curse is broken.

We smile at each other shyly, and I wonder if we'll head into the night, if we'll share a cab and glass of chardonnay. But, as it turns out, he's not really leaving. He's going downstairs to get more hors d'oeuvres. The cute guy, alas, works in catering.

And there you have it: my romantic quandary in a nutshell. Why do I always fall for the help, while my friends are unanimously drawn to white-collar types? It's always been this way: I like men who aren't flashy. Men who work with their hands. Men who prefer pickups to Porsches. There I'll be, attending a hoity-toity event filled with powerful, wildly attractive, potential mates—and invariably I'll gravitate toward the guy pouring drinks and schlepping dishes.

This was not how it was supposed to be. I was brought up like most nice Jewish girls: Hebrew school, shopping malls, summer camp, higher ed. Three things were a given: that I would marry; that I would marry within the tribe; and that my future spouse would be educated, erudite, and articulate—a genial combination of doctor/lawyer/rabbi/saint.

This seemed like a smart idea, except for one minor snag: I never went for men like this. We just didn't speak the same language. Instead, I ended up with suffering artists in paint-splattered jeans, musicians with crazy hair, construction guys wielding ratchets and wrenches. I expected, and still expect, my romantic partners to be handy; it's primal to me, a sign of virility and masculinity.

Part of this, I know, stems from my own rebellious nature. I like people who lead alternative existences, as I have myself. In the seventeen years that have transpired since graduate school, I've had only three office jobs; the longest lasted eight months. Though I knew fairly early on that I wanted to be a writer, I never took a steady gig at a newspaper or magazine. Instead, I chose to be freelance—the operative word being "free"—because I found the idea of someone else dictating what time I had to be at work or when I could take my vacation appalling. *You're not the boss of me!*

This is not to say I haven't worked hard; I am always on call. That's how it is when you work for yourself: you never know when the inkwell might dry up, so you never turn down assignments. But I don't mind: I sleep as late as I want and travel when I feel like it. In other words, I live life on my own terms.

The only problem with this lifestyle is that "freedom" is generally just another word for "nothing left to deposit." Happily, I've managed to sock away some cash—I'm the proud possessor of mutual funds in a Roth IRA—but freewheeling hippies like me tend to live paycheck to paycheck. So unless I hit the jackpot and write a runaway bestseller— or develop a sudden interest in becoming a hedge fund manager—I know I'm never going to be rich. But loving what I do has always been infinitely more compelling to me than making millions. Who wants a job just to make a buck?

And okay, there's this: I've always been taken care of. My family never had great wealth, but my parents managed to send me to camp and college and graduate school—an extraordinary gift for which I'm eternally grateful. And they even bought me my apartment. (I'm slowly paying them back; I expect to make good on my debt sometime in 2089.)

With this kind of financial support, I've always been armed with the courage to be adventurous. When I was nineteen, for example, I did a semester at the University of Tel Aviv. I was supposed to return home after six months, but as soon as I saw the silver wings of El Al glittering in the sunlight, I knew I wouldn't be coming back anytime soon. Instead, I headed south to Eilat, got a job as a hotel waitress, and almost immediately moved into a tent on the beach with a French Canadian named François. I loved "roughing" it. But let's face it: my gleaming green Amex was right there in case of emergency. Not that my parents were sponsoring this little sabbatical—part of the deal was that I had to fund myself—but they obviously wouldn't have let me starve. I never used the card, but I always knew it was there, my friendly plastic safety net. A pauper I wasn't.

And so this leads to a mortifying admission—especially for a feminist who was taught that every woman should possess both her own bank account and the ability to be self-sufficient. On some level, I always believed that eventually someone else would take care of the big stuff. That someone, of course, would be my husband. But here's the rub: what kind of men usually have big fat wallets? Those with white-collar jobs.

You see my dilemma.

One of the more interesting gigs I've had in my publishing career is a column I wrote for the *New York Times*. For five years I covered young people and money, and over the course of my reporting I spoke to hundreds of women. What I learned did not surprise me, although it saddened me: apparently I'm not the only otherwise liberated woman who—*shhhhh!*—expects a man to take care of her. The consistency was staggering: radical or independent, self-sufficient or wildly successful, most of the women I interviewed hoped, ultimately, to be swept off their feet financially. This attitude, I found, resulted from a common upbringing with two opposing messages: women can and should have it all professionally, but we can also opt to find a man who will relieve us of the "burden" of providing for ourselves. (Cinderella, that golden hausfrau, just won't go away.)

Part of this sense of entitlement stems from female hubris. Women *do* want it all—or in any case, we want options: namely, to work, or not work, as we see fit. I remember a 2005 *New York Times* article that focused on a group of Yale University women. Out of 138 female students, 83 were planning to cut back or stop working as soon as they had kids. The piece was controversial—many readers questioned the newspaper's reporting—but the larger point was clear: some of the country's most highly educated women were planning to stay home and let their husbands support them while they raised their children.

I didn't find the story especially shocking, since it echoed the attitudes of most of the women I've spoken to—even those without kids. Take a friend of mine, who just sold her company for millions of dollars. She's earned far more money than her husband, a journalist, ever will. But she still wants to be taken care of—or at least, she wants the illusion of it. When she and her husband had less, she told me, they would split household costs evenly. But soon after the sale went through, she devised a plan: she would replenish their joint coffer once a month, but her husband would pay the bills with that money.

That would include dinners out, rent, food—everything. Why? "It makes me feel like he's in charge," she told me.

"Why is it important for him to be in charge?" I asked.

"He's the guy," she said simply.

I'm not sure how I went from future Mrs. Doctor/Lawyer, etc., to future Mrs. Artist/Carpenter. It certainly wasn't my destiny: I grew up in Brookline, Massachusetts, a Boston suburb noted for its well-heeled, well-educated residents. My folks have been married, happily and unhappily, for more than forty years. They met at a Catskills resort, which was sponsoring a Jewish singles week; legend has it that my father was watching my mother, a babe, reject all sorts of suitors. He finally summoned the nerve to ask her to dance, and three months—three months!—later they eloped. Maybe that's the best way to do it—just plug your nose and jump, without so much as dipping a toe in. After all, if we knew what we were in for, would anyone ever have the courage to be in a relationship?

My parents were radically different. My mother's a native New Yorker who loves classical music, modern art, and roaming around Manhattan. Her parents separated when she was fourteen; my grandmother worked full-time and brought up two kids on a teacher's salary. She survived, but my mother saw how miserable life could be for single women (my grandmother never remarried). So she made it her mission to find a man unlike her father, a man who would "take care" of her. That's what she wanted: to be taken care of.

My father grew up on a farm in Connecticut. Like many immigrants, his parents, who were born in Russia and Germany, did what they had to do to survive: they were educated, but led a relatively simple life. My grandfather built picnic tables and raised chickens and sold eggs. Occasionally, my father and uncle held dances in the coops. This all sounded very romantic: I liked the idea of the family moving here from the old country, crossing the great frontier into the

Diaspora. They pulled themselves up by their bootstraps, and by golly, they survived: *Little Jews on the Prairie*.

After college my father moved to the big city—Boston—and landed an engineering job at Polaroid. And though he was highly intelligent—he has a master's degree in electrical engineering—I think of him as a physical guy, as opposed to an intellectual. At seventy, he still plays tennis and softball; the happiest day of his life was when he scored a hole-in-one in golf. Throughout my childhood, he was always fiddling with something: painting the roof, tinkering under the hood of the car, futzing around in the basement. Anytime I needed something fixed—a broken toy, a game in need of rewiring—my father came to the rescue. That, I learned, was what men did: they fixed stuff.

They also made stuff. My father, along with my grandfather, built us a summer house in New Hampshire. It took years to complete; for about six summers we lived in casual disarray. But that too seemed normal. I thought everyone lived amid Sheetrock and insulation: tool belts, not tuxes.

The fact that I want a man who will support me is disconcerting for many reasons—especially since my role models have always been very strong, independent women. My mother taught piano, trekked from flea market to flea market selling T-shirts, and, in later years, snatched up a bunch of real estate in Boston. This is to say that she kicked in mightily to maintain the family's budget. When I wanted money, I went to her, not my father. When I needed clothes, she bought them. It was she who footed the bill for my apartment, using an inheritance left to her by my grandmother. She wanted me to have assets of my own. "Girls must have their own resources," she always said, and meant it.

Nevertheless, at the end of the day, my mother relied on my father's income. A lot goes on in forty years of marriage, and I'm sure there were times she wanted to check out. But her departure was thwarted by the very real fact that she didn't know how she would raise three kids on her own. She had seen how difficult being alone was for her own mother, and she didn't want to replicate that circumstance. She needed my father's salary to give her kids—and herself—the life she wanted.

With this kind of history, it's hard to imagine that my mother would want me to depend on a man for financial sustenance. But when I announced a few years back that my new boyfriend was a furniture maker living in the mountains of North Carolina, she was silent. "You really don't like bankers or lawyers or doctors, do you?" she said at last.

I felt like I'd been smacked in the face. I'd finally found someone to love, and this was her response? But her message was clear: why are you going out with a guy who can't take care of you?

In the lore of pop psychology, most women end up falling in love with their fathers—except, of course, for those who go out of their way not to. I seem to want to have it both ways: a partner who is exactly like, and nothing like, my dad. The thought of dating someone strictly for the size of his wallet horrifies me; I'm much more interested in Love! Passion! Meaningful Connection! My three most significant relationships, in fact, were with a carpenter, a lighting designer, and the furniture maker. They were good men—trustworthy, disciplined, dependable. Each one came from a blue-collar family and, for the most part, was able to exceed his professional goals. I had enormous respect for all of them.

At the time I never thought money had much to do with the demise of these relationships. But now I'm not so sure. In retrospect, I think it was troubling to be dating someone who might not be able to take care of me for the long haul. My needs are not terribly elaborate—I'd like someone to help me raise my future offspring, maybe take an extended vacation twice a year. But today, only one of my three exes earns more than his wife does. Therefore, to live the way I would want to with any of them, I'd have to bring home a much larger salary than I do now.

You do the math.

So here I am, forty years old and on my own. Obviously, it would be nice if that condition were not permanent, but one never knows. Here's what I do know: I will always have my own bank account. I will always make my own money. My sense of self depends on having a career, so I don't plan on abandoning work, ever. I hope my words will be lucrative one day: I am constantly dreaming up ways to strike it rich as a writer. (I have also been known to buy Lotto tickets—you can never be too safe.)

For the most part, I'm okay with being single. The upside is that anything's possible: my destiny is not yet settled. There's something very exciting about that—that is, when the uncertainty is not painful and maddening. I'd be lying if I didn't admit to occasional sweaty, stomach-churning panic attacks about my future: poor Aunt Abby, the really hip bag lady who wafts from relative to relative, relying on the kindness of family.

I realize, of course, that the struggle between Establishment Rich Guy and Joe Handy resides within me. *I'm* the one stuck in a liminal state between Upstairs and Downstairs. I am still trying to reconcile the bohemian, bra-avoiding hippie chick with the privileged New York Semite who really digs five-star hotels and sixth-row orchestra seats. I love the *idea* of the crazy nomadic painter/musician/carpenter. But maybe—and it kills me to admit this—I'd be happier with the nice Jewish banker. Clearly, the best solution is to find someone I adore, whatever his financial background—and the rest will fall into place.

But no matter who I end up with, what remains is this: I'm just one more Cinderella, hoping for my own happy ending. In my fairy tale, Prince Charming will suddenly appear, his tool belt tucked beneath his Paul Smith suit. He'll beckon to me with a slow grin, and the two of us will ride off into the sunset on his wooden horse, a cloud of sawdust and dollar bills fluttering in our wake.

The Cost of Living

Marnie Hanel

We met at a birthday party the year I lived in London. I was twenty-two. The birthday girl was twenty-seven. And it didn't occur to me that Greg was older than twenty-eight. I noticed that he was handsome, in the strong-jawed way that men are but boys aren't. I noticed that he focused on me, and only me, in the way that men do but boys don't. And I noticed that he didn't try anything—he didn't touch my leg or reach for my hand. He just asked for my phone number and left. I *should* have noticed that his name was Greg. Few guys born after 1970 are named Greg.

On our first date Greg asked me, "What's your earliest memory of a current event?" I told him: the *Challenger* disaster. Greg recalled that the *Challenger* exploded in 1986; it was the year he graduated from high school. (It was the year I started kindergarten.) His earliest memory was of the hostage crisis at the Munich Olympics.

I was only vaguely aware of this event. It happened in 1972. At the time, I was an egg.

Greg paid the bill confidently, without so much as that pause that says, *I'm paying the bill now*. That impressed me. I was just out of college, where once a guy had ordered a bottle of wine at dinner. Not a glass, a *bottle*. I thought it was very sophisticated, almost European, and this reminded me of that.

Greg offered to hail me a cab, but I told him I preferred—and by "preferred" I meant "could afford"—the tube. As we walked to the South Kensington station, I put my arm in his. He told me I was confident, and I thought: *Is there another way to walk with a man?* I kissed him good night, and he smiled, like he'd won something.

I was working then as a legal assistant for an American lawyer who had started his own practice. Business was slow. He had two employees: an associate and me. Ostensibly I was hired to do legal research, but actually I was there to protect his ego. When the phone rang—maybe five times a day, usually his wife—I answered it. I filed papers. I made piles. I straightened them. I actively hated him.

In the grand tradition of entry-level salaries in London, he didn't pay me much. On my meager earnings, I couldn't afford to buy lunch every day, but I also couldn't make it through the week without leaving the office. I became an expert in eating cheaply. I frequented cafés where egg and cress sandwiches and jacket potatoes cost two quid. I ordered everything "take-away" to avoid the surcharge for eating in. In the leanest times, when I'd splurged on L.K. Bennett pumps or a Thomas Pink shirt, I'd pick up an 80-pence pan au chocolat from Marks & Spencer and walk across Green Park to eat it at Buckingham Palace. I told myself I was Holly Golightly, without the powder room money. It's hard to feel poor when you're eating French pastries.

I spent most of my time with a set of ex-pats—bankers and lawyers whose company I couldn't afford to keep. We went to the same clubs that the young royals favored, where there was bottle service and the cocktails cost £15 (coincidentally, just under my weekly lunch budget). Chipping in for the cab to get to these places made my wallet wheeze, but I feigned the nonchalance of my companions.

Most of my friends received an income from their parents. In some cases, this was coyly called a "housing allowance." In others, it was a credit card with a magical bill that never appeared. Personally, I would have rather lived in the West London convent that doubled as a dormitory than ask my parents for money. (And my Maida Vale flat was hardly a convent.) Although I knew that they would be happy to support me, it was a point of pride to earn my own keep. I'd just graduated from college and wanted to prove that I was an independent girl who could move to London, find a job, and make her own way. I had enough money, but I just didn't know how to manage it. Or more accurately, I knew how to manage it, but I didn't want to make the sacrifices necessary to manage it well. I was financially bulimic, binging in the evenings and purging during the day. Penny-wise, pound-foolish. How English.

Although it was hard for me to admit, there was no denying that Greg's company boosted my finances. That knowledge made me uncomfortable. On our second date, I reached for the check. Greg stopped me. I couldn't afford the places he wanted to go, he said, so I had two options: I could either always let him pay and never bring it up again, or I could date someone else.

I continued dating Greg.

I dated Greg on Valentine's Day, when he wore a tie to dinner. I dated Greg at the movies where—grand gesture!—I arrived early and bought the tickets (the equivalent of $44 for two.) I dated Greg when I went to Dow Jones to take the entrance exam for Columbia's journalism school. I called him afterward, rattled, and he suggested I hop in a cab and meet him across London; he would pay the driver. I got in the cab, but I paid the driver.

I fell in love with Greg when he had the chicken pox. He looked so sick, so alone, that all I wanted to do was take care of him. For ten days, I moved into his living room and cooked him breakfast, lunch, and dinner. I planned meals at my desk and shopped for groceries after work. I wore his college sweater and bought him oatmeal for the bathtub. I went to the drugstore and told the pharmacist that *my boyfriend Greg* had the chicken pox. I liked the way that sounded. I liked caring for him. I liked that he needed me. I liked him.

Greg gave me £200 for food and supplies, and I kept the receipts in an envelope on the coffee table. When Greg saw I was saving them, he was appalled. "Do you think I don't trust you?" he asked. "Of course not!" I replied. What I didn't tell him was that I wasn't sure I trusted myself. Each day it was a struggle not to filch £2 coins out of his change bowl for lunch. When I watched Greg count those same coins for his cleaning lady, I realized she made more each hour than I did. I didn't offer to clean his apartment, but the thought crossed my mind.

Greg and I joked that I was the CEO of our relationship and he was the CFO. I was the social chair; he was the treasurer. I booked restaurants, hotels, flights; he paid. We traveled to Malta, went skiing in Switzerland, toured the Chelsea Flower Show, and ate a peculiar fish soup at the Michelin restaurant. My friends were impressed. They constantly enumerated the places he took me, and speculated about the amount he spent. I didn't. I couldn't help but notice that Greg spent only when he was there to enjoy the results, and I knew his lifestyle wouldn't have changed whether or not I was there. As he put it, "It may be twice as expensive to have you here, but I have eighty percent more fun. You have to think about the marginal cost." My friends told me he was handsome, even dreamy. They reminded me that JFK and Jackie had a twelve-year age difference as well.

His friends thought I was young.

And then I got into graduate school. The day I found out, I was so excited I was actually shaking. I'd wanted to attend Columbia ever since I visited my sister at Barnard and saw the campus. I wanted to meet friends on the steps and study in the domed library; I didn't know it was an administrative building. Greg insisted we celebrate. He told me he'd leave the office—just as soon as the markets closed.

School started in August and my lease was up in May, but I wasn't ready to leave London and I wasn't ready to leave Greg. Greg was never embarrassed, never unsure. He made quick, clear decisions that he never regretted. He always trusted his instincts, and never looked back. I hoped that these qualities would rub off on me, and I believed the more time I spent with him, the more they would. So, in June, I sublet a room in Bayswater. I walked through my neighborhood of youth hostels and kebab joints, and Greg walked through his neighborhood of luxury department stores and historical sites, and we met in the middle of Hyde Park. We ate gelato. We held hands. It was much better than the Michelin restaurant.

G reg came to town for a business trip three days after I moved to New York. Whereas a reasonable person might wait until her boyfriend arrived to assemble her IKEA furniture, I didn't. I suspected Greg wouldn't want to put together the pieces. When faced with a similar task in the past—helping me pack and clean my apartment before moving into the sublet—Greg suggested we hire someone else to do it. He had more money than time; I had more time than money. I ended up packing and cleaning alone.

Instead, I spent seventy-two hours with an in-every-way-inadequate IKEA wrench in my fist. I propped would-be furniture against the wall, a poor substitute for his hands. Many pieces of pressed wood came crashing down that weekend. The downstairs neighbors hated me and broomsticked the ceiling. I thought that was *very New York*. I pressed on, and succeeded. I assembled the furniture and unpacked all the boxes before Greg arrived. It looked fantastic.

That week Greg took me to a few classic New York restaurants: the Rainbow Room and the like. Everyone in these restaurants was old, very old. But I figured that was a function of the city, not where we went in it. We ate at a steakhouse with dark walls and an oak bar. (I didn't know it was the last time I'd eat steak until Christmas.) I walked through Central Park, holding Greg's hand, in a series of carefully chosen sundresses. Every place we went was almost cinematically romantic. But the destination I was most excited about visiting was my apartment. Greg's hotel was far away from my tiny place near Columbia, but I convinced him it was worth the trouble. It was my first home in New York and—squealing shower and probable rodent problem be damned—I was going to show it off.

When we arrived, something had changed. It had only been a couple days since I'd seen the apartment, but it wasn't at all how I remembered it. With Greg by my side, all of it—the chest of drawers, the neighborhood—looked a little wobblier than when I'd seen it alone. Greg evaluated the place and very quietly asked me to move a little farther downtown, or perhaps to the Upper East Side. I laughed, but I was embarrassed. This was the best I could afford. I was proud of myself for finding it. I told him it was a good location, across from the law school housing. He told me I'd get robbed here. I laughed harder.

I shouldn't have. Two weeks later, I got mugged.

I wanted to quit school and fly home to my family, but I didn't. Instead, I stayed in that apartment and threw myself into graduate school. I ate $5 udon and $2 black-and-white cookies. I found a coffee shop with free refills and no apparent policy against loitering. I worked hard. I took Greg's calls in empty classrooms and listened to his stories about his trips to Barcelona and nights out with clients. I tried to get him to read my articles. Rarely, he did. Then I stopped sending them. He never seemed to understand the point I was trying to make. He'd follow the facts, but not the ideas behind them. The purpose of writing in the first person eluded him. In truth, the value of pursuing a career with limited earning potential eluded him.

Greg was fond of saying that he would match his niece's and nephew's salaries and build them each a trust fund. When I pointed out that they might have very different trust funds if Suzy was a teacher and Johnny was a banker, he said that it was their choice to pursue more or less lucrative careers. "They have to learn the consequences of their actions," he said. I told him I'd heard that line before, but I was two years old and I'd bitten someone. One shouldn't be punished for helping others, I argued. Greg didn't see it that way.

That year, on a flight, he'd finished his issue of *The Economist* and, at my suggestion, swapped it with my copy of *The New Yorker*. I opened it to an Ian Frazier article that I thought he might enjoy, which is to say, I'd enjoyed. After reading for five minutes, he turned to me and said, "Why is this article so long? I could write this in half the space! What is *the point*?" It was then that I realized he might never get *the point* of my ambition, my writing, my career. He might never understand *the point* of me. We were unraveling.

I visited him in London for fall break, a glamorous move for a grad student. Greg bought my ticket, but when I arrived I couldn't afford to do anything. I took reading to a coffee shop and sat for hours. I walked through Harrods and Fortnum & Mason and touched the pretty things. I took long walks in my favorite neighborhoods. I bought a Cadbury's bar for lunch. It was poverty, but an elegant poverty.

When I returned to school, my friends went on and on about how generous my boyfriend was. This rankled. It's easy enough to give money if you have it. Greg had so much money that buying a plane ticket was nothing more than thirty seconds of typing. It's much harder to give affection. It would have meant a lot to me if Greg had cleaned his apartment, laid out fresh towels, and bought a box of cereal so I'd have a smooth transition after my red-eye flight. But he didn't. When I asked why not, he explained that I arrived on Wednesday, but the cleaning lady didn't come until Thursday.

Greg visited me in New York too. He took my grad school friends to brunch at Sarabeth's, encouraged them to order mimosas, and picked up the bill. He watched the toy boats with me in Central Park. He took me on a train to visit his brother's family. When we arrived in his brother's neighborhood, where one home was more palatial than the next, he asked me to point to the house I wanted. He told me I could have it. He asked me if I thought I could handle furnishing it, or if I wanted to hire a decorator, and how much did I think that would cost? I didn't have the heart to tell him that I had no idea and that I'd recently resisted purchasing a mildew-resistant shower curtain because it was $11.

My double life continued, but there were cracks in it. Financially, Greg and I were both where we were supposed to be. But he was twelve years older, and that made it impossible to keep up. At Christmas, I scrimped for weeks so I could buy him a gift that I knew he wanted: monogrammed poker chips. I researched them extensively, so much so that it became a school joke that I was opening a casino. It was a stretch to pay for the best poker chips, but I wanted Greg to have the right gift. I splurged. I was willing to cut corners in other ways if it meant Greg would be overjoyed on Christmas.

When he opened his gift, Greg told me he liked the chips. "You listen!" he said. Then he asked how he could order more. I started crying. He didn't understand why I was upset. When he said, "I want more poker chips," that was all he meant. But, for me, it meant, *Even when you give me everything you have, it's not enough. You are not enough for me.*

Later that week the argument lingered. When he told me he wasn't going to rent a convertible for our New Year's vacation in Hawaii because it was an extra $15 each day, I balked. I hadn't wanted to leave my family during the holidays and I didn't have time to plan a trip during finals, but Greg wanted to take a vacation so I'd built it up. I'd talked up the adventures we'd have driving in our convertible and the places we'd see. Now, Greg said, I was being frivolous. I insisted there was more at stake. I'd just spent a month refusing invitations to dinner, movies, or anything that required spending money in order to give Greg what he wanted for Christmas. Now he wouldn't spend $60 to give me the only thing I actually wanted, even though the sum was nothing to him. For him, the argument was about practicality. For me, it was about generosity. I could think of a million things I would do for Greg if I had the money, but since I didn't, I loved him on a dime—I sent postcards, hid candy bars around his apartment, printed photos of his family. He had the resources to do something nice for me, but wouldn't. For me, this implied that he would always restrict, always hold back—he would never give himself fully to me. In my family, you give as much as you can, in all ways, but particularly with love and time. I worried that Greg wouldn't. I had a hard time explaining this to him—but then, I had a hard time explaining it to myself. I was twenty-three.

We rented a convertible. It rained.

Later that spring, Greg asked me if I was going to get a summer share in the Hamptons. I cut our conversation short and hung up. I ranted to my roommate, "Hamptons? What is he talking about? I can barely make rent!" She nodded sympathetically and continued reheating the frozen soup that her mom had brought up from Philadelphia. "He doesn't know anything about my life," I said. An older me might have noticed why that was—I didn't *tell* him anything about my life.

Those were our fights about money, which, of course, weren't really about money. When it came down to it, Greg and I didn't understand each other. At least, not in the way that I needed us to.

It's unfair to compare anyone to your first love, but I did. I thought about my favorite college boyfriend. We spent very little money, but we drove down the Blue Ridge Parkway and swam at Jordan Lake and threw our change in the grocery store's Coinstar and bought cheese and wine and watched movies we already owned. We talked incessantly, analyzed everything, and woke up and talked more while he cooked crepes. When I went out to breakfast with Greg, he read the newspaper. And he kept the front page.

Greg thought that everything had a price. In his circle of friends, it was known that he would give $25,000 to the person who introduced him to his wife. Once, I challenged him by saying that you couldn't put a price on a person. He replied that of course you could. He described how he would go about doing it, factoring in education, looks, pedigree. He said you could put a price on anything. But I never thought he'd put a price on me.

Eventually, he tried. As graduation approached, Greg began to ask me if I was going to move to London. I looked into it. I liked London and I liked Greg, but I couldn't see my way around the work visa. It was hard to imagine that a U.K. magazine, or the U.K. office of an American magazine, would sponsor a newly minted journalist. And I didn't have enough work experience to qualify for the kind of visa I wanted—the kind where I wouldn't be tied to an employer I hated. I told Greg that it was impossible, that I'd have to stay in New York. For a moment, I thought he might consider moving back to the States. His firm had an office in the city; his family lived nearby. Instead, he pointed out that it would be cheaper for him to pay my New York salary and move me to London than it would be for him to move to New York. Half-joking, I asked him if he would pay me a lump sum, in case of a breakup. Dead serious, he said yes. He'd even rent an apartment for me.

I explained to Greg that I couldn't legally work in London. Greg said it wouldn't matter, so long as we were together. I told Greg that I wasn't sure what was more insulting, the idea that I could be bought, or the idea that I could be bought for such a small sum. He laughed. He was just being practical, he said. I insisted there was something more at stake. He told me to think about it.

I thought about what Greg was proposing. It was instant adulthood, an Easy-Bake life. At twenty-four, I could have what many women dream of—a gorgeous apartment in London and a handsome millionaire boyfriend. I'd get to skip the struggle of finding my first job, paying dental bills without insurance, receiving rejection letters. I'd skip the apartments with leaky ceilings and water bugs. I'd skip the anxiety of wondering if I'd make it, survive. I'd never have to go on another first date. Instead, I'd be with Greg. Eventually, we'd get engaged. Then married. We'd move to a palatial home, hire a decorator, have kids. We'd have beautiful clothes, furniture, meals. We'd travel the world. Host catered parties. Buy pedigree dogs. We'd read the newspaper at our dining room table; I'd wish I had the front page. We'd look good together, and even if we didn't have much to talk about, we'd be happy enough. I considered his offer. I truly did. But in the end, I couldn't afford it.

The Lost Lexus

Melanie Thernstrom

*L*exus, *Lexi:* I wanted the Lexus. For Christmas, my husband had given me a card on which he had written *Hybrid*—a replacement for my ancient Toyota RAV4. I was newly enchanted with the phrase "carbon footprint" and the idea of lightening mine. Temperamentally, I've never been a light-liver: when I wear clothes they wear out quickly; downstairs neighbors complain of my heavy tread. But I was enamored with the effortlessness of a hybrid—of purchasing one's way into a superior relation to the planet. All I had to do was choose one.

It was the eve of our first wedding anniversary, and I was still trying to understand my husband's financial philosophy—and the extent to which it was a philosophy. I was hoping it was merely habit, because one thing was plain: it was different from mine. Michael was frugal. By chance, I discovered that the Lexus RX hybrid was the same price as the Toyota Highlander Limited hybrid when configured similarly, with GPS. Both had similar reliability ratings, since, in fact, both cars are manufactured by Toyota. But the Lexus was prettier, with a comelier snout, a curvier body, and superior interior decoration. If Michael's thriftiness was simply about saving money, then he would be fine with whichever car I chose. But I had a feeling it wasn't.

"A Lexus!" he exclaimed with dismay. "I'd be embarrassed to drive it." There was a Lexus or two in the parking lot at work, he acknowledged—and Acuras and Infinitis—but he was "glad they didn't belong to me." His was a magnetic gray Toyota Camry with an ash interior: nice, but not *too* nice, and that was the way he liked it. "It's a neutral car—it doesn't make a statement," he explained. "But I wouldn't want to influence you. If I have to drive it to work sometime, I can park inconspicuously," he said glumly. "I guess I just didn't see us as *a Lexus kind of family.*"

When we had gotten engaged, we were financial equals. To be precise, Michael had six times the savings I did—but since six of not very much is still not very much, we were, to my mind, roughly in the same financial category. There was no particular reason to expect this would change. But shortly before our wedding, it became clear that the business he founded—a small, "emerging" software company, as they call it in the business world, or "struggling start-up," as he often described it to me—was going to be acquired by a giant computer company. When that happened, we would become distinctly, dramatically *unequal*. The unhappily paired in his circle counseled him to make a prenuptial agreement.

In relating his rejection of their advice, I understood that Michael wanted me to feel that this money would also belong to me—that we would be financial partners. The first time he referred to the share of the buyout that went to "us," I assumed he was referring to his board. I caught my breath when I realized he meant me. *Our share, us.* He had worked for many years to build the product and the company— years when he had been with other women—and I had met him just when all his efforts had come to fruition. Suddenly, without my so much as having grasped what "scalable, highly-available file serving" or "database consolidation" was, it was all "ours."

"Of course, we're not going to change our spending habits, anyway," he said.

"We're not? Why not?"

"Because that would be bad."

"Be serious."

"What about what I'm saying aren't you taking seriously?"

Perhaps Michael only wanted me to be his financial partner in the same way that I wanted him to be co-owner of our new blue-point Balinese kitten, Crumpet: to share responsibility, certainly, but to do so in the way I saw fit. This meant, for example, hiring a live-in professional pet-sitter when we went away for the weekend to keep her from being bored or lonely (even if Michael was of the opinion that she could amuse herself because "the species survived for thousands of years without humans to amuse them and she will survive the weekend"). She is our cat, to be sure, as long as he is with the cat-care program. But if there is dissent, she is my cat.

I wasn't with the financial program.

"Our income has changed," I said.

"Our income has not changed. I've explained this before. This was a onetime financial windfall."

"Okay, okay, fine, our assets have changed. Our bank balance has an extra zero! Our financial situation has improved by an *order of magnitude*."

"That's not relevant."

"It's not?"

Was it a dim anxiety that we'd need this windfall someday—that we would irritate the gods with frivolity and they'd show us how swiftly fortunes can reverse? Did luxuries strike Michael as unseemly in the face of poverty and increasing financial inequity? Or was his attitude the product of a small-town New England upbringing by serious-minded academics who refinanced their house to send their children to private schools *because education is important*—but bought cars secondhand, shopped for clothes on markdown, and checked videos out of the library? Was Michael afraid that if he bought things his parents wouldn't buy, he'd be rejecting their values—or them?

I had also grown up in an academic family, but with parents who were far less thrifty. My Lexus-driving mother is, however, prone to fits of guilt about extravagances—a problem she likes to solve by taking my father shopping with her. He'll settle into a chair in Saks or Neiman Marcus or Bloomingdale's, reading, munching on cashews, and looking up from his thriller from time to time to nod approvingly at everything she tries on. "Well, I don't know," she'll say, pursing her lips, "maybe it's too expensive."

"Nonsense," he replies, right on cue: if she wants it, she must have it.

When I coyly suggested to Michael that something I coveted was too costly, he simply concurred. When I talked about *want,* he refocused the conversation to *need.* When we first moved in together, I thought we should become a two-iPod household; he thought we should share mine. "Come *on*—everyone has their own iPod," I argued. "Kids in ghettos have iPods."

"Kids in ghettos have automatic weapons and satellite TV," he said. "Do we need those too?"

For me, purchasing decisions have always been guided by a single frighteningly simple criterion: what you can afford. They're not intricate moral decisions—just personal, practical ones. What is it worth to you and what do you have to give up to get it? But now Michael and I could get lots of things and give up nothing, which should have made everything deliciously simple.

A few days after the company acquisition was finalized, I was unloading groceries in the kitchen.

"How much were the clementines?" Michael asked casually.

"I dunno."

"I read that clementines are expensive this year due to the unusually cold winter."

"Hmm."

"You didn't notice?"

"*Sweetie.*" We unloaded in silence for a few minutes.

"Oh, good, you bought wine." He held up the bottle. "How much was it?"

"Four ninety-nine! I bought it at Trader Joe's. Since every single thing at Trader Joe's is something we can afford, there's no need to look at any of the price tags, including clementines."

Michael hates to criticize people, and when he does, he is usually so excessively tactful that it's easy for the other person to miss the criticism entirely. His New Year's resolution was to be more assertive, and I seconded it. But although his tone was mild as ever, I could tell that the suggestion of a blithe state of mind in which price was of no concern perturbed him. I knew he wanted me to reassure him that I agreed in principle that price always matters, because frugality is a principle—even if the money in question wasn't ours.

For example, when he flew internationally for work, despite his company's policy of flying their executives business class, Michael stuck himself in economy, on the grounds that business class was offensively expensive. When I flew domestically, I drained his frequent-flyer miles for an upgrade. Arriving at an airport on an expense account, he looked for public transportation. Arriving on our dime, I looked for a cab.

Yet hundreds of dollars could disappear to charities without a second thought. This included ones I never knew he cared about (Recording for the Blind and Dyslexic), ones I picked because he didn't care about them (Save the Tiger), and ones that obviously needed no help from us (the Association of American Rhodes Scholars). But a $2 call to directory information or a bottle of water *when I was lost or thirsty* caused consternation. For Michael, charity is not inconsistent with frugality; only carelessness is.

I like to be careless. As a writer with no certain income, I had bought boxes of clementines whenever I wanted, even if half of them were rotted; my spending philosophy was based on the idea that one has to take care with major expenses, but little things never add up. "As a former mathematician, I assure you," Michael informed me one day, "*little things add up.*"

As a former mathematician, he enjoyed all that adding—minimizing expenditures, maximizing returns. He enjoyed entering his expenses into his Quicken program and being able to tell you how much he paid for a decaf latte on the second Tuesday in November seven years ago. I refused to keep my receipts—I hated the idea of every purchase being on the record. As a result, his Quicken developed what he referred to as "a gaping hole called Melanie."

"For me, frugality is protection against deprivation," he said. "For you, it is deprivation."

Deprivation, or just a drag. I didn't want to drive to another gas station because he thought the price at the one we had stopped at was a tad high. Even though the alternative was only five minutes away and we weren't in a hurry, it bothered me. I felt those minutes were being *kidnapped* from my life. On my deathbed I would want them back—or I would want to have shortened my life by smoking five cigarettes instead. My fantasy of having money had been that it would render money invisible, like a return to the world of childhood, where everything is free, the clementines in the bowl like fruit on a tree.

My friend Amanda has a system she calls Princess Math, the gist of which is that a penny saved is a penny earned. Therefore, if you buy something on sale, you've saved the savings and you can take that savings and leverage it into a faux-fox-trimmed buttercream pashmina. I had tried to live in the world of Princess Math, but I was always bumping into the limits of my resources. I had wanted to be able to write checks without checking my balance, but I was afraid they would bounce. Now, finally, they would never bounce—if only my husband didn't keep dampening my spending spirits.

When mutual friends bestowed Michael upon me, I knew he was perfect. After two decades of relationships with men who were decidedly or subtly not quite right, I felt entirely vindicated. He was even younger—so much for clichés about older women. They say one must never congratulate a bride, but I basked in congratulations.

Michael's was the kind of beautiful, beguiling mind I had always prized—the kind you can get lost in. The transatlantic phone call after our first date, which took place after he flew back to London, where he was then living, lasted six hours and still felt abbreviated.

The lesson of my excessively long dating life had been that you always paid for fascination. If you wanted someone brilliant and creative, you could also count on him to be narcissistic, difficult, and probably—despite or perhaps because of his brilliance—unhappy.

It's not just that being fascinating and being a good partner are distinct qualities (as intelligence and attractiveness are) and do not always turn up in one person. In men, I decided, they were actually *competitive,* and the drive to be special usually overwhelms the drive to be giving. I dated writers, entrepreneurs, academics, physicians, and scientists for whom relationships were the area in which they least excelled. But if you can't fall in love without being both dazzled and nurtured, you have to wait—and be prepared to stay single.

Michael was sweet, sensible, sensitive, and endlessly good-natured. For the first time ever in a relationship, I was haunted by the sense that I was the difficult one—the one prone to crankiness and self-absorption, the one who, when all was said and done, usually owed the apology. Once, when we quarreled, I declared triumphantly, "You are definitely not perfect." He laughed, and I realized that basically I thought he was. Now finally, with finances, I was almost pleased to identify a definite foible—an area of irrationality.

Unless the irrationality was mine.

I understood that by the standards of Michael's world, his share of the sale of his company had been modest. The business had required a large amount of capital, and as a result, almost all of it was owned by the investors. I knew that, as Michael kept reminding me, *we weren't rich*—not by the standards of rich people, anyway. But by my standards—writer standards, with the multiplications of Princess Math—we were. Rich enough for treats: for clementines, cashmere, champagne, orchids, massage, antique teapots, and Mariage Frères tea ($21 at Dean & DeLuca for a tiny tin, unless you went to Paris to pick it up, which was clearly the thing to do). Rich enough for Highlander hybrids—and now, it seemed, rich enough for Lexi.

"By the way, I think the plural of Lexus is just Lexus," Michael said.

"Or maybe Lexuses. It's not Latin—it's just a made-up word trying to sound like luxury." But to me, it didn't sound like what it probably was: an arid acronym for a luxury export to the U.S. It sounded like *lucky*. It was akin to other appealing *l* words like *lucid, luscious,* and *lovely*. I remember the first ads for the Lexus, where the car was shown with a tower of champagne flutes neatly balanced on its hood—as if the owner would momentarily step out of the car to take down a glass and toast her choice.

The Toyota Highlander owner—who was she? Was she joyous? Was she beautiful? Did she drink champagne? I disliked the name Highlander, which sounded like it was trying to sound Scottish, which seemed absurd for a Japanese car (though why that was sillier than trying to sound like ancient Rome, I couldn't say). Clearly, the company thought the Highlander owner was afraid of *Lowlands* and would buy this big boat of a car to protect herself against vague fears—like the kind of person who voted Republican because it claimed to be the party of national security. Or perhaps she was just a sturdy suburban soccer mom who liked that the back could be turned into a third row of seats for carpooling, and still have room to lug stuff home from Costco.

Certainly, she was not discriminating about color. The Lexus came in special shades: Smoky Granite Mica, Golden Almond, and one I was particularly enticed by, Bamboo Pearl—the palest of pale golds—whereas the Highlander's only distinctive color was Iced Amethyst Mica, a lavender that sparkled in a tacky way, like cheap eye shadow. Even the shades that were common to both cars were inexplicably less nice in the Highlander's version. The Lexus had Black Onyx; the Highlander a don't-bother-to-give-it-an-adorning-adjective Black—not even a modest moniker like Basic Black. Perhaps they just didn't want one to feel too good about a nonluxury line.

Lexus, Lexi, Lexorum. Lexorum Melanie: Melanie's Lexi, unless that meant the Lexi's Melanie. (I could no longer remember how the possessive declension worked.) I realized that I pictured the woman in the Bamboo Pearl Lexus as less likely to be suffering from the early arthritis that afflicted me—as if in buying a new car, I would be buying myself a new body—a bejeweled gold skin over my skin, a sturdy frame over my disappointing skeleton. When I peered through the specially soundproofed windows in my mind, the Lexus driver looked healthier, luckier, more immune to misfortune. *She married an amazing man. The unhappy part of her life was over. The happy, married part had begun. She was exceptionally lucky.*

That part was true. What did the Lexus add?

"It's your Christmas present, so you should get whatever you want," Michael said. I love presents—giving them, receiving them, wrapping them, scattering glittering scraps of paper all over the floor—so it was startling to realize that my husband did not. When wedding presents arrived and I was traveling, they'd still be in their cardboard boxes when I came home. When I brought Michael a present, he'd always want to open it later—after dinner, after he had a shower, later. Why not *now*, I'd say. *Aren't you excited?*

"Maybe they're not always things I want," he finally said, in a careful tone. "Maybe I feel pressure to want them so I don't disappoint you."

"I can get you something else! What do you want?" I constantly had the impulse to buy him presents to show him how happy with him I was. The more I sensed they weren't right, the more I'd want to shop.

"I don't want anything," he said. So there it was: he preferred not to want anything. I know the truth of the truism that truly precious things—true love, bravery, good genes of the sort that for the most part I received, but which were inexplicably overlooked in regard to my spine—are not for sale. But channeling desire into things that can be bought or leased or put on layaway seems to offer a certain beautifully straightforward kind of fulfillment—as long as you make sure to covet things within your means. Desire and the fulfillment of desire: the two parts of pleasure.

Previously, the most expensive thing Michael and I had bought together was an engagement ring. I woke at dawn in excitement the morning of our excursion to Tiffany's—a place I had always gone to buy other people's wedding and baby presents and, once, to model rings for an old friend (who toyed with the saleswoman by pretending I was his mistress while he shopped for his wife). Finally, it was my turn!

But when we got there, it turned out the basic design of the rings was similar, and their respective allure was entirely a function of price. Although the one-carat ring was expensive, it was less than half as nice as the two-carat ring and much less than a quarter as nice as the four-carat ring. (Apparently, niceness and price increased exponentially.) Who wanted a less-than-quarter-nice ring? We weren't going to have a quarter-nice marriage.

The saleswoman helpfully suggested we could consider a *starter* ring and trade up later on—an idea more suitable, I thought, for a starter marriage. The clarity of commerce seemed to quell all the sparkle. The trays of rings began to look like platinum-mounted price tags: lumps of compressed carbon-money whose function was not to express the mystery of your love, but to indicate the size of your portfolio—or (worse) the size you wished to indicate. They were hedge-fund-manageress rings, not Dorothy-ruby-slipper rings; they contained no secret power. In the end, we found a 1920s art deco ring at a little shop in Oregon. It was an artful, intricate creation made from an old mine-cut diamond whose price only we would be privy to. Why the last part was important, I didn't know, but we both intuitively felt that it was.

For Michael, the Lexus was like the Tiffany ring: the imagined prominence of the price tag precluded romance.

"But if you prefer the Lexus and think it's nicer," Michael said, "or, as you say, *more Princess*—"

"Do you think it is?"

"I can't speak to the princess factor. I never wanted to be a princess, or to be married to a princess."

As a little girl, I thought a princess was one who dwelt in a world in which everything was pleasant and the most that could bruise her was a pea. Moreover, a princess wasn't a princess *because* other people were paupers; her fortune reflected her internal worth and could accordingly be reversed. But by middle school I had a dismaying suspicion of a connection: perhaps the princess was rich because *she had more than her share and other people didn't have a ball of string*. Perhaps being a princess was selfish, and one should aspire instead to live modestly and not monopolize resources. These two conceptions—Princess or Callous Consumer—remained vaguely in my head, unreconciled.

The Lexus: Princess or Consumer?

Once, reporting a story in northern Uganda, I found myself at a displaced persons camp. Nauseated by the crush of hungry people, I gave a man all the money I had on me—the equivalent of $60. It was enough, my translator said, for his family of six children to survive on for a year. *This is the call,* I thought, *to change my life. I will never again have a mediocre $60 sushi dinner.* I took off my sweater. It was my favorite, a charcoal gray Tse pullover made of a thin cashmere designed to accentuate the body at the expense of warmth. Retail price at Barney's: $200. Market value in the camp: $2—if anyone would buy it.

When I got back to New York, the call seemed less clear. Friends invited me out to dinner. What was I to say—I'm saving all my money to send to Africa? Wasn't my money a drop in a leaky bucket? I missed my sweater. Even if I sent some money to Africa, surely I wasn't going to send *all* my savings. As long as I had some savings, couldn't I take $200 to buy the same sweater again?

I continued eating sushi and bought the sweater.

"Take a long drive," the Lexus saleswoman said with a soft Vietnamese accent as she handed us the key to the Classic Silver Metallic. It had a black leather interior, like one of those inside-out uramaki rolls. "I hope you give me a chance to earn your business."

We turned off the highway, into an unknown neighborhood. It was Sunday afternoon: families were in the yard, kids played in the street. The car, with its electric engine, was eerily quiet.

Materialism, Empty Status Symbols—Bad.

Renouncing desire—Bad, in a different way, unless you are an ascetic or a saint.

When I bought my first car twenty years ago, my body was good, but I was young and lost. If this car lasts as long as it's supposed to last, by the time I buy my next car, I'll be old and in pain. This is my time. This is my time to be happy.

Not falling prey to luxury car marketing.

Not buying the less nice car in order to avoid the luxury label, which is silly.

Writers don't drive luxury cars unless they are screenwriters.

People who buy new cars of any kind instead of Building A School don't care about Africa.

A rich car is not a rich life. People who think so suffer from Lack of Imagination.

Just stay away from the colors of money, my friend Nicky said, silver and gold. And also black—people who drive black SUVs want to push everyone else off the road.

Buy the car you want to buy, Claudia counseled. Don't worry about what other people think.

People who drive a Lexus are assholes, her husband said.

The price of knowing your car isn't saying something about you behind your back: priceless.

It began to drizzle and the rain-sensing intermittent windshield wipers ingeniously activated themselves. We pulled over to the side of the highway just before we reached the dealer, where the saleswoman would be waiting.

Thinking Too Hard about what kind of car to buy—Ridiculous.

"I don't need it," I said to Michael.

"You don't have to need it. Do you *want* it?" There was an urgency to his voice. "I know I was negative about it at first, but I want you to do what you want. Really, I do. Look at me. Do you believe me?"

The happiness of belief suffused my mind. I leaned into his shoulder and thought, *this is what I want: talking, deciding, turning into our future.* If only we could stay nestled in this space forever, like the ebony inside of a silver egg—a platonic egg in which everything was *us* and *ours,* where I wanted what he wanted and nothing was broken, divided, or different.

The feeling didn't begin to ebb until the Highlander was sitting in our driveway.

PART II

Money and Family

Severance

Jennifer Wolff Perrine

The umbilical cord that linked Zoë to Kelli was plump and fleshy, and as I severed it with a scissor, blood squirted onto my hospital gown.

In the pictures I didn't know my husband was taking, I am cradling Zoë in my arms while Kelli, in the background—a little blurry, a little out of focus—smiles at us from her delivery bed. In other pictures I am handing Zoë to her, and in some Kelli and Zoë are together alone. Kelli loved her instantly; I could tell by the way she kissed her, and grazed Zoë's cheek so tenderly with the tip of her painted fingernail. "You look just like me when I was a baby," Kelli cooed. I envied the knowingness with which Kelli pressed Zoë to her chest; they understood each other's scent, they recognized each other's heartbeats. I felt like an impostor, an intruder, a mercenary.

"Here," Kelli said, handing Zoë back to me. "She's your daughter. Take her."

Kelli and Wayne's car wasn't big enough for them and their two growing boys, plus a car seat with a new baby in it. Neither was their apartment; they feared the government would take away their food stamps if it discovered they were sleeping three children in one bedroom. Once, when they had trouble paying their bills, Kelli pawned her wedding band.

Wayne worked, on and off, driving an asphalt paver, flattening the craggy lots of their midwestern town. His hours depended on the weather; he was out of work whenever it rained or snowed. And he was always off in the winter, when the baby was due. Over time, Kelli had held various low-level secretarial jobs, but constant vomiting and exhaustion, as well as the strain of taking care of her two young sons, had made this pregnancy her toughest yet.

They didn't have much to give their boys, but they gave them what they could: an occasional horseback ride at a local farm, a once-a-summer trip to an amusement park, Transformer robots and books when they could afford them (which wasn't often). Eventually they might choose to have another child—but for now, they just wanted to save enough money to trade their small apartment for a house that the four of them could live in.

Kelli didn't know she was pregnant until one day the previous August, when she went to the hospital after fainting for no apparent reason. Her birth control patch had been giving her trouble; occasionally it fell off in the shower, and when it stuck it gave her cramps and breakthrough bleeding. Now she was four months pregnant, too far along to consider an abortion. After seeing our lawyer's classified nestled in the local *PennySaver* next to ads for tires—the ones on their own car were balding—Kelli and Wayne decided that they would place their third child for adoption.

Kelli and Wayne were poor—but not the kind of poor Steve and I imagined of people who couldn't afford to keep their kid. We'd never imagined a married couple at all; instead, we'd pictured a young woman, maybe a teenager, who'd gotten herself into trouble and had no other way to get out of it. She wouldn't know who the father was, and if she did, he'd be in jail, on skid row, or long gone.

With education—the money that buys it and the money that it provides—Kelli and Wayne could have been us. Without it, we could have been them. We even looked alike. Like Steve, Wayne was fair-skinned and blue-eyed; Kelli and I shared the same brown eyes, prominent nose, and long dark hair. The four of us met for the first time when Steve and I flew from New York to see if they were the kind of people whose child we would want to raise as our own. We had already turned down one birth mother after we learned she'd smoked crystal meth well into her second trimester and that her boyfriend had appeared on *America's Most Wanted*. (We had actually liked that woman; she was colorful and interesting, and the birth father was Jewish and from Brooklyn, like my mother. But we weren't willing to take a risk on a child who could come into the world with central nervous system issues and the murder gene.)

Kelli and Wayne, on the other hand, were as "regular folk" as you could get. They didn't drink or do drugs; they just worked to raise their family as best they could. Like her mother and her two sisters, Kelli was pregnant with her first child by the time she was sixteen; she and Wayne had their second child two years later. At twenty-three, Kelli wanted something else for her life—a real house to live in, a work-at-home job that would permit her to greet her kids when they got off the school bus, and some money to buy new clothes at Target, her favorite store.

Wayne himself had been adopted. His biological father—the man he bitterly refers to as his "sperm donor"—left his mother while she was pregnant with him. The man whom Wayne considers his dad is the man his mother married when Wayne was six months old. He's now married to someone else. But it's this man and his newest wife—two people to whom he is not genetically related—whom Wayne considers his parents. And it's this relationship—loving, loyal, dependable—that has him convinced that placing his unborn child for adoption is the right move. Because he knows that wherever she ends up, she will be loved just as well as blood.

———

Kelli and Wayne entertained themselves by watching a lot of late-night TV. They loved movies, but were also enthralled by get-rich-quick infomercials. When the boys were at school, Kelli sometimes attended seminars that promised participants the chance to learn how to earn millions from home. All she needed was a computer, which she didn't have, and an initial investment of a few thousand bucks, which she also didn't have. Kelli and Wayne could have built new lives on just a fraction of the money Steve and I had spent trying to conceive a child—an amount that, by the time we conceded, had reached into the six figures.

We had come close just once, on our first attempt at in-vitro fertilization. But I carried for only six weeks when the bleeding started and didn't stop. After the miscarriage in 2005, one of my closest friends, a wealthy gay Texan named David, gave me an Elsa Perretti solitaire diamond necklace from Tiffany's. "I don't know what to give a woman in your situation," he said, "but I think you should have a diamond." He told me to regard its sparkle as the soul of the baby who would one day come to me. So I did.

The day after we met Kelli and Wayne—at an Outback Steakhouse where we took them for dinner—they invited us to their home, a small, meticulously neat row-house apartment. The living room was empty except for the television and a huge gray overstuffed couch and love-seat set that Wayne had bought thirdhand for $100. The beige walls were bare, and strips of black plastic covered the stains left on the carpet by the previous tenants. The air stank from the cheap scented candles Kelli lit to hide the evidence of the cigarettes she couldn't quite give up.

In all, we spent three days with Kelli and Wayne in their hometown. For two of those days, Kelli wore the same spotless gray sweatpants and oversize sweatshirt she had bought at a Victoria's Secret

outlet. Her shiny black hair was always brushed into a perfect ponytail, her makeup—foundation, eyeliner, rouge, and lip gloss—always
expertly and abundantly applied.

Kelli and Wayne had chosen us over several other couples a few
weeks earlier, after viewing the photo album that we, like most other
adoptive parents, had put together to show our best face to potential
birth mothers. Steve and I are in our forties, and our goal with this
album was to appear young and healthy enough to convince someone
most likely in her twenties to place her baby with us. We included
pictures of us riding elephants in Thailand, kayaking in Vietnam, and
skiing in Colorado. But Kelli and Wayne didn't seem to care that we
were nearly twice their age or that we took cool vacations. What mattered to them was that our coloring was the same as theirs and that—
from the pictures of us with the children in our families—we looked
like we "really, really loved kids."

Steve and I took a little longer to choose them. It seemed incon-
ceivable to us that Kelli and Wayne wouldn't keep their baby. No,
they couldn't afford to feed another mouth. But they were parents,
devoted ones. They knew the kind of love they were about to give up.
Together, they had an extended family larger than our own. Surely
there was a sister, an aunt, a distant cousin who would step up to keep
this child in the family. We liked Kelli and Wayne, but we didn't know
if theirs was a situation we could trust.

A week after meeting we decided to take the chance. Steve sent
them our first support check through our attorney in California;
though it covered three months of their rent, it averaged out to barely
a week in the Manhattan apartment building where we lived. At the
same time, I began making arrangements for them to head out west
for the birth.

The move was a matter of economics: in many states, the law pro-
hibits adoptive parents from paying for anything more than the birth
mother's medical expenses. But by temporarily moving to Los Angeles, Kelli and Wayne could take advantage of a more lenient California law that, among other things, allowed a monthly stipend to cover

the cost of being out of work. They used the money we gave them to pay their phone bills, along with gas and food and whatever else they chose, including—and very unsettling for us—a video camera, with which they intended to film the delivery and hospital stay. The implications of this arrangement—in essence, that we were paying support money to the biological parents of a baby they might, in the end, decide to keep—made us shudder. Legally they had the right to change their mind at any time and keep all of the money we had thus far funneled their way. We agreed to all of it, though, because Kelli and Wayne could make babies and we couldn't.

They agreed to it because they were broke.

The four of us met again a few months later at the doctor's office in Los Angeles. Steve and I were late and tired, and Kelli was already in the stirrups when we arrived. We'd landed at LAX only hours before, but Kelli and Wayne had been out there for about two weeks already, living in the studio apartment that we had furnished for them, sustained on the groceries we had delivered to their doorstep. Their two little boys were back home with Wayne's parents, and he and Kelli had been talking to them for at least an hour every night. I'd been speaking to Kelli every night too, from our river-view apartment on Manhattan's East Side—making sure she was okay, that she and Wayne had everything they needed, and making a list of what they still needed so I could buy it online for them and have it sent. It was early January, and Kelli wasn't supposed to give birth until the end of the month. But every night before she hung up she said, "You'd better get out here soon; this baby's just waiting for you to come get it." What she was really saying was that she missed her kids and was done baking the one she knew she couldn't afford to keep. So we moved our travel dates up, hoping to have a few days to spend relaxing in the warm California sun before becoming parents. But that girl knew her body; it wasn't an hour after we left the doctor's office that she went into labor.

———

"Shhe has no idea what's about to hit her," our lawyer had told us over the phone several days earlier, after meeting Kelli for the first time. Intellectually, she had processed the fact that she was giving up her child, he said—but her heart hadn't stepped near it. He warned us: "Be prepared."

Over the months, I'd talked to Kelli about this a hundred times. "How are you *feeling*?" I'd ask. "Are you sure you're *okay* with everything?" Truthfully, I hoped that she would express some doubt, some angst; to question her decision and to question me. I wanted to feel that both Kelli and the child she was giving birth to would be like me, at least at their emotional core. I wanted Kelli to tell me how hard it was to give up a child, a girl after two boys. I wanted her to say, if only once, "This really hurts."

But Kelli was nothing if not resolute. If she ever felt even a pang of uncertainty, she never admitted it. "I love you guys," she'd say, again and again. "She's going to have the best life with you." She grew even more excited toward the end of her pregnancy when I started, reluctantly, to buy baby stuff—afraid to hope that this time a child really would become ours. She was especially thrilled when she learned I'd purchased a luxury car seat with memory foam. "We made the best choice when we chose you guys," she said. "She's going to have the best of everything, I just know it."

Kelli went into labor while we were eating lunch at a Mexican restaurant on Ventura Boulevard. She didn't know if she wanted to go straight to the hospital, or if there was time to stop and get the mani-cure/pedicure I had promised her. She took a chance on the mani/pedi—she had never had one done professionally before, and in the last few months Wayne had been painting her toes because her belly had grown too big to reach them herself. At a nearby mall, Steve and Wayne ventured off to a sporting goods store, while we found a salon staffed by some overly curious Vietnamese women. "When are you due?" they asked Kelli in unison. "Boy or girl?" About the two of us, they asked, "Relative? Sister? Mother-daughter?" "No," Kelli told them, "just good friends." They looked at us skeptically and pointed to her face, then to mine. "Same, same," one said. "Yes," said another, "same, same." Kelli and I looked at one another. "Same, same," we both said. It was the first time I saw a tear in her eye.

Kelli was four centimeters dilated by the time we got to the hospital. It would be soon, but not too soon. Steve and Wayne passed the next few hours by making fart jokes and putting rubber surgical gloves over their heads and seeing if they could blow them up. Kelli was contracting pretty hard and seemed to want to be left alone. I didn't know what to do with myself, so I started text-messaging my friends back east. "We're in the delivery room!" I wrote. "It's *actually* happening!!"

When it was time to push, we all got into position. Wayne was on Kelli's left side, and I was on her right, holding her hand with one hand and massaging her calf and freshly pedicured foot with the other. Steve stood behind me, his chest and stomach warm and strong against my back.

Zoë came out red and screaming. When the doctor told me to, I cut the cord. At some point I realized that Steve had been shooting pictures the entire time. I was really happy about that, because then Zoë would always know that she didn't spend one moment in this life without us. She'd see us cuddling her wrinkled ruddy little body, ours the first eyes to gaze into hers, the first arms to embrace her tiny limbs, the first hearts she felt beating outside the one that gave her life. Kelli and Wayne loomed in the background, smiling, approving. You'd imagine sadness in these photos, but there was none. We were a family of five, four parents and one child to whom each of us was utterly devoted, but in markedly different ways.

The hospital set us up with adjoining rooms: Steve, Zoë, and I in one, and Wayne and Kelli in the other. As nurses came into our room to coach Steve and me on the intricacies of bottle-feeding, Kelli recuperated next door, and the baby slept and learned how to use her newfound lungs. Wayne popped in whenever Kelli wanted to spend time with Zoë, and we obliged while she took our child, her child, into bed with her. Wearing a white hospital gown and full makeup, she posed for the video camera they had bought with our support money, kissing Zoë all over her face, telling her how much she loved her. I wondered what Kelli and Wayne would do with these videos. I wondered if Zoë would ever see them.

The next morning and early afternoon we visited together often and talked about the magic of the birth; the four of us even agreed together on Zoë's first and middle names. Zoë meant life; her middle name, Giselle, meant pledge. And that's what the four of us had entered into, a life pledge. Kelli and Wayne brought Zoë to life; Steve and I would carry her through it. At least, that was the plan.

That evening, Kelli and Wayne locked us out of their hospital room, with Zoë inside.

A while earlier, I had tried to introduce Kelli to the pediatrician who had evaluated Zoë. Wayne was rolling her around the hallway in a wheelchair. "She's very healthy," the doctor told Kelli. "She's in great shape." Kelli didn't even look at him. "That's good," she said, barely, under her breath.

"Are you okay?" I asked. When she looked up at me, a coating of frost had come over her deep dark eyes. "Fine," she said. "Can I see her now?" Steve and I wheeled the baby's plastic bassinet into their room and walked out. They said nothing to us.

Hours passed. I walked across the street to the supermarket, where I stood in front of a crate of Granny Smith apples and mindlessly polished them with my shirt while talking into my cell phone. "They're backing out," I told my friend Lyn. "How could they not?"

Now that she had seen her—held her, kissed her—it was unimaginable to me that Kelli would choose to give up Zoë. The only thing that gave me solace—and it was an uncomfortable solace—was knowing that she couldn't afford not to. Kelli and Wayne were entitled

to keep the support we had already given them. But we weren't obligated beyond that point. If Kelli and Wayne kept Zoë, the hospital
bills would revert to them. So would the yet unpaid portion of their
living expenses for their stay in Los Angeles and—since Kelli had delivered so early—the cost of changing their plane tickets home to see
their sons. Most significantly, they wouldn't receive the remainder of
their support check, a hefty chunk of change that for us was a fraction
of the cost of a single IVF treatment, but for them was the foundation
of their new future.

We knew Wayne would talk this kind of sense to Kelli, that he'd
explain they'd made a commitment and they couldn't back out now.
But inside her soul, the conversation that was going on was about
something else entirely. I knew she and I were the only ones who
could have it.

When I could no longer wait, I knocked on her door. Wayne let
me in. I sat on the side of the bed. Zoë was asleep in the bassinet.
Kelli's eyes were wet. I took her hand. "I know this is harder than you
thought it would be," I told her.

"It really is," she said. "It doesn't feel natural."

"It's not," I said, my voice, my body, starting to shake. "It's really
not natural at all."

We sat there, the two of us, her fingers limp in my palm.

I wanted to tell her about everything we would give to Zoë, how
she would go to college, take dance and music lessons, go to horse
camp, and travel with us to exotic places. But at that moment it wasn't
about the material things Steve and I would give her, the things that
she and Wayne couldn't.

"We'll love her, you know," I told her after a few minutes of silence.
"We already do."

"I know," she said. "We love her too."

More silence.

"She's going to know that," I promised her.

"Thank you," she said, finally squeezing my fingers.

The evening after Kelli and Wayne signed the final adoption papers, we took them to dinner at a fancy French restaurant, where I invited Kelli to order a nice glass of wine. She asked for Asti Spumanti. Neither of them could understand the menu, and the waiter kindly obliged in translating it. Throughout the meal, Steve and Wayne continued to make fart jokes as Kelli and I kept peaking into the stroller, checking on Zoë. Afterward, the five of us returned to the house where Steve and I and the baby had been staying, to say our final good-byes.

For months I had been thinking about the day Kelli and Wayne would actually give us their child. And I had wondered, *what will I give them back?* In the end we were all doing one another a favor; they were giving us a child to love, and we were going to love the child they couldn't give to. But the emotional cost to them seemed incalculable.

"Wait," I said, before they left. I reached around my neck to unclasp the chain my friend David had given me shortly after I miscarried more than two years earlier; I had never taken it off.

I fell dumb as I tried to explain to Kelli what I was doing; the words tangled in my throat with the heartbreak of all that failure and loss Steve and I had suffered in trying to make a child of our own. Kelli and Wayne—two people we would never have known if not for the mutual desperation of our very different circumstances—had given me the one thing that up until now neither money nor love nor both of them together could ever buy; the chance to finally be a mother.

I looked imploringly at Steve, and he took my cue to tell her the story of David, the diamond, and the soul of the baby we could never have. As he did, I linked the chain around Kelli's neck.

Kelli cried. I cried. We hugged hard and long. Steve and Wayne, lost for words, looked at the floor and gave us the moment we needed before we could say good-bye, the moment I had needed from Kelli all along. For the last few days we had been two mothers of the same child, but now, as Kelli and I unlocked from each other's arms, there was only me.

As days passed into weeks, there was no doubt in our minds that we had gotten the better part of the deal: Zoë was magic, and we had her and Kelli and Wayne didn't. Steve and I talk about them a lot; we wonder how they are, how their boys are, and if they will ever buy the house they dream about. Mostly, we wonder how they are living without Zoë, because we know we never could.

Recently, Kelli sent me an e-mail from the computer she had bought with some of her support money. She and Wayne had started a home business. The boys were happy. The wound of giving birth to a child they couldn't afford to raise was starting to heal. "Thank you a thousand times for everything," she wrote. "I love you guys and you'll never know how much I appreciate the amazing impact you've made in our lives."

She sent some pictures too, of Wayne and of the kids, but also of herself, standing beneath a blooming magnolia tree, her wedding band back on her finger, the soul of her baby, my baby, sparkling around her neck, catching the light.

Count the Ways

Kathryn Harrison

On the day she discovered she could no longer walk or even stand without assistance, my mother ordered seventeen pairs of shoes, one pair at a time, from various catalogs spread over her bed. Neiman Marcus, Saks Fifth Avenue, Bonwit Teller. Only forty-two years old, her bones crumbling from cancer that had metastasized from her breast, she was a no-longer-beautiful woman whose vanity had long been focused on her size 7AA feet, perhaps the only part of her withered body that disease hadn't marred. In fact, once she stopped using them, her feet became softer, paler, and more slender, immaculately pedicured by an indulgent visiting nurse, her toenails filed smooth and polished red. Upstairs in my mother's closet were—I counted after she died—eighty-eight pairs of shoes. It was 1985, there was no Jimmy Choo or Manolo Blahnik, but I remember the names, some of them, on the towers of boxes she saved: Maude Frison, Charles Jourdan, Yves Saint Laurent, Papagallo, Chanel.

My mother's partner and I stood together in their small kitchen, eavesdropping on her conversations with telephone salespeople.

"You have to take it away from her," I whispered, referring to his credit card, on which she was charging all these shoes she'd never wear.

He shook his head. "I can't," he said. He was a gentle man, soft-spoken. An alcoholic, he drank steadily all day without ever descending into perceivable drunkenness. Like me, he avoided conflict. For eleven years, he and my mother had lived together while he remained married to another woman, fanatically Catholic, who refused to divorce him, just as he refused to initiate proceedings against her.

"Please," I said. "It's your card. She's spending hundreds—thousands—of dollars."

"We'll return them," he said, after a silence.

There was a window between the kitchen and the room in which we'd set up my mother's hospital bed, an opening presumably through which to pass dishes of food, although my mother had never used it for that purpose. The two of us were standing at that small window, its shutters closed, watching her through the wooden slats. I remember her looking almost happy in that moment. What she was doing didn't strike me as a symptom of desperation or panic. Those were my feelings, not hers.

The UPS man brought the shoes to the door, and we signed for the packages and left them on the hall table. We didn't bring them to my mother, confined to her chrome-railed bed, and she never inquired about all the orders that had apparently never been filled. Shoes continued to arrive after her death, and I opened the boxes and filled out the forms necessary to return them, printing the words "purchaser deceased" in the space provided for a reason for their return, other than the wrong size or color or style. I'd wait until there were two or three pairs and then take them to the post office, standing in line with the boxes in my arms.

A day spent squandering money she didn't have on shoes she couldn't wear struck me even then as a perfect coda to my mother's short life. For as long as I'd known her she'd been spending with a vengeance. Not just spending irresponsibly—although she was irresponsible—but spending her mother's money as if it were inexhaustible. Pregnant at seventeen, married at eighteen, and divorced by nineteen, my mother had been pressured by her parents, especially my grandmother, to separate herself from a man they said would never provide her with the kind of living they expected from a son-in-law. Lacking whatever it might have required to thwart her parents—courage, perhaps, or the self-knowledge that might have come in time—she'd allowed herself to be frightened by the picture they painted of life as a preacher's wife, a life of austerity, of always giving and never receiving. A life barren of the luxuries my grandmother had taught her to crave.

1961: I was born, my father was banished; my grandparents, my teenaged mother, and I lived on the steadily shrinking fortune left to my grandmother by her father. There was no other source of money, not really. My grandfather's pension was modest, and he kept his bank account separate from my grandmother's—at her insistence, I'm sure. I've heard stories of incompetent math students who suddenly, once a dollar sign is attached to a number, understand previously confounding calculations in an epiphanic flash, numbers spread across the firmament, orderly and beautiful, like the glorious bright embers of fireworks. For my grandfather the opposite seems to have been true. A math prodigy, he had no instinct for commerce. Most shamefully, he had turned down an opportunity to buy a sizable portion of the Las Vegas Strip. This was in 1942; the country was at war; he thought the place was too vulgar to ever catch on. My grandmother never spoke about this stunning lack of foresight, and never forgave him for it. When I was a child, in the sixties, there were household expenses he assumed, and others that she did, like the cost of the house itself. In the eighties, when I married, her one piece of advice was "Separate bank accounts!"

"But why?" I asked. "We're sleeping in the same bed. Why can't our money be together?"

She gave me a look I'd seen before, one intended to remind the

graduate student I was at the time that there was little of practical
value to be learned in school.

"What if you want to clear out in a hurry?" she said. "Then what?"

"Oh, come on, Nana. I can't get married with an exit strategy."

"Of course you can! That's what those, those what-do-you-call-
thems are."

"Pre-nups?"

She nodded vigorously, all four feet eleven inches of her.

"I think we feel differently about this. I don't think there's much
point in having this conversation. We'll just end up arguing."

"You mark my words," she said.

I haven't, though. Even before we were married, twenty years ago,
my husband and I shared a bank account. I can't imagine living
with a man I didn't trust with my money, what little I had of it back
then. I've never given the matter a second thought. Is this because I
know I can earn money? If I do need to "clear out in a hurry," I can
walk away from what I have and make more. But my grandmother
never had that confidence, and she guarded what she'd inherited. I
don't know what unfolded between my mother and my grandmother
before I was born, but my childhood provided a long object lesson in
the disparate uses of money.

Money was offered as love and withheld as punishment. Dangled
as bait, bestowed in company, withdrawn in secret. It could be made
to seem plentiful, as plentiful as water—which, according to my
grandmother, was the way my mother spent it, *like water*—and just
as suddenly as that substance, it could dry up. Like glue, it could bind
one generation to another; just as easily, it could pry them apart.

As an adult, my mother wasn't without her own money. She worked
as a legal secretary. But she didn't make as much as she wanted. Not
enough to provide for me, not enough to buy the clothes she wanted or
to live as she was accustomed to living—extravagantly. If her mother
had banished her husband because he couldn't give her the luxuries

she wanted, then she would extract them herself, from her mother's purse. She charged clothes and shoes on my grandmother's accounts at various department stores—Saks, I. Magnin's, Nieman Marcus. She shopped for food at the market where my grandmother ran a tab and paid a monthly bill. I never stood with her at the register when she didn't say, "Put it on my mother's account, please." At Saks I watched as she offered up the store credit card, its shiny surface embossed in gold letters with my grandmother's name.

My grandmother allowed my mother to carry duplicates of all her credit cards in her wallet and told her not to use them. Even as a child, I understood how perverse this was, akin to Bluebeard's handing his new young bride the key to the locked chamber that held the corpses of her butchered predecessors. What was my grandmother's motive for what seemed to be a kind of test? Did she want my mother to use the cards so that when the bills arrived she could castigate her? So that she could humiliate my mother by canceling accounts without letting her know? So that my mother would always understand the terms of her imprisonment? My mother was the child my grandmother intended her to be, the one who would never grow up and leave her.

Once I was with my mother when she discovered that an account had been canceled. I was leaning against a warmly lit glass counter, looking at the gloves and scarves displayed within, when the saleslady said she was sorry, the card hadn't been accepted. Perhaps she'd like to pay another way?

Tears at home and remonstrations: How could my grandmother have put my mother in such a position, embarrass her like that? How, my grandmother countered, could my mother put her in such a position, forcing her to close an account by buying things she didn't need, running up bills my grandmother couldn't pay? Often their fights turned ugly, but they rarely betrayed what they were really about: my mother blamed her mother for her unhappiness and intended to make her pay for it. She blamed me as well, the child whose conception had forced her marriage and all that followed, but I had no money, and there were other ways to punish me.

In college, I shared stories of my mother's sprees with my boy-friend. They made him angry. I wanted him to understand who my mother was, and I wanted him to dislike her—to understand our tor-tured relationship. My grandmother had two trust funds, I explained to him. One had been set up for her by her father. The income was hers, but she couldn't touch the principal, which would pass to my mother after her death. My grandmother had also inherited a trust fund from her sister, which my grandmother told me she had willed to me. This was the money my grandmother was whittling away, paying my mother's rent, buying her a car, making her loans she would never repay. Already the money that was supposed to be my inheritance was half gone. My boyfriend looked at me in my thrift-store sweater and army surplus pants. In protest against my mother's profligacy, as a means of accusing her, I spent as little as I could on clothes.

"That is totally selfish and unfair. Criminally selfish!" He paced and waved his arms around. "You're going to confront her," he told me. "This Christmas, when you're home for break, you're going to tell her that she can't spend your money. It's your money. Security for you."

"No," I said. "It isn't mine, not really, not yet. And anyway, I wouldn't do that. It's not the kind of thing I'd do." In fact, I couldn't imagine myself saying such a thing, voicing what didn't preoccupy me as it did him, talking about money as I'd been taught never to do, be-cause like sex and politics it was vulgar, like religion it was private. But day after night after day, my boyfriend harangued me. I was passive, he said, I was subservient. I always let my mother have her way. Ev-eryone did. No one ever held her accountable for anything. I'd never grow up, I'd never have a life, I'd always be a child if I didn't confront her. So I did. And we fought. Generally, the hostility between my mother and me was not articulated. At least not directly. Instead of telling me I was fat—I wasn't—she gave me clothes a size or more too small. "Oh," she'd say, when she'd coaxed me into trying on whatever it was, "Oh, I didn't realize you were that big." She never said I was ugly, not exactly; she just mentioned that she preferred brunettes to blondes and offered me a nose job for my sixteenth birthday, a gift I didn't accept. In any case, my grandmother would have paid the bill. But this time my mother attacked me straight on, stepping toward me until she was only inches away.

"You," she said. "No one owes you anything. Do you understand that? Do you?"

"I . . . I didn't—"

"Nothing. Nothing. You don't deserve a thing. How dare you suggest that my mother's money—my mother's—might be yours?"

"I didn't mean—"

"I know exactly what you meant. And you're wrong."

I wish I could remember the end of the fight. I know I was frightened by the violence of her reaction, very sorry I'd let my boyfriend convince me to voice what had been his worry, not my own. And I was shocked that all the things he'd said about my mother—that she was uncaring and jealous and destructive—seemed to be true. Even as I'd solicited his sympathy, I'd defended her to him. I'd said she was thoughtless, not mercenary, but I was, I guess, wrong. The money meant more to her than I did.

In the end, what remained of the trust fund I was supposed to inherit was spent on medical bills, as my mother was uninsured when her breast cancer was diagnosed. She'd taken the money my grandmother gave her to pay her health insurance premiums and spent it on something else. Something that made her feel safer, perhaps, more properly armored, than insurance ever could. Shoes, I imagine, beautiful shoes made by Maude Frison. I remember a dove gray pair I admired most of all, but none of her shoes fit my feet, which were larger than hers. When she died we gave her shoes away, most of them to the home health aide. What the aide didn't want went to Goodwill.

And here I sit, twenty-three years later. I don't know how much money is in the account I share with my husband. I don't know what we pay for electricity each month, for oil, on the mortgage. I work—I work hard and take great satisfaction, sometimes even joy, in the work I do—but I don't know how much money I made last year, or how much I'm likely to make this year. We owe taxes, but I don't know how much.

I do know what milk costs, and apples, dry cereal, laundry detergent. I know the price of kitty litter and of a gallon of gas, and how much is too much to spend on a week of day camp. But I don't open or pay the bills I set on the sideboard. In our marriage this is my husband's task.

On a winter afternoon in 2008, I go shopping with my older daughter, and she finds a pair of expensive jeans—too expensive. But she loves them, and I want her to have them. Eighteen years old, off to college in the fall, she's as delightful to dress as she was when she was three, even if I have no say in what she chooses to wear. Besides, I tell myself, it's not as it is with the younger two, whose clothes sometimes last less than a season. Sarah has stopped outgrowing her things. She could, as she says, have these jeans for many years. And another part of the calculus: she has my mother's beautiful eyes, but filled, as I never saw my mother's, with love for me. Not always, of course, but right now they are, as I give her this gift she doesn't expect. Was this a look my grandmother got from my mother? Was it something she bought? Is it something I am buying? I don't believe I am, but what if I'm mistaken?

I hand the salesgirl my credit card, and then I say, "Wait," and count out five twenties and place them in her hand. "I don't want the whole thing on the card." The salesgirl smiles, as does Sarah. I smile too. I find it funny when I catch myself in the kind of deceits practiced by Lucy Ricardo or some other sitcom housewife, little obfuscations to prevent arguments with my fiscally responsible husband, a father who would be rightfully outraged by the amount of money it's possible to spend on a pair of jeans.

I married a man who, unlike my grandfather, has a good head for business. He likes keeping track of our money; perhaps he likes it as much as I like not having to. It's an aspect of our partnership that most of my friends would find sexist, anachronistic, infantilizing. It would be, if I discussed it with them.

A number of years ago a friend said that if a novel ignored money, if it failed to address the economic aspect of its characters' lives, it was fundamentally dishonest. I remember her words when I write because they correct my tendency to do on the page what I do in my life—ignore money. Fail, as much as possible, to take it into account. I spend money, of course, on food, clothes, books, travel, birthday presents. And I earn money, deposited automatically to our shared account, freelance checks I receive and endorse and hand to my husband. In life I rely on him to address my failure; in a book I must correct myself.

I've yet to recover from my mother's turning on me and saying I deserved nothing. Often, when I accept a writing assignment, I forget to ask how much it will pay. "How many words?" I inquire. "When do you want it?" But never, "What will you pay me?"

A part of me is still standing in line in that post office, boxes of shoes in my arms, trying to figure it out. I spoil the children, my husband complains. They'll grow up not understanding the value of money. I hope that isn't true. I don't think it will be. Their father will teach them, and the world will teach them. I can't, because I haven't yet unlearned my mother's lessons.

The Cheapskate

Amy Sohn

The first time I realized my dad was weird about money was when I was eleven and he made me duck the turnstile at the subway. "But I'm too tall to duck anymore!" I cried. "Just give me a token!"

"Shh," he said, eyeing the station attendant through the glass. "Just do what I say."

So at four-foot-ten, I ducked, trembling, certain we would be chased by a plainclothes cop and hauled off to jail. It wasn't until we were on the subway, on our way to go shopping for cheap kids' clothes on the Lower East Side, that my heartbeat finally returned to normal.

To be my father's daughter was to play by his sociopathic rules, even if they terrified you. He was like a Jewish Clyde Barrow, albeit with no gun and no driver's license. Little did I know, as I endured his vehement frugality throughout my childhood, that I would inherit his neurotic attitude about money—not the conniving necessarily, but the obsession. Most women live in fear of becoming their mothers. I have turned into my father.

His mendacity in the interest of penny-pinching knew no bounds. My younger brother Josh and I were required to age ourselves down not just on subways and buses but also in movie theaters to get child admission prices. When my family flew on PeoplExpress to New England for winter vacation, instead of just booking our already cheap tickets under our name, my father would book a party of ten under some strange pseudonym like Schmonz. (This was in the eighties, when you didn't need a credit card to book a ticket.) We would get to the airport half an hour before takeoff, unticketed, and I would stand there cringing as people boarded and the airline worker paged "the Schmonz party" again and again. When the mysterious passengers inevitably failed to show up, my father would step up to the desk and get four standby tickets for half the price.

Josh was too young to understand what was going on, and my mother, too powerless to do anything, just smiled uncomfortably at my dad's eccentricity. As we stood there listening to the Schmonz page, I wanted to disappear into the rug, convinced that my father would be found out by the cops and hauled off to jail in front of us. For those endless twenty minutes, my father never looked afraid or in the slightest bit guilty. He relished the adventure, a level of excitement he didn't have in his work as a computer programmer. When we finally settled in our ill-begotten seats, he seemed elated and exuberant. He had tried to pull a fast one—and succeeded.

Beyond being thrifty, my father was also zealous about home maintenance, even though we lived in a modest three-bedroom apartment in a middle-income building in Brooklyn Heights. To stain anything, spill a drink, or hurt the rattan bottoms of the dining room chairs was a personal insult. Once, while watching *Cheers* and eating a bowl of Ben & Jerry's, I accidentally dropped my spoon on the floor. My father must have heard the clatter all the way down the hallway because he raced in.

"Why can't you be more careful?" he cried when he saw it, lunging for the ding.

"Don't be silly," my mother called wearily from the other couch, used to his tirades. "It didn't make a mark."

He snatched the spoon, blotted the smudge of ice cream with his shirttail and spent the next two hours sanding and re-staining that square of the parquet until it was several hues darker than the rest of the floor. Now when you walk in, it's the first thing you notice.

My mother tolerated my father's neurotic attitudes with a roll of the eyes. She controlled the checkbooks because she balanced them, and every once in a while when he became obsessed enough to look at them, he would harangue her about various expenditures. She would wait patiently for him to finish; eventually, he'd get caught up in something else and leave her alone.

As his daughter, I was an easier target. One afternoon he came into my bedroom to find me on the phone with an operator, trying to get a number for a movie theater. Like a murderer preventing his victim from calling for help, he slammed his finger on the receiver and shouted, "Throw seventy-five cents in the toilet, why don't you? Didn't anyone teach you to use a phonebook?"

I was agog, not only because we'd already paid for the call and now I didn't have the number, but because he could get this irate about a couple of quarters. I told myself he was crazy and I would never care so much about money when I grew up. Who knew that, years later, I'd be haranguing my husband, Charles, about unnecessary directory assistance calls on our AT&T wireless bill?

My father was not senselessly cheap; we were not rich, and some thrift was necessary. Though my mother always worked, first as a teacher and later as a small-business owner, my father earned most of the household income as a programmer: good money but not great. Josh and I attended private school for elementary school, which was expensive, and we took family vacations each winter. My parents bought a house in the Berkshires with money they inherited from my father's mother, and in the city they went out frequently to dinner and the theater. But even when they went to see plays, my father had his own strange calculus for what they should see.

Most of the time my parents bought discounted off-Broadway tickets from the Theater Development Fund, which meant they frequently came home at intermission because the play was so awful. The only time we went to Broadway shows was when we had relatives in town; my father would stand on line at the half-price TKTS booth and pick a second-rate show that no one wanted to see because those were the only plays available at TKTS. In his mind, the family's needs came second to cost control. Ideally, he could keep costs low and still find quality entertainment, but if anything had to give, it was the quality.

One weekend when my mother's eighty-five-year-old parents came to town, he dragged them to a matinee of an off-off-Broadway musical version of the Patrick Swayze film *Roadhouse*. Why? Because he got $3 tickets from Audience Extras. The show had nudity, vulgarity, and pulsing rock. That night at dinner, when my grandparents described the show, they seemed both offended and befuddled.

It took me years to see the connection, but I believe one of the reasons my father was so insane about money was because of his some-times erratic employment. He would toil for years at some investment bank without incident, and then suddenly, one day, he'd be around in the mornings. If the phone rang, he'd scream at me not to answer it. When I got up the courage to ask what had happened, he would always allude to an impossible or "ball-busting" boss and then say he didn't want to talk about it anymore. A month or two would go by and he'd get a new assignment, and a few years later the whole process would begin again.

Once, when I was about twelve, my father called in sick at a job he didn't like so he could go on interviews. I had the day off from school and was at home. "If a guy named Mr. Gray calls," he said on his way out the door, "tell him your father has shingles and won't be coming in today."

"Tell him you have what?"

"Shingles. It's a skin rash."

Around nine-thirty, the phone rang. "Is your father home?"

"Who's calling?"

"Mr. Gray."

"He told me to tell you that he can't come in because he came down with . . . um . . . bricks."

"What?"

"Bricks." He chuckled and hung up.

My father had such a basic hatred of authority that he had no compunction about gaming the system, whether by lying to his boss or swindling to get a deal on something he felt was overpriced. He saw himself as an underdog, which meant he saw his family as underdogs too. The big guys (his employers, PeoplExpress, the MTA) were colluding to persecute us—and we could either tolerate it (be weak) or buck the system (be smart).

Although he himself had a rocky professional path, my father compensated by investing in my career, early on. At ten, when I was bitten by the acting bug, he enrolled me in theater classes and took me to them every Saturday. Eventually, he suggested I get professional headshots and a talent agent. After I signed with one, he took me faithfully to auditions and play rehearsals. He always seemed overinvested in my success—disappointed when I didn't book an important gig and delighted when I got a callback. I didn't know then how much of his pushing me had to do with money—but he seemed proud when I got my Actors' Equity card and crowed when he showed me my tax return.

I never made significant money—theater and NYU graduate films don't pay much—but I always wondered if part of the reason my father wanted me to act was because of the hope that I might strike it rich. Even if he knew he couldn't take the money for himself, it had to be about more than just the work—because had I been more successful, I could have paid part of my own college tuition.

When I graduated college, I decided to pursue acting. But that spring, after booking precisely one paying acting role—as a feminist protester on *Law and Order*—I realized I didn't really want to be an actress. I began writing stories about my bad dating life, which eventually led to a job as a columnist for an alternative newspaper. Six months later, at age twenty-two, I got a contract to write a novel based on my column, for a six-figure advance.

When I told my parents about this development, at a dinner out to their favorite restaurant, they were thunderstruck. My mother was always supportive in the way you want a parent to be—proud without being overinvested. She seemed happy, and more interested in the publishing details than the money. My father wanted to know how I would invest the cash and when I would get the bulk of it. But there were no furtive signs of jealousy. His face showed only *naches,* pure joy at the accomplishments of a child.

Still, from the moment I told my dad about my book deal, he assumed I was rich. If I let it drop that I had splurged on a handbag or a pair of jeans, his face would get tight and uncomfortable—even though it was not his money. I remember one weekend when I was visiting at their country house. My father was expecting a call from a headhunter, and when he found me checking my home machine once too often, he blew up. "I'm out of work," he said, "and you're making long-distance calls!"

What my father probably never anticipated was that by raising me to believe I could do anything I wanted in the world, he was also ensuring that I would never marry for money. At twenty-nine, I fell in love with a poor, struggling painter who had no steady income and two defaulted student loans. He supported himself selling his paintings and didn't work a day job, even though he was living hand to mouth. I had found a man with my father's inability to tolerate the nine-to-five. We married a year later, and now that we have a toddler, I am the family breadwinner.

When it comes to money, I consider myself extremely lucky in that I've been able to support myself, comfortably, doing something I love for thirteen of my fourteen working years. But now that I have a family that relies on my income, things have become a little more complicated. For the past few years I've been able to get lucrative jobs writing for television, but the money doesn't stretch as far as it did before I had a mortgage, part-time nanny, and nursery school bills.

Because Charles suffers from the bizarre condition of caring too little about money, I make all our financial decisions. (We joke that he has champagne eyes and a beer pocketbook. Despite his poverty, he could look at an ad for handbags in the *New York Times,* point to the one he likes best, and nine times out of ten it will be the most expensive.) The benefit to our arrangement is that I am a control freak who has all the control. The downside is that I feel burdened by the financial pressure.

In the same way that my father would harangue my mother about the occasional splurge, I bray at Charles when he makes international calls or buys our daughter a $150 cashmere sweater. I pore over cellphone bills like I'm reading Talmud and spend hours of my time recovering $10 overages when I could be writing spec screenplays. I cringe when Charles says things like, "I *know* I had a twenty in these jeans."

Part of my money craziness is due to the incredible seductive power of procrastination. During one dark stretch when I was struggling with my second novel, I decided to start a novelty T-shirt company. Because I had a clever concept and knew people in media, I got early press and wound up grossing $5,000 in a year before closing the business. But when I think about how much time I put into the T-shirts, I feel like a moron. Instead of sitting alone with my characters, I went to the post office to check the mailbox or logged onto Paypal forty times a day. Novelists have emptied basements, answered every letter in their inbox, and even masturbated to avoid writing, but I think I am the only one who started a business.

Charles says that I would spend fifteen hours to earn two dollars, and he's right. I'm like the woman who won't have sex with her husband until she straightens the apartment. She knows that the sex will yield her more pleasure, but she cleans because it gives her a sense of control.

Because I cannot control the instability of my career, I am obsessive about controlling what little I can. The cable bill, the weekly grocery bill, the utility costs. Maybe the work I do to recover "lost" money is easier than the work of having difficult conversations with Charles about how we could be a better financial team. We don't like to communicate about the difficult topics because the conversations lead to finger-pointing about who works harder and who's less appreciated. Instead, I act like a baron. I lord my fiduciary authority over him when I'm feeling anxious about money, telling him, "We're really strapped right now," and then, a week later, taking him out to dinner because something good happened that I want to celebrate. Because Charles doesn't have much concept of how much money we have, he's always scratching his head at my seemingly arbitrary fits of cheapness. "I don't get it," he'll say. "Are we rich or are we poor?"

My money neuroticism reached a nadir when I found myself procrastinating on my third novel by trying to settle Charles's defaulted loans. Every month during the time I'd known him, he would get a letter in the mail from a collection agent; in large letters, the first line would always read, "It's not too late to settle your account." Each month the five-figure sum would grow larger and larger.

If Charles got to the mail first, I would find these letters torn up on the top of the trash pile. But if I got the mail first, I would save them in a manila folder entitled "Charles Default," a folder it pained me to possess at all. Even though his debt was incurred long before he met me, I saw it as "our" problem—if only because loving someone means wanting him to have better credit. And then one day, he got a notice that said if he didn't settle his account, the agency would "have no choice but to litigate." I told him he should settle his debt. His response? "You can't get blood from a stone!"

Agonized at the prospect of my spouse being sued and sadly cognizant of the fact that he didn't care, I forged his signature on a letter that gave me permission to speak with the agent. I was able to get him a good settlement, just 60 percent of his total. But Charles was furious that I had deceived him, and said he'd prefer the money to go to our daughter's future college tuition.

My father knows that I am the breadwinner in my marriage, even though we have never discussed it explicitly. I think it irks him, because he's afraid Charles is taking advantage of me—a fear that I have never (all right, only occasionally) shared. I imagine that the male chauvinist in my dad doesn't like the idea that his daughter is supporting her spouse, even though our financial arrangements are not that different, ratio-wise.

I would have guessed that my father's financial anxiety would have lessened over time, especially now that his children are self-supporting. But recently he proved me wrong. It was my mom's birthday, and as she does every year, she invited Josh, Charles, and me to have dinner with her and my dad at their favorite restaurant. We agreed and even hired a sitter so we could enjoy ourselves. I bought her jewelry as a gift, and she loved it. When the dinner bill came, I put down my card without really thinking, expecting my mom, if not my dad, to wave it away. Josh didn't put down any card—because he's younger he still gets away with murder. Within seconds, my father scooped up my card, as though aware I might reconsider, and told the waitress to put half on my card and half on his. This meant that I wound up paying not only for Charles and me but for half of my brother, even though my mother had asked us to join her and I always thought the asker pays.

I spent the entire car ride home griping to Charles about my father's behavior. Then we got home and had to pay our nanny $100, which included sitting, her takeout dinner, and carfare home. I tossed and turned in bed, feeling angry about money. And then it struck me that maybe my behavior was on a par with my father's. True, he had acted greedy, cheap, and gauche. But I was letting a few hundred dollars keep me awake.

The next morning our daughter slept late, and we woke up after eight. "The car!" shouted Charles, bolting upright in bed. He ran out to move it across the street, but it was too late. He came back with an orange ticket for $45, our second that week. I wanted to scream at him to set an alarm and get on the ball. But instead I sighed and put it on top of the other bills. Then I went into the kitchen and made the coffee, skimping on the scoops.

Money Matters

Julia Glass

Two weeks ago, my older son asked me if he could have his allowance back. He asked calmly, without loud declarations about oppression or injustice. Alec is twelve, and about a year ago I decided to suspend his allowance for three reasons: he was refusing—almost willfully, it seemed to me—to improve his dreadful manners; he was consistently forgetting to do the simple chores his father and I had assigned him a few years before; and he was chronically losing mittens, hats, and even footwear, in response to which I was chronically deducting small amounts from his weekly pay. (He was also being especially brutish toward his little brother, though I told myself this was irrelevant.)

Bottom line: I had become a consummate nag. Nags who hate being nags are in danger of becoming something even worse (harridans? harpies? green-eyed monsters?), so in desperation and self-defense, I pulled out what I thought would surely be a powerful weapon: money. I also typed out a list detailing (1) Alec's household responsibilities and (2) behavioral and hygiene goals suitable for the so-called higher primates. Together, we agreed on the best place to post the list—at the foot of his bed—and he vowed that he would make a better effort to follow it. "When you show me that you can make progress on these things, we'll talk about your allowance again," I said. No tears, no shouting. I walked away from this civilized exchange feeling proud of myself and my rational authority. Well, we all know about pride.

Lo, these many months later, Alec is taller, and his voice is deeper, but he still hunches at the table, knees drawn up to his chin, consuming his food with orchestral sound effects and using his left hand as the companion utensil to his fork. Worse, his hair (a hill I will not die on) is so long that it swings through the spaghetti sauce when he dips his mouth toward the plate to slurp up the noodles. He never—and I mean *never*—brings down the upstairs garbage or sweeps under the kitchen table without a reminder. The one big change is that I no longer nag him about these tasks, perhaps because nagging is now reserved for homework. As for my having deprived him of any disposable income, the generosity of two grandmothers and assorted aunts and uncles has blunted all the incentive I hoped to create with my grand moratorium. He seems to receive hefty checks not just on his birthday and at Christmas but on Armed Forces Day, Canadian Thanksgiving, and every third full moon.

I'm not sure exactly when I started giving Alec an allowance: first grade, perhaps. I did so almost entirely because of peer pressure from Alec's friends. The dirty truth is that as much as I did not want Alec to feel unfairly deprived, I did not want his friends to see me as a miserly witch or to pity Alec for having that miserly witch as a mother. Basically, I caved. I started out giving him a dollar a week and said I'd increase the amount by another dollar at every subsequent birthday. On most Saturdays for the next five or six years, Alec had to remind me to pay him. The whole arrangement felt vaguely silly and definitely unconsidered.

Like many older, well-educated parents, I read way too much child-rearing advice before Alec was even out of my womb. Very quickly, having absorbed a terrifying surfeit of information about death by SIDS, breast-milk toxins, and choking on small objects, I moved ahead to reading about every subsequent stage my child would achieve if he should survive his perilous infancy. And I found myself lingering over the issue of allowance. Why? Because neither my sister nor I ever received an allowance from our parents. Of course, we badgered them intermittently about the injustice and humiliation: all our friends received an allowance. But Mom and Dad held firm: chores were simply a part of our family responsibility, not paid jobs, and if either of us needed or wanted money to buy something, we should go straight to them and say so. All reasonable requests would be granted. My parents, for all their flaws, never succumbed to peer pressure. They maintained a unified front, and they held fast to their beliefs about how to raise their children.

Me? I'm Mommy Insecurest, the queen of indecisive. So when I got to the experts' advice on children and money, I was excited. At last I would learn the truth about the allowance conundrum. Well, think again. Although most child-rearing gurus—or the ones I read— seem to agree that allowance is not a reward or a wage, they varied greatly on the issue of when and why to withhold allowance and on whether and how a parent should guide a child's way of spending it. One author counsels that while this money isn't a wage, you should definitely revoke part of it if jobs around the house are neglected (part of the allowance should be "irrevocable"). You may also do so if school performance becomes truly and chronically abysmal. Others claim it should never be withheld. One guy suggests that the money be divided into fourths, as follows: immediate use, short-term savings, long-term savings (e.g., college), and charity. (Yikes!) Some see allowance as a "teaching tool," others as a concrete expression of respect for the child's independence. Or both.

The problem is, in part, this: although I have always kept my nose above the rising tide of bills (if barely) and am, as of three years ago, paying a mortgage and supporting my family—I've even made a will and set money aside for the retirement I'm sure I'll never earn—at the core of my soul I believe myself to be a financial cretin. Alas, despite the superficial solvency, it's true. Don't ask if I understand how my mortgage *works;* I chose the "product" a trusted and very conservative adviser chose for me. As for things like amortization, credit ratings, and all those weird switchback columns on the federally sanctioned torture instrument known as the 1040, my obdurate befuddlement has me so cowed that I do everything I can to pay off my credit cards in full every month, and I attend to my quarterly taxes far more assiduously than to cleaning my house. Call it the upside of fear. Every April I go over my accountant's handiwork with glazed eyes and crossed fingers. (I can't believe I'm confessing this.)

I am not opposed to capitalism, perhaps because I don't have to be. I am one of the rare and lucky individuals who, at least for the moment, can make a living from my art—essentially, the art of daydreaming. If I'm diligent, you'll find me sitting at a desk all day making up convoluted stories about people who never existed. At make-believe—a skill I've had since before I even embarked on my excellent education—I'm apparently pretty darn good. If the most essential kind of allowance we were told to give our children were an imagination allowance, a "teaching tool" for make-believe, then I'd be the one giving the advice, not the one desperately seeking it.

Thinking about money and education always means revisiting my childhood. You are probably assuming that every time I wanted to buy a book or a candy bar, a Beatles album or a mood ring, I had to go to Mom or Dad. But after fifth grade, I rarely did. Because when I was ten—two years younger than Alec is now—I started working as a page in my local library. Actually, I loved this job; I'd have done it for nothing. But I made a meager wage that, over a few years, grew to a savings of several hundred dollars. I would cash my checks at my parents' bank and put the money in a tin box decorated with a photograph of kittens. Eventually, my father persuaded me to open a passbook savings account.

Other than books and those mammoth turquoise jawbreaker gumballs (what is it about candy that turns your tongue blue?), I bought very little. I made my first purchase of a record album in college, and I never wore much jewelry; I didn't even have pierced ears. Meanwhile, I grew fond of watching my bank balance grow in that little red passbook. Does this mean I grew up to be a frugal, fiscally wise young adult? No. I did not even follow my father's advice to take one, just one, course in economics while at college (which I now regret). I majored in art, moved to New York, and spent too much money on art supplies, more books, and meals out with friends. I lived hand to mouth for nearly two decades, right through Alec's toddler years.

His father lived this way too. Dennis is a photographer, and despite working the hours of a corporate lawyer through most of our seventeen years as a couple, his profit margin has always been slim. For thirteen of those years, we lived together—like, on top of each other—in his small rent-stabilized apartment, where we stayed until Alec was nine and Oliver four. To this day we have never merged bank accounts or made a household budget. We've never even married. There are advantages to this form of financial denial; for one thing, we never bicker about who spends more money on what. Between the two of us, through our many lean years in New York and beyond, somehow we've paid the bills—though back in our pseudobohemian days Dennis maintained the childishly rebellious habit of paying them late. (More than once, we flirted with eviction sheerly because he took pleasure in withholding the rent from the faceless but allegedly evil landlord of our apartment building. I did not find this funny.)

And then, five years ago, my first novel met with astonishing, unexpected success. Suddenly, I was earning more money than I needed to pay the bills. At first, I spent some of the surplus in extravagant ways: I had a few party dresses custom-made for the black-tie literary soirees to which we were suddenly invited. I bought my children eco-friendly toys from Vermont and tickets to upscale puppet shows. Dennis and I went out to dinner a bit more often, paying the cutthroat price of babysitting in Manhattan.

Recently, I've become somewhat more frugal—mainly because I own a house (or, to be more exact, I've put myself in debt for the rest of my life). But still, we do not budget. Money flows in and out of my bank account in quirky, unpredictable ways; I'm not sure I comprehend royalties much better than I understand hedge funds or the alternative minimum tax. But it's clear, nevertheless, that I'm the parent who will be the one to teach our children about money. (Can kids be sent away to money camp?)

One source of frustration for me is that because laws have changed to protect children from exploitation through labor, there are no paid jobs for Alec like the one I had at my local library. (At his age, I'd been working eight or ten hours a week for nearly two years.) I'm not even sure there's such a thing as a "paper boy" anymore, and he's too small to shovel snow or even push a mower—never mind that the average lawn around here is about the size of a beach towel.

In the quest to find out, once and for all, the "right" attitude toward allowance, I called the mother of Alec's best friend. She and her husband both work in finance. Yes, she told me, both of her sons receive an allowance, which they spend as they wish—how else do you learn how to handle money?—and it is unconnected to chores. Of course they must be reminded, she tells me; what red-blooded boy remembers to take out the trash? For extra chores, they can earn extra money. Yet they can lose allowance if they misplace something valuable; say, a pair of glasses. "I talk about money whenever we buy something," she said. "I compare the relative cost of one thing to another, so they understand how different things are valued in this world."

So far, so good. But then she went on to tell me how, at a certain age, each child will be given $1,000 with which to play the stock market. "They will learn about compound interest, taking risk, evaluating what you invest in. No one should reach adulthood without understanding how compound interest works." Uh oh.

"Do you know," said this mom as an aside, "that if you invest four thousand dollars in the market when you're sixteen, and if over time the market behaves as it has historically, at age sixty-five you'll have a million dollars?"

My legs turned to jelly. Well, I thought, that's what I get for asking an ex-banker about allowance. But after I got off the phone, I realized something. Buried in this woman's shrewd, highly educated

knowledge of money was a nugget of humble, sensible advice—advice
that's wise when it comes to almost any challenge of raising a child:
Just talk. Talk about money. I am a word person, and though I may
have struggled at the task, I've had no shortage of things to say to my
sons—when they've asked—about mortality, politics, emotions, God,
and sex. Tough subjects, but as a parent you expect to talk about them.
Why did I think I shouldn't talk about money? Allowance is just the
green herring.

It looks as if my preoccupation with this subject, however, has
become a bit of a lightning rod. Two weeks ago, a classmate of Alec's—
a boy who's in his larger, less intimate circle of friends—came home
from school with Alec to hang out for a while. They threw their books
on the floor and draped themselves on the edge of the kitchen table
while I made them a snack. Out of the blue, the friend declared, "I
wish you could see my dad's house. It is so sweet. Really huge. I mean,
he really scored." (This boy's parents have been divorced for several
years.)

Alec smiled and looked approving, but he said nothing. The friend
went on to describe to Alec the humongous TV screen his dad just
purchased—as well as some kind of super-deluxe Xbox game station.
"It cost over a thousand dollars, but it is so totally cool, it's really worth
the money. It's an investment," he said. He giggled. "We are loaded."
(Yes, he used that word.)

I watched Alec. He seemed fascinated. Was he covetous?

I couldn't help it. I had to say something. As I poured oyster crackers into a bowl, I said to the friend (totally failing at my efforts not to
sound like your Big Square Mom), "Wow, I guess your dad's really
successful. What does he do?"

"Yeah, he is," said the friend. "He's in insurance."

"Good for him," I said cheerily. My snooty artistic inner voice
sneered, *Oh, insurance salesman. Bet* that's *a rewarding job at the
end of the day.* I thought of Willy Loman. Except that Willy Loman is
a failure. And what did I know? Maybe selling insurance—or super-
vising people who do—*is* rewarding. The more I let my stealth critic

hold forth, the more nauseated I felt. (We won't go into my unspoken comments on the rumor that the insurance dad is currently dating a "dancer.")

So I couldn't help it. Once again I spoke. "You know," I said, "I'm glad your dad's got all that great stuff, but there's more to life than money."

"Oh yeah," the friend said loudly. "Like *luh-uhv* and *frrrriend-ship*." I felt like I'd been punched in the gut. Or landed in a Quentin Tarantino movie.

"Actually, yes," I said, my voice trembling. I served the crackers and juice. I shut my trap. I'd asked for it, hadn't I? The appetites of two growing boys brought a merciful end to that conversation.

Later, I called the money-wise mom to report this conversation. "Listen," she said at once, "there is a lot of sadness there. You have to remember that. Don't think his bragging is unconnected to the divorce. But yes, it's terrible."

She was right, and I felt guilty. I thought of the nasty tone with which that boy uttered the word "love." And yet I felt I had to discuss it with Alec—the money stuff, not the love stuff.

So, the next day, there we were driving somewhere together: as always, me, the chauffeur, up front; Alec in back. I asked what he thought about the friend's remarks. (Has anyone else noticed how today's automotive safety consciousness facilitates all those difficult parent-child exchanges in which eye contact would be the kiss of death? I wonder how many kids now learn about the facts of life in the backseat of a car. Quite a rich intergenerational irony there.)

"No big deal," said Alec.

"What did you think when he boasted about his dad's house and the Xbox thingy?"

"Nothing."

"Does he talk about money a lot?"

"No."

"Has he asked you stuff about, like, how much money we make or what our house cost, or—"

"No!" Actually, it came out more like "no-WUH!" That extra syllable of pure disgust.

"Just asking," I said.

For the next few days, whenever I was alone, I found myself running through all the clichés we're fed about money and wealth.

Money isn't everything. . . . Money makes the world go round. . . . Money is the root of all evil. . . . It's as easy to fall in love with a rich man as a poor man. . . . Money can't buy me love. During an idle moment, I went to Google and typed in MONEY PROVERBS. Normally, my rare efforts at searching the Web meet with only moderate success. Well, not this time. It seems that money does, literally, make the world go round.

Interesting how many of the proverbs come from China. *I have money, you have money; so we are friends.* And *Money can buy a lot that is not even for sale.* What, like love and friendship? *The day your horse dies and your money's lost, your relatives change to strangers.* Good thing we don't own a horse. *He that has no money might as well be buried in a rice tub with his mouth sewn up.* Don't show that one to the folks in the CIA.

Denmark: *A single bag of money is stronger than two bags of truth.*

France: *A man without money is like a wolf without teeth.* And *Money makes even dogs dance.* I guess canines loom large in a country where they get to dine in restaurants.

Holland: *A man without money is like a ship without sails.* Imagine a life without teeth *or* sails.

From the Arabic: *Money can build roads in the sea.* Yiddish: *With money in your pocket, you are wise and you are handsome and you sing well too.* Hebrew: *Marry for money, my little sonny, a rich man's joke is always funny.* Cute. *Money purifies everything.* Well, that's a relief. I *knew* the oil companies would do the right thing with their runaway profits!

From Portugal: *Give me money, not advice.*

From India: *Money hides in the tiger's ear.* Come again?

And we mustn't leave out the Greeks. *Money is the wise man's religion.*

The more of these bizarre sayings I scrolled through (on one site alone I read a list of 185), the more I began to feel, in my gut, what I've known all along but refuse to face in the most practical of ways: I'm simply afraid of money. Not of having it but of mastering it . . . and of recognizing its power—in particular, its power in the realm of love.

Yesterday I told Alec that he will begin getting his allowance again. "Thanks, Mom," he said. Not effusively, and that was a relief.

I said, "We need to talk about money more than we do."

"Okay," he said gently, as you might to an invalid.

I was about to start in with various codicils and hedgings, but I left it at that.

I *do* think it's time to talk about the value of things. Not what they cost, but what they're worth or what we've come to assume they're worth (diamonds, anyone?). How and when money matters; how and when it doesn't. It matters more than I'd like to believe it does—and I owe my sons that knowledge. I will always wonder if, perversely, my deep discomfort about finance was part of what enabled me to take the risks I took (many of them foolish) that led me to be an artist. But Alec and Oliver—thank heaven—will follow their own paths and take their own risks.

I suppose it all comes down to this: I want my children to thrive without being acquisitive; to have enough prosperity that they can be generous; to feel self-sufficient enough that they may never be bought. Let them be sensible enough to care for themselves—and, one day perhaps, for children of their own.

Meanwhile, Oliver, who's now in first grade, overhears me concede that it's time for Alec to get his allowance again. "When do I get *my* allowance?" he asks, his smile more hopeful than greedy.

Give it up, I tell myself. Chill. I take heart from the Belgians, who offer me this bit of wisdom: *Money buys cherries.*

My Brother's Keeper

Elizabeth Williams

My little brother is a con artist. And when I'm being honest, I worry that I'm partly responsible.

David was born when I was thirteen, two years after my mother remarried. I'd be lying if I said that I was excited, or even happy, about his arrival. The reality was that I felt sick to my stomach about the whole idea. In the midst of what would prove to be an adolescence fraught with fear, pain, and crushing disappointment, I had no desire to give up the one role I felt most comfortable with—being an only child. But I held out hope that when my brother came home, I'd fall instantly in love. The truth? I looked down into his brown eyes, and felt . . . nothing. But over time I softened, and one day, without even realizing it, I felt as if I'd passed through a mirror. Suddenly, I wanted to spend every waking hour with him, making goofy faces through the slats of his crib.

Awash in teenage hormones and already a perfectionist prone to smugly correcting grammar missteps, I was in awe of each developmental hurdle my brother crossed and determined to document his every movement. David smiled. David graduated from breast milk to cereal. David pooped. Without any real cognition, my obsession with my perfect little brother became my way of keeping the focus off my other problems. When I was with David and marveling at his growth, I didn't have to face my awkward teenage face—or the fact that I was not only clinically depressed but bulimic. Loving David in the most perfect way that I knew how made me feel normal. Nothing made me happier than the moments when I'd take him for a walk in our neighborhood and people would assume he was my child. Inwardly, I'd shiver with delight at the thought.

Before I knew it, I was a sophomore in high school, living the anti–John Hughes existence—neither cool and composed nor quirky and nerdy. I was ordinary. So it was with great glee that I realized, sometime after David's second birthday, that he returned my outsourced affection.

All of a sudden, when I came home from school, I no longer had to drop my knapsack and run to his bedside. Instead, I'd put my key into the latch, turn it, and find this sweet little boy waiting for me, arms wide open—the personification of approval and acceptance. Two things I felt were lacking in the rest of my life.

It was with this newfound confidence that I applied to various colleges, determined to be a writer. Thanks to my grades and the late eighties push to integrate college campuses, I found myself with several offers. I chose a large East Coast university—because, frankly, their financial aid package was too good to ignore.

As I stood in front of the arts and sciences building, alone and afraid but ready to start college, I said a tearful good-bye to my mother and stepdad. But my thoughts were with David. How would he fare without me? I told myself he would be just fine.

Not surprisingly, my fragile existence was tested under the weight of the expectations I had set for my college career. While home for Christmas break during sophomore year, I found myself stuffing back a handful of ibuprofen. Since a suicide attempt is a clear indication of a cry for help, it was decided that I would stay home for a semester to get the care I needed. So, at my mother's insistence, I told my friends that I was forced to take off a semester due to illness. With that, I was back at home, sleeping on the couch in our crowded one-and-a-half-bedroom apartment that I would now share with my mother, step-father, brother, and—the newest addition—my little sister.

My time at home was awful; I was embarrassed and depressed. The only thing that seemed remotely worthwhile was the chance to spend quality time with David. But I soon discovered that the sweet little boy I'd left when I went off to college was no longer present. Instead, a lying, angry, sometimes violent six-year-old had replaced him.

How could this be happening? I wondered. And why weren't my mother and stepfather more alarmed? But, cleaving to the family position of avoiding any discussion of real issues, I never shared my concerns with my parents. Instead, I focused my energies on David in a misguided attempt to "fix" him, while avoiding my own problems. This mostly entailed massive amounts of quality time; I thought that museum visits and babysitting would magically ameliorate his issues. But the net result was an inordinate knowledge of the intricacies of the Power Rangers on my part, and not much more. I returned to college the following semester—but not before I witnessed my brother steal money from our mother's purse. Explaining away his behavior (hey, sometimes kids do the wrong thing!), I chose not to tell my parents what I'd witnessed. That decision haunts me to this day.

Five years after what I've come to admit was my nervous breakdown, I moved to Los Angeles to write for television. Wide-eyed, naive, and armed with scripts that I'd soon discover were terrible, I got off to a rough start. My driving skills were tenuous at best; within a week of my arrival, I'd plowed my car through the front window of a restaurant. Although I technically wasn't at fault, I was forced to pay for the damage. Knowing that my family didn't have the cash to bail me out, I dipped into my meager savings and paid my debt. With my money and emotions depleted, it was time to face a harsh reality: I had bills, lots of them, and they needed to be paid.

So I entered the very large pool of recent college graduates struggling to make ends meet, and I found a PA job on a Fox TV sitcom.

I approached my new gig with vigor, all the while fantasizing that one of the show's writers would read my stuff and declare me too brilliant to fetch coffee and high-fat snacks for a living. It only took a week of grime and lack of sleep for me to realize there would be no white knight riding to my rescue. The only person who'd rescue me from my life and fix my unfortunate financial circumstances would be me. Which meant, in addition to working sixty-hour weeks schlepping scripts around town, I took odd jobs. I tried everything from walking dogs (hampered by my allergy to dogs) to transcribing porn (yes, the average porno has dialogue) in order to dig myself out of my financial hole.

At the same time, my little brother, now a high school student who had moved with our family to Atlanta, Georgia, went a different route in order to solve his financial woes: theft. One night, awash with guilt, David called me to confess that he wanted more cash than typical after-school jobs could provide. In his sixteen-year-old mind, the best way to achieve this was to steal cars in Georgia and drive them over the border into Alabama for parts. He claimed that he'd now seen the light and wanted to turn over a new, honest leaf. Desperate for this to be true, we as a family closed our eyes (and ears) and went on with our lives. I'd soon discover that he was lying.

After a few years of living in Los Angeles, I was still on my quest to achieve a fulfilling career as a writer. This meant taking a series of laborious and soul-destroying low-level jobs during the day, while I honed my writing skills at night and on the weekends. It wasn't an easy existence, but I'd developed a hardened pride about my ability to support myself.

In the midst of my "I'm Every Woman" lifestyle, I still found the time to call home and check in. Often, the news wasn't good. "Your brother took the car and stayed out all night. We were just about to call the police when he showed up," my mother said. "What the hell? Where'd he go?" I asked. I could feel my mother's shrug through the phone. It was clear that my brother was having problems, but it wasn't clear how to address them, or if it was even my job to address them.

So I took the easy way out and ignored the situation, choosing instead to focus on my career. And then one day—finally—I wrote something that demonstrated I had a modicum of talent. I got an agent, and within a month I was a working, well-paid television writer.

Anxious to leave my cat-obsessed roommate behind, I packed up my belongings—and like George and Weezy before me, I moved on up. My fifties-style apartment had a mold problem and was hardly in the sky—but it was a mere two miles from the beach. And it was all mine. After years of struggle, I relished the opportunity to finally live like a proper grown-up.

Money doesn't buy you love, but it does buy you choices. I traveled to Paris on short notice. I upgraded my car. I discovered art, and before I knew it my apartment walls reflected my love of collecting. But I didn't blow everything I had on culture and travel. I also indulged in a less noble passion—the pursuit of the perfect designer shoe.

Though I'm single, I wasn't alone when I spent my money. In my head, my family was always along for the ride. Every time I threw down a credit card at Barney's, I'd see my mother's face. Or hear my stepfather's voice: "Things have been a little slow. They cut back on my hours, so your mother and I can't take a vacation this year." I'd sign my name, and my throat would choke with guilt. A tape played in my brain on a constant loop. "Guess what, Liz, you're not just a disgusting daughter. You're a disgusting human being. How can you achieve financial freedom without giving your family the same opportunity? Yes, your work is sporadic, and you haven't saved for retirement—but it's up to you. Free your family from the bonds of middle-class life."

And so, a year into my success, I began to send my parents monthly checks. But because I'm passive-aggressive, I never used the word "guilt" to explain my gifts. Instead, I emphasized my need to "help out." Certainly, because of my status as a daughter (and a black daughter at that), no one would question my motives. As a member of the black middle class, I was raised with the ghosts of relatives past. "Uncle Lester never did get that house 'cause the white folks wouldn't give him a loan." "Aunt Ella scrubbed the white folks' floors to send her boys to college." "They run Cousin Shadow out of town just for looking at a little white girl wrong." There was always the sense that what was "mine" was "theirs." I achieved a little bit of success, and I had an obligation to those family members who never had that chance—not only to succeed but to spread the wealth.

Two years passed. I couldn't seem to figure out a way to meet a decent guy, but my career was moving at a steady clip. Though most of my television shows were canceled within the first year, I always managed to get another job. For the most part, I had everything I wanted in life. I considered myself lucky. And then my luck ran out.

David's life had been moving forward like a stock flow chart. Sometimes the line would head upward (he got a D+ instead of an F), and sometimes it would head downward (he was arrested for selling drugs). I watched my parents and little sister manage the indemnity visited upon our family because of David's poor life choices. Throw precious, hard-earned money out the window to bail David out of jail. Do it again when you pay for David to retake a failed class or when you spot him extra cash so he won't resort to anything illegal to order to make extra funds. The whole thing made me sick. But I was consistent. I said nothing.

One day, during my weekly phone call home, I caught my mother in a moment of candor. "I'm afraid David will be another black male statistic," she said. "Behind bars and broken." "No," I said. "That won't happen. I've got money now. Whatever David needs, he can come to me." As usual, I was playing the game that I'd played since childhood, "Liz to the Rescue," in which I offer myself up financially to family and friends and then secretly resent them for accepting my benevolence.

A few months later, when my cell phone rang with a familiar area code in the display, my heart sank a little. I answered the phone with a smile in my voice. "What's up, little brother?" Not surprisingly, David wanted to do more than reach out and touch his big sister. He wanted to borrow some money. Confronted with actually having to do something, I wanted to curl up and die.

My family's pathological, passive-aggressive relationship with money often turns smart, educated people into robot actors. Whenever money is the topic, our conversation exists in the small space between quotation marks. We use words like "borrow" and "lend" instead of "give," "take," or "have." It's a great way to ignore the truth, it's a great way to ignore our feelings, and it's a great way to live in denial.

Turns out David needed to borrow $200 ASAP. (Whenever he needs money, it's always urgent.) "Sure, David—no problem," I said. "What do you need the money for, by the way?" I asked partly because I was worried. Though he was now a college student, my brother had always been "criminally minded," and I wanted to make sure I wasn't funding something illegal. I instantly felt better when he explained that he needed the money to cover business he'd incurred from throwing a party.

During this time in his life, David fancied himself a mini-mogul (think P. Diddy but without a job or a realistic plan), promoting hip-hop-style parties for the local college kids. Occasionally, the parties would be a huge success. Most of the time, they'd fail miserably. Weeks and then months went by, and I'd continue to receive imploring phone calls from David to support one thing or another. The truth was, I never denied him, and I never discussed these monetary transactions with my mother. In retrospect, I should have, because it certainly would have helped to know earlier on that he was working both of us.

In high school, I was obsessed with Madonna. Couldn't read enough about her. Couldn't memorize enough stats. Madonna's mom died of cancer when Madonna was still a little girl. Madonna had a difficult relationship with her father. When Madonna went home for a visit, she slept on the family couch, and though it wasn't a king-sized bed at the Four Seasons covered in 1,000-count Frette sheets, she relished the normalcy. I remember reading that last bit of information and being horrified. Why is there a family couch at all? Madonna is rich beyond belief; why hasn't she purchased a large home for her family to live in? Why don't they benefit from her success? Once I started handing out cash to my brother on a regular basis, I finally knew the answer. The moment you start "helping" family, they grow to expect it. It's downhill from there, because being regarded as the family bank puts a strain on your relationship, no matter how loving it is. My feelings of guilt and shame about the situation I'd found myself in made it almost too difficult for me to bear.

As time went on, the support I provided to David came only in fits and spurts. In the meantime, I managed to love and be loved by various, mostly cynical men. I managed to lose those last ten pounds—only to see them return with twenty additional pounds as a bonus. And most important, after my dad died, I managed to get it. I ran, not walked, into therapy.

What I learned was this: it seems that I use money to buy familial love in the same way that others use food as a means to give or receive love. Given my past experience with bulimia, I heard it, that distinctive sound when something clicks in your brain, after my therapist made the food-money connection. But comprehension and action are two very different things.

When David was a junior in college, he got into trouble with the law, again. This time, they found enough drugs to charge him with a felony. My mom and stepdad were left with no choice but to hire a lawyer to negotiate the plea agreement. The lawyer did a great job, and David was spared jail time. But his attorney's fees were through the roof. Oddly enough, I didn't offer to pay them. It was the first time since I'd started this frenetic money dance that I was able to admit a certain truth: I was angry with my brother. In fact, I almost didn't know what to do with my feelings, I was so angry.

My mother, our mother, had sacrificed so much to make sure that she raised David in the right environment. The move to Georgia was prompted by her fear that raising a black son in a nineties-era urban setting would be a recipe for disaster. Frankly, the statistics supported her fears—and so she convinced my stepdad to transfer jobs and move the family away to a smaller city. Now her son was proving her decision wrong by selling drugs. It was an outrage.

I could no longer extract memories of David's childhood sweetness. The tiny hands and feet that I used to kiss now belonged to an angry man, whose attitude sent a clear message: David didn't give a damn about me, or the rest of our family.

With the support of therapy and a new understanding of David's issues, I found it easy to cut him out of my life. Though it displeased my mother, who would always find a way to justify his bad behavior, I decided I would love him, but from afar. Maybe not forever, but certainly for the time being.

That was, until the night I got a 3:00 A.M. phone call, a blubbering David on the other end. I had never heard him so upset before. He was desperate, depressed, and, most of all, sorry. I calmed him down, and we spoke for two hours. Primarily, he was upset about the direction his life had taken; the stealing and lying horrified him. He apologized to me for all the trouble he'd caused the family. He apologized for his lack of gratitude toward my mom and stepdad. He apologized for scamming me out of money and promised to pay it all back. Content to hear that he was growing and healing, I forgave all of the "loans." He was a poor college kid; the money was a wash. The only thing that mattered was that David made a true effort to live the best life he could. Certainly, hindsight affords me the opportunity to realize that my pseudo-Chopra musings did nothing to help my brother. In fact, by keeping our conversation to myself and not telling my mom and stepdad that David was depressed, I may have made things worse in the end.

With his depressive "episode" behind him, David somehow managed to convince the dean at his college that he deserved to graduate. My brother literally conned his way into a diploma. After the typical ups and downs that befall most college grads, he finally landed a job in the record business. As a family, we breathed a collective sigh of relief, hoping the job would be the start of something new for him. After we'd shared the late-night confessional, I felt especially relieved. That sweet little boy who trusted me implicitly was back.

David and I talked on the phone more often, about everything—

the cadre of my idiotic boyfriends, the similarities between working in television and the music business, his desire to make amends for the past and move on in a positive direction. Flush with the excitement of renewal, I didn't hesitate when he asked me for a little bit of cash to tide him over between paychecks. I was once twenty-three, and familiar with how difficult it could be to live on a meager salary. Plus, David was working steadily, which meant he had the resources to pay me back. Before I knew it, I was back on the merry-go-round. The reasons for why he needed the cash grew more and more elaborate. But each time he asked, I complied, knowing full well that it would make things worse and not better. It was the coward's way of living.

A couple of years later, my bank account was $7,000 lighter as a result of all of the money I'd loaned my brother. I felt like a fool, but was helpless to stop. And then his lies caught up with him. Our cousin, who lives not far from David, began complaining that he owed her quite a bit of money. At the same time, my parents started to receive less-than-pleasant phone calls from bill collectors looking for him. My mother began to investigate. It became possible that the job in the record business didn't exist at all. It began to look like David was making a habit out of borrowing money from attractive women and leaving them high and dry. It was likely that the fabulous loft apartment in which he claimed to be living was, in fact, a bug-infested studio.

As the lies and half-truths began to unravel, David held fast to the narrative he'd created for himself. Desperate to believe that her son was not a pathological liar at best and a sociopath at worst, my mother made more excuses. I was fed up, but too paralyzed to address my frustration. Luckily for David, I prolonged the pathology and contin-ued to give him money.

One weekend, David sent me a text message saying he needed $300 ASAP—something about his company not giving him enough petty cash to drive around the artists he was trying to sign. For the first twelve hours, I ignored the text, my stomach churning. The texts became more urgent. "RU gonna help me out, or what? I need this

$$$. Very, very important." He left several messages on my home and cell phones, but I didn't respond for an entire day. Early the next morning, I wrote him back: "Do you still need the $?" "Yes" was his almost instant reply. I read his words, lost in thought, until I realized I was texting back: "sorry, can't help u." Immediately, David called me.

Finally, I had the opportunity to tell my brother how I felt. I could have confessed how disappointed I had been by his behavior. I could have confessed my hatred of the ease with which he lies to his loved ones. I could have confessed how mortified I felt to know that he seemed to specialize in scamming women. But I said none of that. Instead, I made up a lame excuse about a change within the entertainment business, explaining that it meant I could no longer afford to support him or anyone else in my family. We finished our conversation and hung up—but not before I said my usual "I love you." That, at least, I truly meant—no matter what.

Months after our conversation, I went home to celebrate my mom's birthday. During my visit, I noticed secret, closed-door meetings between my parents and my brother. Though my sister and I speculated on what could be happening, we mostly ignored it, as party-planning duties overtook our curiosity.

At the party, as old friends and family flocked around my mother, I watched my brother sitting silently, very much alone in the crowd. His face was awash with jealousy and shame. He never noticed me watching him.

As I was leaving for the airport the following day, I got the real story. David had lost his job, and because of the ensuing financial difficulties, he'd be moving home to begin again. Immediately, I flashed back to a conversation I'd overhead between David and a party guest where he confessed, somewhat confidentially, that he was days away from a huge promotion and about to sign a lease on an apartment.

He moved in with my mother and stepdad a week later. Within a month, $300 was missing from my mother's checking account. In typical denial mode, my mother chose to believe she'd been a victim of some type of bank fraud. My sister and I whispered furtively to each other over the phone, each of us certain that our mother was instead a victim of her son's fraud. We were proven right. My mother and stepfather gingerly confronted my brother with their evidence. For three straight days he kept up the lie. Finally, when my mother cried, David confessed. Despite his promises to the contrary, he has yet to pay her back.

Most of the time, I'm able to take ownership of my role in shaping David's life. Busy with work or errands, I can admit to myself that I set a terrible precedent with the way I handled money and family. But the quiet days, without work or a relationship to distract me, are the worst. I remember the little boy whose face I covered in kisses; I remember how I drank in his soothing baby smell. I remember, and I am profoundly sad.

Planned Parenthood

Lori Gottlieb

In the end, I had to choose between my two children. Admittedly, this wasn't on a par with *Sophie's Choice*—nor did I actually have two children. But that's how I felt when I considered shaking the already tenuous financial ground on which my son's survival depended by having another child. I don't mean simply that he'd be splitting the proverbial pie with a sibling. I mean that he might not have a morsel of pie to eat. In order to have a second child, it seemed, I'd have to sacrifice the first.

Oddly enough, money was never a factor in my decision to have my son. If I thought about it at all, it was in a nebulous sort of way—which is to say that I was in complete denial about the costs involved. I was single and thirty-seven, and although I'd heard that having a child was "expensive," I didn't have time to waste analyzing bank statements or the cost of college tuition. I knew I wanted to be a parent, period—and I figured that like the gazillions of people who somehow made it work on modest incomes, I would, too. *You can't put a price on a child*, I thought. So without hesitation, I shelled out thousands of dollars for donor sperm and two intrauterine inseminations at a local fertility clinic. Later that year, I became a mom.

But then—along with the round-the-clock feedings and diaper changes—came the bills. My son was born five weeks early, and his weeklong hospital intensive-care tab was a staggering $25,000 after insurance. At the three-month mark, his pediatrician bill had reached $5,000. I took no maternity leave because, being self-employed as a freelance writer, I had to finish the work I'd been commissioned to complete before his premature delivery. So I spent $500 each week for full-time child care. I had no choice: if I didn't do the work, I wouldn't get paid. And I desperately needed the income, given that the medical bills plus the day-to-day expenses—clothes, bottles, burp cloths, bouncy seats, swings, toys, swaddling blankets, sanitizers, strollers, car seats—were burning through my savings.

Looking back, I'm astounded by my naïveté. I wasn't much different from a teenage girl who gets pregnant by her high school boyfriend and goes around telling everyone, "Oh, we love each other, we'll make it work"—to which any rational adult would reply, "With what, fairy pixie dust?"

But my desire wasn't rational. Even if I'd known that having a baby on my own would nearly bankrupt me, I would have done it anyway. I wanted a baby at—literally—all costs.

Six months after my son was born—when he was cooing and laughing and I'd fallen recklessly in love with him—I wanted a second one. If the first time around I was in denial, this time it seemed I'd gone insane. By that point, of course, I'd learned that fairy pixie dust doesn't buy diapers or pea puree; you can't barter it for babysitters or Baby Bjorns. Whereas the first time around I separated money from love, this time I realized they were inextricably linked. If you love your children, you need to be able to provide for them.

One night, while my son babbled himself to sleep in his tiny room, I sat down and crunched the numbers. Not the numbers prospective parents in my neighborhood on the west side of Los Angeles might use when considering the costs of raising children. My numbers didn't include new clothes (I figured hand-me-downs would be fine), private school, Gymboree, music enrichment classes, or even a separate bedroom in our 1,400-square-foot condo. They didn't include vacations or restaurant meals or entertainers for birthday parties. They were about scholarships and cutting corners and making do. I already had the start-up costs—the baby gear, the supplies. I already had full-time child care. In some ways, this kid would be less expensive than the first.

Meanwhile, I dismissed the figures I read on the Internet, which put the cost per child up to age eighteen at anywhere from a quarter-million to one million dollars. *Few people can afford this,* I thought. *You don't need that much money to raise a well-adjusted kid.* Case in point: my son's babysitter—the one I was paying $500 per week—had not two but three kids, all of whom were lovely. Granted, it wasn't the same; her mother watched her kids, and her quality of life was vastly different from mine. But still. People like Sandra Day O'Connor grew up with modest means. She turned out okay. So what if I had no idea how I'd afford to raise two kids past age five? Maybe Sandra Day O'Connor's parents hadn't either.

A week later, I was back at the fertility clinic, sitting across from the doctor as we discussed my plans for baby number two. My labs looked good, he said, but not as good as the previous year—so I might waste a lot of time and money if I didn't up the ante. I was now thirty-nine years old, and while I'd gotten lucky the first time around with the simple turkey baster method, the odds of getting pregnant in a timely manner with frozen sperm would be significantly better if I did an in vitro fertilization. The difference? A 7 percent versus 30 percent success rate per try. The tab? Twelve thousand dollars. I asked about a payment plan. The clinic didn't do payment plans. The first time it hadn't even occurred to me to inquire about one. Now money wasn't just a vague number—it had specific value. Twelve thousand dollars equaled six months of child care, or a year of tuition. It equaled mortgage payments on a future house where my "home office" wasn't a laptop and papers strewn across my bed, and my kids didn't have to share an eight-by-eight-foot room that could hold only a twin bunk.

On the drive home, I complained to a friend about the cost of getting pregnant.

"If you think that's expensive," she asked, "how are you going to pay for the actual kid?" It was a good question. Ignorance coupled with intense desire had worked in my favor before. But this time around, I knew what it was like to see my bank account balance dwindle to zero, to sell assets to make ends meet, to miss quality time with my son because I had to take on too much work at once to pay the bills. I knew that I didn't have the means to support another quarter-million-dollar kid. And so, on the day I was supposed to go in for my day-one ultrasound, I canceled.

Growing up, I never thought I wouldn't be able to have two kids because they'd be too expensive. I may have imagined not affording a nice house, or nice clothes, or certain material possessions. But what girl grows up thinking she won't be able to afford a child? Now I saw clearly how something as impersonal as money could determine something as personal as pregnancy; how, without money, we don't really have free will to live our lives the way we want to; how even free will isn't technically free. It comes, like everything, at a price.

When I asked friends with two kids how they made ends meet— friends who worked in public radio or as teachers, friends who didn't have the kind of incomes that would support a child to age eighteen on anything close to a million dollars, much less a quarter of that—the answer was always the same: *There are two of us.* You have to have either physical resources (a spouse to provide child care while the other spouse works) or financial resources (to pay for child care while both spouses earn money).

I had neither.

The word "resources" came up again and again. "We didn't really have the resources to have Luke," a friend said of her younger son, "but we couldn't live with the idea of not giving Gabe a sibling." When

I told her I felt the same way—I didn't have the resources but couldn't imagine not giving Zachary a sibling—she said, "It's not the same."

She was right. Having just one child is viewed differently, depending on your marital (and thus financial) status. If you're single, you're considered selfish if you have another kid (because you can't afford it); if you're married, you're considered selfish if you don't (because you aren't giving your only child a sibling).

But would I be selfish (because I couldn't afford it) or selfless (because I would have to sacrifice so much more) if I had a second child? And what if my financial situation changed? What if I got married one day, or landed a lucrative work project, or moved to a less expensive city? My son didn't have any choice in my decision to conceive him without a dad. Would he later feel resentful that I also chose to deny him a sibling? How could I explain this to him? *It wasn't infertility, honey. It wasn't even selfishness. It was . . . lack of financial security.*

And that would be the truth. It wasn't that I wanted more "adult time" than a second kid would allow—or that I wanted to spend the money we had on me. (After all, 90 percent of my clothes come from Target.) I just didn't want my son to struggle so much. I wanted him to have opportunities—like going to summer camp or doing an unpaid internship—that would be closed off to him if I also had to support his little brother or sister. I didn't want him to have to see my anxious expression each day as I picked up the mail and leafed through the bills. I didn't ever want to have to tell him that we were having leftovers for the third night in a row because we had to wait two more days for Mommy's paycheck to arrive.

Lying awake at night, I ran through the litany of only-child clichés and tried to play devil's advocate to justify my decision:

Question: Won't your son be lonely without a sibling?
Answer: He'll be lonelier if Mommy is working eighty hours a
week to support two kids.
Question: Won't he be spoiled?
Answer: Are you kidding? On my income?

Question: How will he learn to share?

Answer: Easy. We buy a cookie. I say, "That's a big cookie. Let's share." He gives me half. He eats half. I say, "Nice sharing, sweetie!" He just learned to share. (Besides, his friends with siblings have so many toys they don't have to share. This isn't the emperor in the palace; this is a kid who knows about compromise.)

Question: Won't he feel the burden of taking care of you when you're older?

Answer: That's what insurance is for.

Just weeks before, I was so sure I would have a second kid that I charged $3,000 on my credit card for extra vials of my son's donor's sperm so that he could have a full biological sibling. But as I lay there at night, something started to shift. I still craved the two-child family—but suddenly nothing felt more urgent than protecting my son's stability. I didn't go to the clinic the next month. And to my own amazement, I felt pretty sure that I could, in the long run, come to some sort of peace with my decision.

Until, unexpectedly, my will arrived in the mail. A few months before, all of this financial pondering had motivated me to update it. But the minute I saw the actual document, I knew that I had to have that second child. On the one hand, I noted how little by way of "resources" I could leave my child. *Hey, kid, your mommy's dead, and not only that, you're broke!* I wanted his guardian to have money so that at least as he struggled with my absence he wouldn't struggle with opportunity. Besides, who wants to inherit a kid who comes without child support? It's enough to ask a friend to raise him; it's quite another to ask a friend to finance him too. I'd chosen some older cousins with college-age kids as his guardians—loving cousins with a house and a pool and a basketball net in the backyard—but as I imagined Zachary growing up there, dribbling the basketball up and down the court by himself, with grandparent-like guardians and no other kids around, I began to weep.

And then I thought: even if I live to seventy-five and Zachary doesn't need guardians to replace me, who will be there for him after I'm gone? If he ends up single at nearly forty like me, where will he go for Thanksgiving? If he gets taken to the emergency room, who will the paramedics call? I imagined Zachary reading my will one day—he's sitting by himself, a grown man now, facing a strange lawyer in a strange office—and I picked up the phone to book an appointment at the clinic.

Two days later, I drove into the clinic's lot, pulled into a space, and couldn't take my hands off the steering wheel. Frozen in my car, I felt like I was about to make or break the fate of my son's happiness. I knew, of course, that a sibling guarantees nothing. I have a brother whom I see only at family occasions, who has never been there for me, and who will not be there for me when my own parents are gone. I also knew that money guarantees nothing. In fact, I grew up with both money and a sibling, and neither made me particularly happy. But would I have been even less happy had I grown up with neither?

As the security guard eyed me suspiciously, I sat in that parking lot for half an hour, with an imaginary cartoon above my head: a sack of money in one frame, and a newborn baby in another. The caption read: "Which will make you happier, Zachary?" At eight months old, he'd probably point to the more "fun" picture, the one of the baby. But at thirty-nine, with my son's livelihood on the line, I had to be more practical. I picked the sack of money and drove home.

Before I had a child, I didn't care about money beyond earning enough for the basics—rent, food, utilities, transportation, and a rare splurge at a sushi restaurant. I lived frugally, and I honestly can't recall desiring anything material and thinking, *Wow, I wish I had the money for that.* Now, though, everything had changed: money was what it all came down to. In the span of three months, I'd gone from being a person who was indifferent about money to one who had become obsessed by it. I checked my net worth online every day. I bought only generic items, or used ones on eBay. I read the labels on the supermarket shelves that listed the price per unit, and at home I made sure all the lights were turned off in unoccupied rooms. One night I dreamed I'd won the lottery, then lost it all in a stock market crash. In the dream, I had two kids, and my son was saying, "Mommy, I want pancakes!" and my daughter was saying, "I want waffles!" and I was saying, "I'm sorry, kids, but we're out of milk for the week," and they both burst into tears. I thought about going to therapy, but I didn't want to spend the money.

I remembered an incident with a boyfriend a few years back. One morning he announced that he wanted to have a lot of money. Not earn a lot of money, mind you; just have it in the bank. I thought his comment was out of character, because he worked for a nonprofit and wasn't materialistic.

"Why?" I asked. "Since when do you care about money?"

"Money is freedom," he said simply. And while I probably made some dismissive comment back then, I know now that he was right. With money, you can afford better child care, you can afford to take time off from work to *be* the child care, you can drive a safer car, live in a safer neighborhood, get a better education. If you fall ill, you can get better medical care. It wasn't about jetting off to Tahiti. It was about having security. It was about having options.

Another friend, who works as a public defender, told me that she doesn't care about money. I'm skeptical. She has a small trust fund, so she can afford not to care about money. She can live a bohemian lifestyle in her tiny apartment and with her beat-up car because she can leave it for a more comfortable one at any moment. *Poof!* I want to live in a safer neighborhood! *Poof!* I want to buy healthier food. *Poof!* I want to have a baby. *Poof!* I want a second one. *Poof!* I want to take time off from work to raise my children while they're young. *Poof! Poof! Poof!* She may not care about money until she truly needs it. Or, like me, she may never care about it on her own behalf—but I'm betting she'll care about it on her kids' behalf.

Money is freedom.

O ver the next year and a half, like a crazy person, I drove to the clinic on the first day of my period each month and sat in the parking lot, paralyzed: unable to go in, unable to go home. I'd sit there for half an hour, the security guard nodding at me like an old friend. One day I wondered if he was an only child, and when I asked, he said he had three brothers—he was close to two, one he didn't like very much. "I love my brothers," he said. "Except the little one. He's trouble, but maybe that's because nobody paid attention to him."

I realized I'd been thinking about my son all this time—but what about the second child, born into such a financially strapped family? What if I harmed not just one child's life, but two children's lives by opting to raise them when I couldn't really afford them? The problem was, I could make a convincing case for either side of the argument: *My kids will live in cramped quarters,* I'd think, only to be followed immediately by, *but when they're little, they'll have no idea their room is so small.* Or, *My son is so happy,* I'd think, *but one day he'll likely ask me for a sibling.* Or I'd think how nice it might be for Zachary not to have to share me with a sibling, given that he's only got one parent to begin with—but then I'd think of a study I read about how kids with the buffer of a sibling do better than those without it, especially in single-parent homes.

There were so many what-ifs: what if it was a girl, who would be likely to feel the effects of not having money more strongly than a boy? The clothes, the proms, the girly things that cost so much and seem so important to school-aged kids? I remember the stigma attached to the two girls in our elementary school class who grew up "poor." They both had younger siblings, and they both lived in dingy apartments across from the school instead of in comfortable houses half a mile away. I remember the birthday parties they couldn't have in their homes because there was no yard and no space inside for guests. The used jeans one of them wore. The expensive dress the other wore to the middle-school dance and her mother's public tantrum after the girl "ruined" it by spilling red punch on the lace. I didn't want either of my kids to bear the burden of that kind of shame.

Partly, I didn't want my children to become a stereotype: single mom and deprived kids. But there was also the sense that if I gave my son a sibling, he'd feel more normal. If he didn't have a father, at least he'd have more of a traditional "family." My married friends had all kinds of mommy guilt—from being away at work too much to losing their tempers every once in a while—but nothing, I think, compared to the guilt I felt about not making the right decision for my son. When I chose to have a child on my own, I assumed I'd have two. We'd be a family of three instead of a family of four. A family of two felt complete now, but I worried that later it might feel small and empty. Then again, was that an absence my child might feel? Or an absence *I* might feel and project onto him?

That cartoon bubble from the parking lot haunted me: a sack of money, or a baby. You can have one, even though the latter depends on the former. If you save the money, you lose the baby; if you have the baby, you lose the money. It was an impossible choice.

I sat in this limbo until just before my forty-first birthday, when my son was a delightful two-year-old, when nearly all of his friends were joined by newborns at home, and when he started referring to his favorite stuffed animal as his little brother. My income was flowing, but as a freelancer, I knew it would never be stable. If I had another child, I'd make almost nothing that first year. It didn't make sense to have a second child, but it didn't matter. I was old enough now in fertility years that if I couldn't make a decision, perhaps fate would. I figured I'd give it one shot—one $12,000 gamble with a 30 percent chance of success—and if I got pregnant, it was meant to be. If not, ditto.

So at nearly forty-one years old, I walked into the clinic, paid $500 for labs and an ultrasound, and spent an hour going over the medication protocol with the nurse. I called the pharmacy, ordered the fertility drugs, and instructed them to charge the $2,500 on my credit card. I had my sperm shipped out for another $300. I turned down $5,000 in work that month because of the appointments and two procedures and bed rest an IVF would entail. I was glad to relinquish the decision, to let not my bank account but biology figure it out.

Later that day the nurse called with news that my labs looked great—this time, they'd come back with the same "very fertile" numbers I'd had when I conceived my son three years before—and, coupled with the fact that I produced more eggs than usual that month, my chances of success went up significantly. I was elated, but by the time I was to give myself the injections that night, the terror I'd felt in the parking lot returned.

I opened the box of hormone injections, got out a needle, and remembered my mother's blunt reaction when I'd told her, many months back, that I wanted to have another child. "It's not fair to the child!" she wailed. "That child will have *nothing*!"

At the same time, I considered how intensely I love Zachary—how he does indeed have something, and how if my mother had said the same thing the first time around, she would have been wrong. Maybe she was wrong about the second kid too. But what if she was right? Could I take that risk with my kids' lives?

Money, of course, isn't insurance—and, in a perverse way, having more than one child has often been used as insurance against the unthinkable. In the old days, after all, you'd have four kids to end up with two. If anything ever happened to my precious son, I don't know how I'd survive—unless I had a second child for whom I'd be forced to go on. On the other hand, would I feel more secure with a second child? Or would I feel as though I'd have two to possibly lose—or leave as orphans without resources? In one sense, our family would be stronger. In another, it would be weaker. But if I didn't try to have a second child, would I be putting all my eggs, so to speak—all our family's eggs—in one basket?

As I dipped the needle into the vial, and watched the pricey liquid fill it up, I realized that if I didn't push the plunger, money would become to me what my son's plush dog that he carries around has become for him—a security blanket. Its presence in my retirement account would reassure me that my son wouldn't be faced with choosing to have only one child someday, like I was. For the rest of my life, money would have particular resonance for me, and its value would never again be the literal number written on each green bill or the electronic printout of a brokerage statement. Money would represent a different kind of cost—an emotional one with intangible value.

I knew all that, and yet I didn't give myself the injections that night. Nor have I been back to the clinic. Ironically, in my year and a half of ambivalence, I spent $10,000 on a baby I ultimately, painstakingly, decided not to have. Ten thousand dollars I could have spent on education funds, or soccer camp, or Little League, or hundreds of trips to Sea World. Despite the occasional pang of grief, I feel I made the right decision—but still, I pay $30 per month to store that frozen sperm I'll never use. Each time I see the automated charge on my credit card statement, I contemplate canceling but never do. Like a lost loved one's clothes hanging for years in the closet, the sperm—$3,000 worth—will be the last thing to go.

The Price of Admission

Leslie Bennetts

When our son entered fifth grade, he transferred to a new school where his classmates had been together since prekindergarten. Concerned that it might be hard for him to penetrate long-standing cliques and make friends, my husband and I encouraged Nick to initiate a playdate. After some parental prodding about who seemed nice, he finally came up with a name, and we handed him the phone.

Finding the boy required a couple of calls; his family had two primary residences, a Park Avenue apartment and a suburban estate. Nick finally located him, talked for a moment, and then returned. "We're having a playdate," he said, "but it's in Palm Beach."

Further questioning elicited the news that the boy's family went to their house in Palm Beach every weekend, and they'd invited Nick to join them. Owning a weekend place in the Hamptons or upstate New York is taken for granted among much of the well-to-do professional class in Manhattan; our children had often spent time at their friends' country houses. But Palm Beach was a new one on us, and getting there would clearly require airplane flights. Nick needed friends, however, and so—hoping the cost wouldn't be prohibitive—I phoned the boy's mother to ask about coordinating the reservations.

"Oh, that won't be necessary," she said cheerily. "We have our own plane, so our driver will pick up the boys after school on Friday and take them straight to the airport. All Nick needs is a bathing suit, tennis whites, and a blazer in case we go to dinner at the club."

Umm—okay. Great. Thank you so much.

When Nick phoned from their oceanfront estate in Palm Beach, he could scarcely contain his astonishment. "David doesn't have a room," he exclaimed. "He has a wing!"

As it turned out, David's family couldn't have been nicer, and Nick had a wonderful time that weekend. My husband and I were left with a mildly disorienting mixture of gratitude for their hospitality to the new kid in class, bemusement at their lifestyle, and concern about where we ourselves fit into this picture. How do you reciprocate a playdate like that?

Such feelings were all too familiar. Ever since our children entered school, my husband and I had been dealing with a peculiar form of culture shock whose proximate cause was the extreme wealth of their classmates' families. In the rarefied world of Manhattan's elite private schools, where the parent directories included a bumper crop of newly minted billionaires and multimillionaires, my husband and I—both journalists—had always been out of our league financially. The lifestyles of our children's fellow students were characterized by conspicuous consumption at a level so extreme as to resemble parody; in some circles, the bestselling *Gossip Girl* books and the television series chronicling the ludicrously profligate antics of its teenaged characters seemed more like reportage than social satire.

Although I too grew up in Manhattan, I was raised with different values, and the city my own family lives in today bears little resemblance to the one inhabited by my parents during the 1950s. Their attitudes were more bohemian than conventional, and both chose artistic careers. They had little interest in money or material things, and even less regard for people who flaunted their wealth. They respected intellectual and creative achievements, and they were not impressed by the extent of anyone's financial assets. No one ever suggested that my brother and I select our professions, much less our spouses, with economic considerations in mind. As a result, I rarely gave money much thought; as long as I could pay the bills, it simply didn't matter to me. It was only when I embarked upon parenthood that the need for significant financial resources began to dawn on me.

When I got pregnant and my husband and I confronted the necessity of a bigger home, real estate sticker-shock provided the first trauma—one familiar to virtually all New York City parents, no matter what their socioeconomic level. But for us, the really tough stuff began with the decision to send our children to private school— an issue that placed our professed values on a collision course with our personal goals.

My husband believes strongly that white middle-class families should support the public schools by enrolling their children and working to improve the system. I agree in theory, but I wasn't willing to sacrifice the quality of my children's education to abstract principles, no matter how admirable—and I feared that public school, at least in New York City, would represent such a sacrifice. It's hardly news that money buys children the kind of advantages that encourage academic achievement; even in the best of circumstances, the public school system can't compete with the small classes, individual attention, abundant resources, lavish facilities, and extraordinary opportunities offered by first-rate private schools. Others might disagree; I know many parents who reached different conclusions on this issue. But I felt strongly that my own kids would fare best in private school, and I was determined to find a way to afford it.

My husband suffered far more guilt about this choice than I did, but we were equally daunted by what it would cost. Private school tuition may not represent much to investment bankers and hedge fund managers—"Tuition is chump change!" scoffed one man I knew who earned an eight-figure income—but for two writers, the price of admission seemed horrific.

And so we made a deal. We wouldn't buy new clothes. We would eschew luxuries. We wouldn't own a country house—or even a car.

We would take vacations only when they were work-related trips financed by a paid assignment. We would do whatever we had to do to make money, and somehow we would scrounge together the tuition for private school.

Managing this challenge has ranged from difficult to excruciating, but we've never regretted the decision. Both of our children received a fantastic education in an intellectually stimulating environment, and they've also benefited from the rich array of artistic, cultural, and other opportunities afforded by their schools.

But the social milieu accompanying such privileges was considerably more challenging than my husband and I anticipated. Our first exposure to the dramatic income gap between us and our peers had come when our daughter was four and we enrolled her in a private school where many of our friends had sent their children. It was a comfortably homey place known for its relatively unpretentious style and its emphasis on values, and all went well inside the classroom. But the parents were also expected to get to know each other, so we dutifully showed up for a parent-teacher dinner given by the family of one of our daughter's classmates.

Their apartment was impressive—enormous and luxuriously renovated, with a huge kitchen that could have accommodated the entire grade. Thinking about my own galley kitchen, I couldn't help but feel a pang of envy. Further economic distinctions came into sharp focus at the end of the evening. As a group of departing parents crowded into the building's elegant mahogany-paneled elevator, I looked around and realized that every other mother was wearing a glistening floor-length mink. I was the only one in a modest cloth coat.

Although I felt a momentary pang of self-consciousness, for the next few years we coexisted alongside the super-rich parents of our children's classmates without undue discomfort. We were admittedly startled to realize that our daughter's class enjoyed a private visit to a major new New York City institution because another student's family had given the money to build the institution, which accordingly bore their name. Nobody related to my husband or me has ever earned, let alone donated, the kind of money that gets a building named after you. But such civic generosity is admirable and has contributed immeasurably to the betterment of the city I love so much.

Other manifestations of family wealth were less visible, but more pervasive. I was surprised to learn that many of our friends routinely received financial help from their parents to pay their kids' tuition bills. "You're the only person I know who's paid for private school on their own," one friend told me a couple of years ago.

Since the day we graduated from college, neither my husband nor I have ever taken any money from our parents—a fact that has left each of us with a complicated mixture of pride at what we've accomplished on our own, the self-respect earned through self-reliance, and the occasional twinge of envy toward those whose circumstances are cushier.

But the excessive wealth of people who rub your nose in it can really challenge your character. It's easy to sustain a tolerant, live-and-let-live attitude about rich people who are gracious and respectful of others. And yet privilege can also breed arrogance, a sense of entitlement, and condescension toward those of more modest means. Some people wield their money like a weapon, and when I've found myself on the receiving end—particularly from those who have not actually earned their good fortune—there have been times when I've had difficulty maintaining my emotional equilibrium.

In my experience, people who inherited or married their money seem to disparage the nonrich more frequently than hardworking entrepreneurial types who made their own fortunes. The careless putdowns range from insensitivity to outright insults, and they can carry a memorable sting.

I still flush with embarrassment when I remember the surprise birthday party I gave for my husband years ago. Because it was held in our own apartment—I couldn't afford to rent a larger venue—I had to wait until he left for work that morning before dashing out to do all the shopping for the food and supplies whose sudden appearance in our home would have made him suspicious. The day sped past in

a frantic whirl of cooking and preparing for eighty friends and colleagues. My husband's birthday is in mid-August, and that year it fell
during a brutal heat wave. When the first guests started arriving, I
was still frantically trying to finish up the last-minute tasks. Sweating
and breathless, I hadn't even put on my makeup or changed into my
party outfit.

One of the early arrivals was a friend whose family is worth hundreds of millions of dollars; their palatial homes are maintained by
fleets of servants. As she watched me desperately tearing around, she
started to laugh and make fun of my disheveled state. "Look at her!"
she exclaimed. "Can you believe this?" Finally, after she had gotten
all the other guests focused on what a mess I was, she delivered the
coup de grâce. "My God, Leslie, this is ridiculous!" she said, her tone
withering. "Haven't you ever heard of caterers?"

I felt as if I'd been kicked in the stomach. It obviously didn't occur
to her that some people lack the money to hire caterers, just as she
hadn't thought to ask if she could do anything to help. In her eyes, my
do-it-yourself-on-a-budget efforts were worthy of scorn, not respect.

It's been hard enough to manage my own emotions at moments
like this, but making sense of them for my kids is a bigger challenge.
Living in a world whose social norms are dictated by the unthinking
assumptions of the ultra-privileged, my husband and I have struggled
to translate our conflicted reactions into a coherent philosophy, not to
mention consistent household rules.

One of our priorities was impressing upon our children that their
education was a privilege, and that they should never take it for
granted. We made it clear to them that we worked hard to provide
this privilege, and we expected them to earn it by doing their best, as
we were doing our best on their behalf.

But when they transferred to their second private school, they
joined a world characterized by such extreme wealth that the income
gap between our family and many of their peers reflected a corre-
sponding gulf in values. A far more high-profile institution than their
first school, this one boasted a reputation for intellectual achievement

and academic rigor that was accompanied by an equally daunting reputation for the inordinate wealth and power of its parent body. In this world, private school was a given—along with a mind-boggling array of other luxuries.

I can't pretend that we didn't know what we were getting into; when we took Emily to her admissions interview, the girl ahead of her—a fellow fifth grader—was wearing a Prada backpack. My own purse was a $20 microfiber bag from Target.

By middle school, many of the girls were taking $100 facials, $150 haircuts, and $250 worth of highlights for granted. Regular manicures, pedicures, and Brazilian bikini waxes were regarded as basic requirements. But all that paled in comparison with the rituals and expectations we encountered when Emily entered seventh grade. With a bar or bat mitzvah virtually every weekend, that year hit us like a hurricane, and we were instantly sucked into the maelstrom.

Most of these events were high-end affairs, and many had clearly cost hundreds of thousands of dollars. Every Saturday night Emily headed off to the Rainbow Room or the Pierre Hotel ballroom for yet another black-tie extravaganza, replete with a staggering array of expensive entertainment. Many of her friends wore a new Betsey Johnson dress to each party, and Emily quickly realized that repeating the same outfit was looked down upon.

Not only did her classmates' parents fork over hundreds of dollars for each skimpy little dress to adorn their gangly thirteen-year-old, but they also spent lavishly on the gifts for every event. Unfamiliar with the unspoken rules, I started out buying real presents—only to be informed by my daughter that nobody wanted an actual gift. This was different from little kids' birthday parties. What was expected here was a check.

Since she would ultimately attend scores of these occasions, I settled on a very modest amount to give the children who were mere acquaintances, with a bit extra for close friends. Five years would pass before my daughter admitted to me how embarrassed she was made to feel for giving such small checks. Her classmates routinely amassed tens or even hundreds of thousands of dollars as their bar mitzvah haul, and our gifts had been ludicrously inconsequential, even though the cumulative cost represented a considerable financial sacrifice from my point of view.

When Nick entered seventh grade, the frenetic schedule started up all over again. By the time he was finished, our kids had attended somewhere between 100 and 200 bar and bat mitzvahs. Fewer than half a dozen children—one of them the boy with the house in Palm Beach—had requested that their friends make charitable donations instead of giving them money. Perhaps other kids' parents made them donate some of what they received to worthy causes. But among the kids, glee about spending their bar mitzvah loot was the prevailing theme.

As usual, my husband and I felt painfully ambivalent. Our children certainly enjoyed the nonstop partying provided by these occasions, and because both were still relative newcomers to their school, we were grateful they'd been invited. Since I'm not Jewish, this whole scene was new to me, and I was astounded by the level of material excess that characterized every aspect of the bar mitzvah phenomenon.

But my husband, who is Jewish, was furious. His own bar mitzvah had been an intimate, deeply meaningful event, attended only by family and close friends. His mother did all the cooking for the party after the ceremony, as she did for each of his three brothers. Forty years later, he was appalled by the news reports on families who spent a million dollars to have some rock star sing at their child's bar mitzvah.

As he pointed out, however, such spectacles were not confined to spiritual occasions. Among people of every religious, ethnic, and racial description, conspicuous consumption had become the norm throughout American society—from over-the-top sweet-sixteen parties to lavish "destination" weddings that often saddled a young couple with crushing debts. The bling culture seemed to have overtaken the whole country, and the old-fashioned enterprise of parenting had been transformed by the frenzy of getting and spending.

The lifestyles of the new gilded age were seductive, to be sure—and our children were often the beneficiaries of great generosity. Nick was invited to vacation at a friend's house in the south of France. On two different summers, Emily was taken on a grand tour of Europe by a friend's family. My husband and I debated whether to let her go; we were quite uncomfortable about accepting such an extravagant offer. But Emily took Latin, French, and Italian in school, dreamed of studying in France, and talked about becoming a translator when she grew up. Since we couldn't afford to take the family to Europe, it seemed heartless to deny her the opportunity to broaden her horizons on such a spectacular scale.

Broaden them she did. She spoke French in France and Italian in Italy; she went to fabulous museums; she learned firsthand about great art and architecture. She also dined at Taillevent in Paris and stayed at five-star hotels in Italy, France, Germany, and England. Hearing about all this, my mother made nervous jokes about the expectations such experiences might engender. "After this, aren't you afraid the rest of her life will seem like an anticlimax?" she asked.

We were indeed. Nor were we alone in harboring such concerns. Our children's school boasted one of the most extensive scholarship programs of any independent school in the country, along with one of the most diverse student populations. A significant number of children came from families with far more limited financial resources than our own. As time went on, our kids developed friendships with students from a wide range of backgrounds and socioeconomic levels, and my husband and I got to know parents who worried about the same things we did.

But others seemed utterly oblivious. In raising children, it is axiomatic that parental overindulgence can lead to a sense of entitlement among their offspring. And yet some of our fellow parents appeared to give little thought to the long-term impact such coddling might have on their kids.

At one school fair, Nick and another fifth grader were dashing off to enter a sports game when the other boy asked me to hold his cell phone.

"Don't forget to take it back from me afterward," I told him.

The boy shrugged. "I've already lost sixteen of them," he said. "If I lose this one, my parents will just get me another one."

Nick looked stunned. His father and I had thus far refused to buy him even one cell phone, let alone sixteen of them. That night he asked me what I'd do if he got a cell phone and then lost it. I told him it would depend on the circumstances, but unless he'd been grossly negligent, we would probably replace his first phone. If he lost another, however, he'd be out of luck; we would consider such carelessness to be proof that he wasn't yet responsible enough to handle that privilege, and we certainly wouldn't continue to buy him new ones if he kept losing them.

Nick sighed. By this time, he and his sister were keenly aware of the chasm between their own parents' values and those of many of their friends' parents. Whether the subject was an early bedtime or required chores or the question of why other kids got to have a TV in their room, our mantra was the same: "We don't care what everybody else does. We have to do what we think is right."

But this was a constant challenge. The city was awash in the multi-million-dollar bonuses of the Wall Street warriors whose wealth had spawned an explosion of demand for luxury goods. By middle school, our kids were struggling with the relentless pressure to keep up with hordes of designer-clad eleven-year-olds. Even as prepubescents, all the girls were suddenly wearing a certain Tiffany necklace, or carrying a particular wildly overpriced handbag. By the next season, of course, the must-have status signifiers had been replaced by new ones, leading anyone who bought into such fads to become enslaved by ever-escalating demands.

When Emily hesitantly asked for the item-of-the-moment as her thirteenth birthday present, we finally broke down and gave her a small Tiffany silver necklace. But such concessions were rare. Far more common were our heart-to-heart talks about why she wanted

certain things and what it meant to spend hard-earned money on fri-
volities that briefly seemed necessary, just because "everyone" had
the same thing, but would soon become obsolete. The way I see it,
a child's every request offers a teachable moment. When she wants
something she doesn't really need, a responsible parent can help her
explore that desire—and hopefully steer her thinking, as well as her
aspirations, in a different direction.

While Emily was in middle school, I often felt very guilty about my
refusal to accommodate the prevailing habits of her peer group. But
as she got older, I noticed that she was increasingly making such distinctions on her own. The Tiffany necklace was retired to her jewelry
box; she no longer wanted to wear the same thing "everyone else" was
wearing. She began to examine the values that exalted such expenditures, and to understand what they represented. Instead of hanging
out with the shopaholic girls who thought nothing of dropping $1,000
at Barney's if they had half an hour to kill, she made other friends
with more down-to-earth values—and budgets.

And when she fell in love for the first time, it wasn't with one of the
rich boys who had wooed her; instead, she chose a young man whose
amused disdain for materialism-run-amok helped to reinforce her
own growing disapproval of the stretch limos, the parties on parents'
yachts, the expensive drug hobbies and heedless profligacy of so many
of her peers. In high school, one boy they knew had a black American
Express card, which—as every kid was aware—required a minimum
annual expenditure of $250,000. When a friend of his—not even a
girlfriend, just a friend—expressed the desire to have dinner in Paris
one day, they hopped on a plane and were soon dining in Paris. Emily
and her boyfriend just rolled their eyes.

In the meantime, my husband and I tried hard to make our children understand that good fortune confers responsibility. Their high
school required every student to perform eighty hours of community
service in order to graduate, so our family started volunteering at the
neighborhood soup kitchen. After graduating, Emily continued to volunteer there during her college breaks. Last summer she worked as a

waitress in a café for $7 an hour. The job was hot, sweaty, and hard, but she loved it. Her brother is three years younger, however, and just when Emily seemed to have evolved into a young woman with responsible values, it was Nick's turn to navigate the social minefields of early adolescence.

Throughout Emily's school career, I dutifully attended every parent discussion group, eager to find out what her peers were up to and learn how other parents were handling various issues. The gatherings weren't really parent groups at all; the fathers never showed up, and working mothers were woefully underrepresented, probably because they were too busy working to devote their weekday mornings to such activities. The discussions were attended almost exclusively by stay-at-home moms whose husbands—or fathers—had made enormous amounts of money. When Nick reached thirteen, I gave up on trying to participate.

The last meeting I attended was held at the opulent Upper East Side town house of one of Nick's classmates. When another mother suggested that we go around the room and discuss how much money we gave our kids for their allowances, the conversation turned to what the boys in the "in" crowd were doing on weekend nights.

To my surprise, I learned that they were gathering for poker games that cost $50 to $100 just to enter. Most of the mothers in the room apparently gave their sons a $100 allowance every week, but they were now wondering whether to double this amount so that poker night alone wouldn't deprive their boys of disposable income for the week's other entertainments. The same question was raised in reference to the girls; while the boys were gambling, it seemed the girls were getting together for $100 dinners at swanky restaurants.

I was incredulous. Even if I were a billionaire, I wouldn't want my thirteen-year-old to grow up thinking such activities were an ordinary part of daily life. But these mothers, although they complained about the high cost of their children's social lives, seemed to assume there was nothing that could be done about it. The moral questions inherent in spending money like this never even came up.

When the discussion reached my end of the room, I said, "I don't give my kids an allowance."

"What do they do for money?" another mother asked.

"They work for it," I said.

Every head in the room swiveled around as the other women did an exaggerated double take. "*Work?* What do you mean, work? What do they do?" one demanded.

"They babysit. They walk other people's dogs. They take care of the neighbors' cats and water their plants when they're away. My son does computer troubleshooting. They both do all kinds of things to earn money."

The mothers all seemed scandalized. "Well, *our* children are very busy," one said primly. "They play sports, and they're much too busy to—to—*work*." The very word made her mouth pucker, as if it tasted bad.

I refrained from adding that Nick, who plays four instruments and three sports, is busy too. There was clearly no point. Their disdain made me feel like the proverbial skunk at the garden party, and their values were so different from mine that there didn't seem to be any way to bridge the gap. Although I have worked for pay since my senior year in college, most of the other mothers in the room hadn't worked in many years—and some had never supported themselves in their lives. "I mean, who are we kidding? I was on my father's payroll till I was past forty," one woman said. Presumably her husband has since taken up the slack.

I never went back to another parents' discussion group. But I often wonder how these people's children will turn out. I have many affluent older friends whose kids are now young adults, and some are having trouble making the transition from dependent child to self-sufficient grown-up. They can't seem to cope with the idea that they're actually supposed to support themselves, let alone figure out how to do it. My friends report conversations in which their adult children grow indignant about any parental reluctance to take care of the financial obligations they incur. Somehow, they grew up expecting that somebody else would always foot the bill. Such young people are often notable for many fine qualities, but these don't necessarily include a strong work ethic or a sense of personal responsibility.

And yet some families apparently don't regard this syndrome as a problem. From John D. Rockefeller to Warren Buffett, America has spawned a long series of self-made men who thought it unwise to hand down their fortunes on a silver platter. Instead, these old-fashioned tycoons upheld the character-building effects of controlling their children's spending, making them work for what they got, and limiting their inheritances. But among today's nouveaux riches, very different values frequently prevail.

When our sons were in middle school, another mother and I fell into a conversation about the boys' respective interests and abilities. Her own father is worth hundreds of millions of dollars; never serious about a career, she herself had quit working years before she had children. She saw no reason for her son to bother with earning a living either. "He'll never have to work, so he can do whatever he wants to do when he grows up," she commented.

Her complacency astonished me. It seems like a terrible risk to let your kids think that somebody else will always support them. What if their circumstances change and they have to take responsibility for themselves? Family fortunes rarely endure over the long haul, if history is any guide. In China two thousand years ago a scholar wrote: "Wealth never survives three generations." During the Middle Ages, the European proverb warned: "Clogs to clogs in three generations," a formulation echoed in nineteenth-century America as the saying: "From shirtsleeves to shirtsleeves in three generations." Adam Smith spelled it out in *The Wealth of Nations:* "Riches, in spite of the most violent regulation of law to prevent their dissipation, very seldom remain long in the same family."

Unencumbered by vast wealth, my own kids have always understood that they will need to make their own way in life, a challenge they seem increasingly ready to take on. At fifteen, my son started his own Web design company, and it's flourishing. A passionate guitar student, he wanted to buy an expensive guitar, but his father and I thought it cost too much. So Nick figured out how to repair a broken computer and sold it on eBay for $1,500. He spent the money on the guitar, which he plays every day.

Emily survived the fierce competition of the college admissions process despite the fact that it wasn't exactly a fair contest, as other parents sometimes made clear. "Of course Stephen will get into Brown—we gave them half a million dollars last year," one father told me condescendingly.

Emily and Nick have had no such illusions about their own prospects. "Guess how much money we've given to any of the colleges you're interested in? Zero," I informed them. "You're going to have to earn your way in on merit." What a concept!

Emily nonetheless got into the Ivy League university of her choice. When she arrived, she noticed that more than one building bore the family name of a high school classmate who was also accepted. But for now, my children still believe that hard work and high performance can get you where you want to go in life.

At college, Emily immediately made friends with a fascinating group of students, mostly foreign. They grew up all over the world, from Singapore and Beirut to Paris and London. They were all smart and sophisticated—and most of them came from wealthy families, whether Chinese or Iraqi or French.

A few weeks into her first term, Emily asked if she could bring her new crowd home for fall break. Before they arrived, she e-mailed me an adorable photograph of half a dozen girls, all dressed up and on their way to a special event, and then phoned to tell me about each one. After describing their personalities, interests, and family backgrounds, she added, "I know you don't care about this stuff, and you probably didn't even notice their clothes, but every girl in this picture is wearing an unbelievable outfit. Marc Jacobs, Dolce & Gabbana, Gucci—"

She went down the list, identifying each designer getup for her oblivious mother. Every outfit had apparently cost thousands of dollars. At the end of the line was my daughter with a radiant smile on her face, looking so happy it brought tears of gratitude to my eyes.

"And I'm wearing that cute dress I got on sale at H&M for seventeen dollars," she said, laughing delightedly. "Isn't that great?"

By the next semester, however, she had also made other friends, most of them on far more limited budgets. "It's really nice to be around people who can't just go out and drop a hundred dollars and not have to think about it," she said to me one day. "It puts things in perspective. Money has meaning. There's a finite amount of it, and if you do one thing with it, you can't do another. The world I grew up in is not how normal people live. It's not reality." She grinned. "It's really refreshing to be around people who are dealing with reality," she said.

Am I proud of my children for growing up with realistic values about money? You bet I am. Do I feel some satisfaction about the job my husband and I did in helping to foster those values? Yes, in all honesty, I do.

But mostly what I feel, as my children prepare to leave the nest, is the combination of hope and anxiety that has always characterized parenting for me. Life is fraught with so many unforeseeable challenges. As a parent, you want more than anything to protect your children from harm, and knowing you can't always do that is excruciating.

So I try to find comfort in the idea that my husband and I have given our kids the tools to cope with whatever lies ahead. These days the headlines are full of dire news about the economy; our protracted national spending spree has collapsed in mountains of debt, foreclosures, layoffs, and bankruptcies. Those who thought the joyride would never end may find their sense of well-being battered by hard times; self-esteem that derives from wealth and possessions can vanish all too readily with reversals of fortune.

I can only hope that my children have learned to build their lives on a sturdier foundation, one fortified by self-reliance, hard work, independent thinking, personal responsibility, and pride in accomplishment. When such traits are embedded deep in your character, nothing can take them away from you, or so I tell myself. If my children aren't spoiled or addicted to self-indulgence, they'll always be able to fend for themselves.

Won't they?

The Inheritance

Dani Shapiro

"Someday you're going to die." I was on the phone with my mother when she issued me this existential news flash. I crouched on the stairs of my brownstone in Brooklyn, the receiver pressed so hard to my ear that my head hurt. My mother was just a few miles away, in her apartment on the Upper West Side. "Someday you're going to die," she repeated, as if one reminder might not be enough, "and Michael will remarry."

Michael, my husband, was at that moment in the kitchen feeding our eighteen-month-old son, Jacob, his green beans. I had walked out of the kitchen when the phone first rang, the caller ID flashing my mother's name. As far as I was concerned, caller ID was what God had created on the eighth day. I climbed farther up the stairs and tried to keep my voice to a whisper. Even though Jacob was just a toddler, I didn't want him to hear the tone I used when speaking to my mother. I knew I sounded cold, withholding—like a complete and total bitch. But it was better than the alternative, which was where I was headed. I could feel my insides dissolve, my bones shrink until I was a bewildered little girl once again.

"How can you *say* that?" I wailed. I wasn't sure which was more disturbing: that my mother was gleefully informing me of my future demise or that she was certain (*gleefully* certain) that my husband would make quick work of finding a new bride.

"Because it's true," my mother said. "And that's why I'm redoing my will."

Fuck you fuck you fuck you. It was a little song in my head.

"Michael will start a new family with a young wife," she went on, as if she were a psychic looking into a crystal ball. "He will pay attention to his children from that marriage, and Jacob will be left out in the cold. I need to protect my grandson."

"He *is* protected!" I screamed into the phone. "Michael would never do that! He's a wonderful father! You don't even know him!"

"And whose fault is that? You've kept us apart! You've kept me out of your life, Dani, which is your choice. But I feel sorry for you."

I closed my eyes. We had reached the *I feel sorry for you* stage. My mother tended to pull this one out of her arsenal when all else failed, followed closely by *someday I'm going to die and you're going to feel very, very guilty.* Like many of her best shots, she had used it so many times that it had pretty much lost its power.

But everything between us was different now. Now, my mother was actually dying. She had been diagnosed with terminal lung cancer and had perhaps a few good months left. This was a shock to us both. She was seventy-nine years old, and I was forty. I had fully anticipated that she would live past the century mark and that I would be an old woman by the time she died. That is, if I survived her at all—which neither of us really expected I would. My mother was a gale force, a hurricane, a tornado. Being her daughter involved finding any available branch and holding on for dear life.

"I want you to come see Dena with me," she said.

Dena had been my mother's fancy New York City attorney ever since my mother started pursuing legal action against various individuals and corporations a few decades earlier. Dena had drafted letters on my mother's behalf against, in no particular order, insurance companies, investment banks, rabbis, shopkeepers, and relatives. Just

in the family department, Dena had maintained an expensive cor-
respondence with my mother's brother, her brother-in-law, her sister-
in-law, and her stepdaughter—my half-sister Susie. My mother, when
she got wound up, could talk for a long time. When I was in college,
I used to put down the phone, head to the dormitory kitchen, get
myself a drink, and come back to the phone to find my mother still
talking. I doubt that Dena ever cut her off. I wouldn't have either if I
had been billing $600 an hour. Many nights, as I tossed and turned, I
pictured the lavish addition to Dena's suburban New Jersey home that
my mother's dollars had built.

"Why do you want me to come to Dena with you?" I asked.

"Because I've redone my will," my mother said.

I bit my tongue to stop from saying, *again.*

Later, I would come to understand certain things. When my mother
no longer was able to answer her own phone and it fell to me to
check her messages, I understood that the only people who called my
mother were people she paid. For years she had put her apartment on
the market, then taken it off. So real estate brokers regularly called. *Hi,
Irene, it's Bob from Brown, Harris. I have a lovely classic six to show
you on West End Avenue.* Travel agents checked in. *Mrs. Shapiro,
Lori from Silver Seas Cruises, calling to see if you're still interested
in the Galápagos trip.* Her stockbroker, her accountant, salespeople in
various department stores who worked on commission. The lady from
the Chanel counter at Bergdorf Goodman, offering a special gift box
with a purchase of $150 or more. The man from the Armani Boutique,
calling to say that the navy skirt in her size had just arrived.

Changing the fine points in her will—something she had done at
least a half-dozen times during the past few years—must have en-
sured her a decent flurry of contact with the outside world, without
which she would have been lonely and lost. Silence and introspection
were out of the question. She couldn't possibly face the wreckage she
had made of her life. She had alienated all of her remaining family

and most of her friends, so instead, she kept moving, surrounded by paid professionals. Redoing her will involved multiple calls and meetings with Dena, with her investment advisers, and, ultimately, with me—her angry, hostile, exasperated, *ungrateful* only child.

The offices of Weil, Gotshal et al. tower high above Sixth Avenue in Manhattan. One of the most prestigious of all the white-glove law firms, it has many departments: entertainment, litigation, real estate. But the Trusts and Estates Department, where my mother and I sat waiting for Dena in a wood-paneled conference room, would have to be the sine qua non of wealthy familial dysfunction. As in a shrink's office, a box of Kleenex sat on the gleaming table.

My mother was, at this point, visibly ill. She had been undergoing radiation for the cancer and walked with the help of a cane. Still, she had managed to get a blow-dry (she hadn't yet lost her hair) and put on some makeup. She was wearing a glamorous, fur-lined coat and a suit, as if this were a charity luncheon rather than a meeting to discuss what was going to happen to her stuff after she died. I, on the other hand, had dressed carefully for this meeting in faded blue jeans, boots, a yoga T-shirt, and a long, lightweight cashmere sweater made by an Irish designer friend. It would appear that I had thrown my clothes on without a thought—but in fact I had thought about it plenty. I was forty years old and still trying to differentiate myself from my mother.

Five years later, it's hard for me to recall what, if anything, my mother and I talked about in those minutes as we waited for Dena. I do know that we never spoke of anything emotionally substantive from the moment of her diagnosis until her death. We didn't talk about my future, or our shared past. This didn't strike me, at the time, as being strange. We had never been able to speak of important things. She railed at me for my many flaws, and I cringed and ducked, evading her in ever-newer and more ingenious ways. She got angrier, I withdrew further. She hated me and she loved me, and the feeling was mutual.

I was all she had in the way of a daughter, and she was all I had in the way of a mother. It was pathetic and sad and irrefutable: this was how the story was going to end.

"Good afternoon, ladies!" Dena strode into the room, a sheaf of papers in a folder under her arm. She was a small woman, chubby, with frosted highlights that belied her salary and position. We had met a few times over the decades. I—who have a great memory for faces and almost never forget where I know someone from—would not have recognized her if I passed her on the street.

My mother adjusted herself, sitting taller in her upholstered chair. She seemed to grow more queenly in this conference room, at home among the legal briefs.

"Dena, you remember my daughter, Dani."

I could barely look at Dena. What had my mother told her about me over the years? Before my mother became ill, I had almost entirely stopped speaking to her. It had become impossible to navigate her presence in my life—particularly once I became a mother myself. It felt like a profound personal failure that I couldn't maintain a relationship with her; the fact that she had repeatedly threatened to disown me was the least of my concerns. Money had never mattered that much to me. I willfully made a point of not understanding my finances. My father had worked on Wall Street until he died, and my mother was obsessed with money, using it as her one and only weapon. Each month she pored over her utility bills, checking each line item to be sure she wasn't being ripped off by the electric company or AT&T. I preferred taking the stance that it was meaningless—even though on some level I understood that money could only be meaningless if there was enough of it. So I worked hard, made a good living (for a writer, anyway), and never balanced my checkbook. I didn't *need* my mother's money—certainly not enough to put up with her treatment of me. I was, however, upset by the idea that I wouldn't inherit the *stuff* I had grown up with: my grandmother's lamps, the paintings, the midcentury modern furniture that I didn't even like but that was a part of my childhood.

But all that had changed with my mother's cancer. Her cancer had pulled me back into her orbit, which meant that I was once again restored—with Dena's help—to being her beneficiary. The root of "beneficiary" is *bene:* good, well, gentle. But I already knew that there was nothing good or well or gentle about my mother's estate planning. It was simply this: I was her only child, and she couldn't quite bring herself to leave her money to United Jewish Appeal.

"Has your mother discussed with you the terms of her new will?" Dena asked, opening her folder in front of her on the table and handing us each thick copies of "The Last Will and Testament of Irene R. Shapiro."

"I thought it best if we did that here," my mother interjected.

"Fine. I'll lay it out simply," said Dena, and then proceeded to speak in paragraphs of legalese involving generation-skipping trusts and asset allocation that made my head spin. I felt sleepy. Dena was speaking slowly. Six hundred dollars an hour, I thought. Six hundred dollars an hour divides into ten dollars a minute. I'd speak slowly too. I'd take long, dramatic pauses just for kicks.

My mathematical reverie was interrupted when something Dena said registered with me. My son's name.

"Here, in paragraph seven, item B, Jacob will receive the distribution of the first quarter of the principal at age eighteen," she was saying. "The next at twenty-five. Then thirty—"

"I'm sorry—what?"

"There will, basically speaking, be two trusts," Dena backed up. "One from which you will be able to draw income during your lifetime, the principal of which Jacob will receive upon your death. And the other, which will be in Jacob's name."

I glanced at my mother. She was staring intently at a paper clip. Why hadn't this occurred to me? Of course—it made perfect sense. *Generation skipping.* She would leave her estate to Jacob, skipping over me as much as she possibly could.

I was now wide awake.

"Who will be the trustees of these trusts?" I asked Dena.

"A private bank," she answered. "You and the private bank will be co-trustees."

"And if something happens to me?"

"Then the bank will continue to oversee the trusts."

"What about Michael?" I turned to my mother. "He's Jacob's father. You can't just—"

And then I stopped. Her words came back to me: *Someday you're going to die and Michael will remarry . . . out in the cold . . . just trying to protect my grandson.*

We are at the point in this story where I fear I may be misunderstood by the reader: it would be reasonable to think that we're talking about vast sums of money. After all, the fancy lawyer, the private bank, the multiple trusts, the Corleone-like suspicion. We are not. While not insubstantial, the size of my mother's estate did not justify the hiring of white-glove lawyers and private banks. In fact, when I looked up the institution in question, I saw that my mother's estate was the lowest that their "wealth management" team would even consider. It was sheer foolishness and grandiosity—the chance to sweep into wood-paneled conference rooms with a fresh blow-dry and be offered coffee in a porcelain cup—that drove my mother. In the end—years later—I estimated that this grandiosity cost the estate more than a quarter of its worth in unnecessary executor's fees and commissions.

And another thing: I was happy to hear that Jacob would be my mother's beneficiary. More than happy. I was relieved and delighted. Michael and I would never have to worry about sending him to college or graduate school, which, for two writers, was a huge weight off our shoulders. But the thought that Jacob would automatically inherit a large chunk of cash at the age of eighteen, or twenty-five—his trust growing and compounding over the years—that seemed, to me, a very bad idea. I had known trust-fund kids over the years, and it rarely turned out well.

"If I had been handed that kind of money at eighteen," I said to my mother and Dena, "I'd be dead." I appealed to my mother. If I could accomplish just one thing here, let it be this. "Take the age limits out," I pleaded. "Let distributions be at the discretion of the trustees. And please—please, make Michael a trustee."

My mother ceded on the first count, but not the second. She wasn't going to give in on the subject of Michael—my future jolly widower, deadbeat dad.

"There's another important clause I want to point out to you," Dena then said. She flipped to the final page of my mother's Last Will and Testament, and my mother and I flipped along with her. "About Susie," Dena said, referring to my father's daughter from his first marriage, my half-sister, with the intimacy of someone who had been discussing her with my mother for decades. "The language here is very clear. Susie is explicitly named as someone who can make no claims whatsoever to your mother's estate."

My mother had a graduate degree in social work, a postgraduate degree in family therapy, and was a card-carrying member of the Step-Family Association of America. She had written articles about the relationships between stepparents and stepchildren and had appeared on *Good Morning America* as a stepfamily expert. She even had her own website. In her private practice, she counseled stepfamilies about how to get along. But when it came to her own stepdaughter, she had a bit of a blind spot. She hated Susie and, since my father's death twenty years earlier, had taken pains to ensure that Susie would inherit as little as possible. She had *left Susie out in the cold*. With sudden clarity, I understood exactly what my mother-the-family-therapist was unconsciously doing in her will: she was protecting Jacob against an evil stepmother just like her.

Susie is fifteen years older than me, and over the years we had managed to maintain a careful, but still somehow loving relationship—a triumph, I think, for both of us. I had taken her side against my mother many times, sensing the injustice that had been done to her. "Susie is going to be furious," I told Dena. "She's my half-sister, and I don't want this to be ugly."

Dena looked at me with a small, condescending smile, as if to suggest that the time to avoid ugliness had long since passed. "Everything is very clear," she said. "Of course, Susie can try anything she wants."

The rest of the meeting slipped by me. Their mouths moved, pages were turned, the heating vents blew recycled air, but I barely registered any of it. What else could possibly matter? My mother was messing with the very foundation of the family I had built, doing everything she could to create an imbalance of power. Later that evening, back home in Brooklyn, Michael and I would be giving a tantrumy Jacob a bath. As Jacob's little face scrunched into a beet-red scream, Michael would turn to me: *Imagine that*—pointing at Jacob—*with money*. In the coming weeks, Michael and I would buy life insurance policies on me, with Michael as the beneficiary. But in this case, the word "bene" would be restored to its true meaning: *good, well, kind*. If something happened to me, Michael would not be put in the position, by my mother's will, of having less money than his trust-fund son.

And in the coming years, Michael and I would work ourselves to the bone, writing books and screenplays, scrambling as fast as we could to render my mother's choices moot. But when it came to Susie, my mother's destructiveness would truly assert itself. All the ugliness would rise to the surface; more lawyers would be hired, fancy ones, when Susie eventually contested my mother's will. Susie wouldn't win, of course. Dena had been right. The will was perfectly clear. But after the lawyers were finished, tens of thousands of dollars and many hostile letters later, Susie and I would fall into a deep and permanent silence.

On that late winter day, in the hushed corridors of Weil, Gotshal, as my mother and I walked slowly together toward the elevator, I tried to imagine what my world would be like without her. I thought about my half-sister and how we might not be able to rise above the way my mother had left things. Pain and miscommunication between us seemed inevitable. I thought about my son and the money he would someday inherit, whether it would be good for him or not. I thought about my husband and how my mother had tried to erase him. And I thought about my mother, who seemed to be shrinking with each slow step we took away from the Trusts and Estates Department. She once again looked old and sick. But back there in the conference room, she had summoned all of herself with the last bit of strength she had. She was incandescent, burning with the knowledge that she had succeeded in leaving her mark on all of us.

Till Debt Do Us Part

Rebecca Johnson

I didn't have a regular cleaning lady until I was thirty-seven years old. I would have loved to be free of the daily drudgery of sweeping, dusting, and the Saturday scrubbing of the toilet, but paying another person to clean up my mess felt wrong. Overindulgent. Spoiled. Excessively first world. If I, a grown woman with no children, could make my own mess, I could damn well clean it up. Or so I reluctantly told myself.

Then I married and inherited three stepchildren. Pretty quickly after that, I got pregnant and had two children of my own. Suddenly, a cleaning person, like a nanny, felt essential. Who was I kidding? Betty Friedan was right—housework is endless and thankless. If I didn't outsource it, how was I going to keep working a job that paid good money and engaged my mind? Plus, I was beginning to feel my age. No more nights out on the town or late-evening workouts. By ten o'clock, I was in bed, exhausted.

So one day at the local library I took down the number of "Ivona. Polish cleaning lady for hire." She has been with me now for six years. She's a bright, lovely twenty-nine-year-old who works like a demon for me a few hours a week, and I pay her three times minimum wage. In another life, she'd be president of this country. The rest of the week, my husband and I try to keep on top of the Cheerios smashed into sofa cushions or the greasy macaroni-and-cheese fingerprints left on the walls by our two toddlers.

It all worked relatively well until the summer my eighteen-year-old stepson lived with us. Because my husband has always wanted his children, who mostly live with their mother, to feel at home in our house, we live in a place about twice the size of what we need. On the rare occasion when all five children are home at the same time, the space feels warm, filled up, and alive. But mostly those empty bedrooms are a waste, an echoey reminder of what we don't have and miss on a daily basis. (Plus, you should see our heating bills.) My husband and I both looked forward to having his son living with us full-time—me because my young sons adore him, and my husband because nothing makes him happier than having his children around him.

The summer fell between his freshman and sophomore year of college. During that time my days followed a similar routine. I'd get up with the kids around six-thirty in the morning, play with them until nine-thirty, when the babysitter arrived, then start my workday. My stepson's days also followed a routine: he'd wake up around eleven, eat some lunch, doodle around on his computer, maybe read a book, then head out around five for his nightly Frisbee game.

To be fair, he did look for jobs. A promised construction job fell through. Camp jobs were filled by the time he started looking. But when nothing landed in his lap, he seemed to shrug his shoulders and settle into a carefree existence bound only by the pleasures of the day.

I watched his life with bemusement. When I was his age (I can't believe I'm using that phrase . . .), I worked two jobs—the day shift at the Metropolitan Museum of Art gift shop, then waitressing in the Village at night. Home was a two-bedroom apartment on the upper Upper West Side of Manhattan shared with three roommates. Money was so tight, I'd pack my lunch and ride a rickety bike through Central Park to work. Whatever I saved went into a bank account for expenses the next year. Looking back, I see those days as some of the best in my life. Having my own money made me feel deliciously independent, master of a destiny that suddenly seemed wide open and filled with possibility. Paying an electric bill would never again be so thrilling.

The fact that my stepson was not tortured by his joblessness seemed odd to me. But one of the beauties of stepchildren is that you aren't overly invested in their decisions. My parents were poor, so I had to work. My stepson's tuition bills were paid for, as was his housing, his clothing, his food, his medical insurance, his books, his iMac, his iPod, the gas and insurance for his car, and the entrance fee for his Frisbee tournaments. Why would he knock himself out looking for work? If that's how he wanted to live his life, who was I to question it? Live and let live. Or so I told myself.

Then one afternoon, as I was eating my lunch and he was making his breakfast, he asked me why Ivona didn't clean his room.

"Why would she?" I asked, genuinely puzzled.

"She cleans the boys' room," he said.

"They are two and three years old," I answered, trying to suffocate the indignation beginning to rise up in my throat. If there's one thing I've learned living with teenagers, it's that they do not respond well to outrage.

"She cleans your room," he replied.

"I'm an adult," I sputtered.

"So?" he asked.

"I work. I make the money that helps run this house."

"Whatever." He rolled his eyes and left the room. I took a sip of coffee and tried to understand what I had found so intensely irritating about the conversation.

The next day my husband asked me if Ivona could clean his son's room. I said no. I don't remember the exact parameters of the fight that followed, but it basically went like this—Him: you're a bitch. Me: you've spoiled your children by expecting nothing of them. For the next few days, a frosty distance settled on the house. It was my stepson and my husband against me.

I contemplated giving in—it would only take Ivona ten minutes to run a vacuum over his rug and pour some bleach in his toilet—but something in it violated all the unspoken, grandchild-of-Depression, Protestant-work-ethic principles that constitute the invisible web of my personality. It wasn't so long ago that children were brought into this world for the sole purpose of helping out. My grandfather came from a family of nine where romantic illusions about childhood were as rare as the rain that fell on their West Texas farm. As soon as you could work in the fields, you did. My stepson is not a bad kid. He works hard at school, gets good grades, and struggles with the moral questions that bedevil all human beings. But if I ever suggested he plow the back forty, the way my grandmother did to make her college tuition, he'd laugh in my face.

It's not even his fault. Only once you are a parent do you begin to understand the precise ways in which children are formed by the actions of the people who care for them. Some of it is nature—one of my sons came out of the womb watchful and reserved, while the other came out ready to be amused by the world. Beyond that, every day is an opportunity to train them by shaping their expectations. At the table, when my four-year-old announces, "I'm done!" I tell him that's wonderful, now put your dish in the dishwasher. If he balks, I stand my ground (mostly). Life would be a lot easier if I just cleared his plate for him—God knows every babysitter I have ever hired does—but I am in this for the long run. I don't want my child to expect others to clean up after him. And I definitely don't want to be cleaning up after him when he is eighteen years old. Divorce mucks all this up. Because my husband saw his children so rarely compared to a full-time parent, the last thing he wanted to do was insist they spend their time with him on unpleasant chores like cleaning.

After my own parents divorced, I watched, horrified, as my mother's standard of living plummeted. Overnight, we went from living in a grand southern house with white pillars and the remains of servants' quarters out back to a two-bedroom apartment on the edge of town with walls so thin I could hear *Three's Company* on the neighbor's TV. Money, I learned, was something to be feared and hoarded as a bulwark against the great uncertainty of life. I began to obsess over my allowance, stacking and restacking the quarters in neat little towers on my dresser, wondering if those piles would be enough to ease the financial worries that seemed constantly to beset my mother. Money isn't everything—as a wise friend once said to me—unless you have none of it.

As a result of those early experiences, I became an ant, furiously saving and constantly worrying. Ants are not, I have to admit, the funnest people in the world. An ant would no sooner spend her last nickel on a good meal than fly to the moon. Restaurant owners like to say that nobody actually orders the cheapest bottle of wine on the menu—I do. It doesn't matter how much money we have, ants love a bargain. We shop at garage sales, buy extra when things are on sale, and even take a certain pleasure in sniffing out the cheapest way to do something. We buy our Christmas decorations the week after December 25 and really, really hate to pay for parking, dry cleaning, and wrapping paper.

Grasshoppers are the opposite of ants, which is why credit card companies love them. Grasshoppers don't think about what things cost, they think about what they want. They buy strawberries in the dead of winter and popcorn at the movies. They buy hardcover books and extra-large lattes at Starbucks. No surprise, I suppose, that I fell in love with and married a grasshopper. Who wouldn't prefer the generous big spender to the cramped Scrooge?

But there can be a dark side to people who are so carefree with their money.

I got my first inkling that life with my grasshopper husband would not be all smooth sailing the weekend I picked up the phone at his house and couldn't make an outside call. He handed me his cell phone. To be helpful, I called the phone company on his behalf. There was nothing wrong with the phone, the woman on the other end said, someone simply hadn't paid the bill. I told her that had to be a mistake. Freelance writers don't pay their phone bills. Actors, dancers, musicians, people with spotty income, people who are poor, people who have fallen through the safety net, don't pay their bills. My husband is an investment banker. He has a Ph.D. (well, almost, if he ever gets around to turning in the dissertation). He makes many times over what I make. There had to be a mistake. When I told him what the woman said, he did not seem surprised and blamed his assistant for not paying the bill.

At the time, I believed him. I now know better. We split our time between two houses, one in the country, one in the city. I pay the city bills. He pays the country bills. At least, that's how it's supposed to be. In reality, bills pile up unpaid in the country because he forgets them. Or all the money is in one account when it should be in another. Or, frankly, he just doesn't seem to care all that much. Every time I open one of those bills marked URGENT we have one of these terrible fights that are a recurring motif in our marriage. Every couple has them, those issues that flare up over and over, forcing people into intractable corners from which they feel helpless to move. For some people, the issue is sex; for others, it's time away from the house ("Golf *again*?"); for others, it's drinking or drugs or temper. It could be anything. For us, it's money.

About a year into our marriage, when we were having a particularly difficult time on this subject, we went to visit a couples counselor for a few sessions. (At $175 a pop, there was no way I was going to make it a regular occurrence.) At my darkest moment, when I genuinely questioned whether two people with such radically different views of the topic could possibly stay together, I turned to the therapist and said, "I can't believe that we could break up over the topic of money."

"Are you kidding?" she answered. "It's the number one reason couples break up."

It only made me feel marginally better to hear that my misery was not original.

Over time, I have learned to live with these differences between us. I try not to open the bills, my husband and I maintain completely separate bank accounts, and I file my taxes separately. What I don't know can't hurt me. (Okay, I'm not that naive, but I want to preserve my marriage, so I pretend.)

Truthfully, I think I have learned some things from him. When I look back on my mingy twenties, I see someone not unlike an anorexic battling a dysfunctional relationship with food. Every time I spent a lot of money, I would literally feel nauseous, like I had eaten too much. At thirty, when I decided to buy a house on my own, I searched and searched until I found one that was both charming and within my budget. Nevertheless, after I gave my real estate agent the go-ahead to make an offer, I literally had to lie down on my bed. My pulse was racing so fast, I wondered if I was having a heart attack. I must have picked up the phone to cancel my offer ten times before I finally made peace with the notion of so much money leaving my bank account in one fell swoop. With my husband, I have learned to enjoy the pleasures money can bring—the joy of renting a house on a beach or staying a full week in one of those mindless resorts where the big decision of the day is whether to snorkel in the morning or the afternoon.

More important, my husband gave me the courage to experiment with my work. All my life, I have wanted to write a novel. In my twenties, I watched with envy as friends from wealthier families went to graduate school in creative writing, while I worked at building a career. Once I was established as a journalist, I found myself addicted to the steady drip of income that kept me afloat. Taking the time to write a book would mean forgoing an income, something that terrified me way too much to consider. With him (and his income) at my side, I no longer felt so afraid. When editors called with stories I once would have accepted just for the money, I found myself saying no. And when my book was done, I dedicated it to him.

I like to think I have also helped change him for the better. The other day, my husband shocked me by coming home from the grocery store with seven pounds of porterhouse steak—way too much for our little family.

"Why?" I asked, mystified, as package after package of red meat came out of the shopping bags.

"It was on sale," he answered. I was pretty certain I recognized the joy of a bargain in his eyes.

Who's Your Daddy?

Amy Cohen

A few months ago my father called with something great to tell me.

"Did you hear the news?" he said, barely able to contain his excitement. "I just saw it on TV, and I had to call you immediately!"

"No. Hear what?" I said.

"Are you sure you're ready, because this is so wonderful!"

"I'm sure," I said, but actually I was a little worried. (The last time my father had good news, it was that I didn't look "nearly as exhausted or sallow-skinned as usual!")

"What is it?" I said now.

"Some old lady in Spain gave birth to twins! She's sixty-seven. It means you've got twenty-five years! That's good news, right?"

"Great," I said. "It's good to know I've got so much time. At sixty-seven, my baby and I can bond over mashed peas and long naps. And even better, the nanny can double as my attendant."

"Wiseacre," he said. "I thought you'd be happy."

"No, I am. Thank you. I just—" I thought about what I really wanted to say. "I just still can't believe I haven't had a child yet."

———

I knew my father was just trying to make me feel better. After all, it had been a rough year. I'd broken up with my fiancé—the only man I'd ever been engaged to, and at age forty, no less—in part because he'd decided he didn't want children. Hoping to get me to see things his way, my ex-boyfriend was constantly offering up stories intended to scare the maternal instinct out of me.

"Gretchen and Theo blew through more than $100,000 on in vitro. *A hundred thousand dollars!*" he said, referencing a friend who worked for a university press. "And that was only three tries. Gretchen doesn't even make thirty thousand a year, so she had to borrow the money from her brother-in-law, who she hates. Then they finally have a kid—I met him, he's really pale and hyperactive—and he ends up having all these allergies. He's always in the emergency room. So now they both work two jobs to pay the medical bills, and they never even get to see the kid!"

He waited for me to announce that he had finally changed my mind.

"That's fucked up, right?" he said.

"I think it's worth it."

"A hundred grand for one kid?"

"Worth it."

"Dogs," he said, pointing his finger in my direction. "They're cute. They're fun. They love you unconditionally. Think about it: dogs. That's the way to go."

We ended things a few months later.

R ight around my forty-first birthday, I decided that I would have a child—no matter what it took. Since I worried that my age might factor into how easily I would be able to conceive, I asked a friend who'd recently undergone fertility treatments to brief me on how much I could expect to spend. Remembering the scary story of

Gretchen and Theo, I asked if IVF really was $30,000 per try.

"Oh, *easy*," she said. And that, apparently, was if you used your own eggs. ("I hear donor eggs cost more than some cars," she told me gravely.) Health insurance, naturally, covered nothing.

Undeterred, I continued exploring sperm banks and insemination. But fearing that my uterus was a barren field where no seeds would grow, I also began investigating adoption—specifically, a little girl from China. A woman I knew had just brought home her daughter from Beijing, so I figured she would be well versed in the costs I would be facing. "Are you sitting down?" she asked when I called. Between fees, flights to meet the baby and bring her home, incidentals and various forms, she revealed, I would be looking at approximately $40,000.

I was amazed. It seemed like an incredible amount of money, and I wasn't exactly sure where I would get it. But I had already begun to picture my life with this little girl—down to her jovial pigtails and my futile attempts to get her to eat meatless chicken nuggets. In my fantasies, my daughter was plum-cheeked and charismatic and a far better student than I ever was. We would be very giggly together. I could almost see her.

I have often joked that my approach to life is "I fear, therefore I am"—and having a child proved no exception. I worried about how I would support my daughter on a writer's salary. I worried that my one-bedroom apartment would be too snug for two people, especially if one of those people was a teenage girl. I had even started to worry that I was developing a perimenopausal beard. (Apparently, I was worrying about everything.) But it seemed that I'd left out the one thing that actually was a cause for concern. A month after I began filling out adoption forms, I received e-mails from several different agencies, informing me that because I was a single woman, I was no longer a viable candidate. The Chinese government had changed its policy and was not allowing unmarried women, or people they deemed obese, or anyone with a severe history of depression, to adopt. "If I gain a hundred dred pounds because I'm so depressed about not being able to adopt a Chinese girl, then I'll really be out of the running," I joked. But the truth was that I was devastated.

In the last few years my eighty-one-year-old father—who once sug-gested I get a job as a social worker because "you want a job you can give up easily when you have kids"—has had to adjust not only to my not being married, but to my changing ideas of family. Because my life is so different from the one he imagined for me—marriage and a few children—he figures the sky's the limit in terms of what family means.

"I wanna get you a big dog," he said recently, when we met for our weekly lunch.

My father wears large, square glasses, and his wavy, white hair was cut short. In profile, his nose leapt out from between his eyebrows, curving into what looked like a juicy fig surrounded by nostrils. My grandmother used to have his nose airbrushed in photographs so that it would look small and straight.

"Would you let me do that?" he said. "I think you'd love it."

"Would everyone please stop telling me to get a dog?" I asked. "I like dogs, but I don't want a dog. Besides, I'm allergic."

"She's allergic," he said, shrugging. "What's a little sneezing? Do you know what the number one growing industry in America is right now? Pets! People have gone crazy about their pets. You can become part of all the pet people. The dogs get massages. They go to psychia-trists and hairdressers. Marilyn Tanzer's daughter, who's a few years older than you—but not much—has two golden retrievers, and she calls them her children. It's a billion-dollar industry! And with a dog, who knows? You might meet some nice man who also has a dog."

"Ah, so that's what's behind the dog."

"Or the dog is just a dog. It'll spend time with you. I just hate to see you being alone so much. A dog could help with that."

I looked around the restaurant. We were regulars there and more often than not ran into women with whom I'd gone to high school or summer camp. They were polished blondes with hair the shade of mild Dijon mustard; they wore Lanvin ballet flats and pushed elaborate double strollers, introducing me to fellow stay-at-home mothers they'd met in their toddler's music class. Once, I assumed I'd end up like these women I knew growing up. I would be taken care of. But now their lives couldn't have seemed further from my own.

"Dad, I'm still looking into adopting a child," I said. "I don't qualify in China, but supposedly Vietnam or Ethiopia will have me." I took a deep breath. "Most of the agencies have told me that it will cost at least thirty thousand dollars. Minimum. And that doesn't even include the cost of the flights to go pick up the baby, or the cost of the hotel when you're staying there for three weeks. And I might have to make more than one trip to—"

My father interrupted me. "That's going to be a long flight, sweetheart. Do you have the miles to go business class?"

That was my father. To think of the flight and, more specifically, my comfort first.

"Dad, it's years away," I said. "The process takes years."

"Okay, so clearly you've got some tsuris around adopting," my father said, using the Yiddish word for anxiety. He looked at me more closely. "I think maybe you've got some tsuris about your life."

"Ha," I said, rolling my eyes. "Just a little."

I watched as my father fished into his afternoon martini, circling his index finger along the bottom of his glass to retrieve a stranded olive.

"Okay, I've got something to tell you," I announced.

"There's more?" He laughed. "Do I need another drink?"

"You might," I said, taking a deep breath. "First, I'd like to try to have a child. I mean, have, as in give birth."

"So you're—" He searched for the right word. "Investigating?"

"Very seriously. And having a child of my own would cost a ton of money too. Huge. Sorta mind-boggling, actually."

"But how does it work?" he said. "After all, you're not the Virgin Mary."

"Dad!"

"What I mean is that you can't produce a baby by yourself. What do you do about getting the sperm? How does it work? Do you go pick up the sperm and then take a cab home?"

I explained that I had chosen a lab in California known for its carefully screened donors, and that the specimen could be sent directly to my doctor. Once directed to the website, I could choose from dozens of candidates, listed by height, weight, age, college major, and ethnic background. Each had answered questions about why he became a donor, what foods he liked (sushi and burritos were very popular) and sports (I was always drawn to men who wrote "surfing"). The more information you wanted about your donor, the more you paid, as all information was à la carte. A detailed family history was $60. A baby photo: $30. A taped interview: $50. It added up.

Choosing a donor, as I found out, was more complicated than it seemed. At first, I went for the classic physical ideal, typing keywords like "blond," "blue-eyed," "6'2" and over," and "extremely athletic" into my search. But none of the genetically perfect specimens seemed right. Soon, I began looking simply for a guy I liked. Was he funny? Menschy? Was he close to his family? His mother? I had recently tried online dating for the first time and was struck by how similar the process was. Both online dating and looking through a sperm bank registry involved reading profiles, looking for a spark of humor or charm. Both processes asked you to think about how much love is worth purely in terms of dollars.

And then, after weeks of looking, I found him: half Chinese, half Swedish. A writer. I listened to my donor's voice, which was soothing and melodic. I studied his baby picture, in which he grinned from underneath his long, blond bangs. And perhaps because I looked for a donor the way I might a boyfriend, I realized I was starting to think of my potential donor *as* my boyfriend. I would compare him to the men I was dating. *Donor 6735 doesn't say our relationship is moving too fast. He doesn't have commitment issues,* I would think. *He's ready to have kids right now!*

Soon, it became clear just how attached I was to this man I knew so little about. Oh, sure, I knew his sister was a horse trainer and he had dust allergies. But I barely knew him, even though he would be the future father of my child. Or so I thought.

"All bought up," the woman at the sperm bank informed me when I called to order. "I can't explain it either. He's been available for months and then—poof—someone buys up all the vials."

She went on to explain that often lesbian couples ordered twice as many samples from the same donor so that both women could try for siblings. But by that point I'd stopped listening. Now I was thinking about the hundreds of dollars I'd spent getting detailed information on number 6735: the pricey baby picture, the essays, the detailed family history.

My father had thoughts on this too.

"Sweetheart, you need to be very picky about your sperm," he told me. "This is a major life decision. I know you like to save money, but you don't want cheap sperm, am I right?"

"Let me tell you, it's not a cheap process," I explained. "You pay for the sperm, and the older you are—"

"You're still young," he said.

"Dad, in the fertility world I'm the Rosetta Stone," I said, sighing. "Anyway, the older you are, the more vials you have to buy, because it's more likely you'll have to try more times. You pay the doctor each time it doesn't work. And that's just for insemination. If *that* doesn't work, then I might have to try in vitro, which is a fortune. And that's if it works on the first try, which I can't bet on."

I could feel a panic attack setting in—my heart was thumping as if there were a mosh pit in my chest.

"Is there any way we could set up a savings account for my kid?" I asked. My father had set up bank accounts for my four nieces and nephews, which went toward sending them to college. "I mean, could we do that?"

"Well, sweetheart, I'd love to help you, but the government doesn't let you set up a bank account for a vial of sperm."

For most of my thirties, whenever I would indulge in buying something expensive, I had an instant rationale: "If I had kids, I would have spent this money on them: on outfits they would adamantly refuse to wear or expensive summer camps they would remember as traumatic. But since I *don't* have kids, I can spend it on myself." Now, as I tried to envision supporting a child on my own, I was angry at my lack of foresight. What was I thinking, taking tennis lessons? Why did I book that trip to Vietnam? How could I not have at least planned that I would end up alone? All I knew now was that I wanted a child more than anything in the world. I vowed to make it happen—even if I had to work around the clock, even if I had to borrow from my family.

In the following weeks, feeling overwhelmed and a little lost, I sought solace in movies about single mothers: *Alice Doesn't Live Here Anymore* and *The Goodbye Girl*. When I'd seen these movies in years past, I'd thought, *Wow, single motherhood. How exotic.* But now I found myself watching and thinking, *They didn't have a lot of money, but they did okay with heavy sarcasm and a diet of hugs.*

Watching these mothers made me think even more about what kind of mother I would be. And then I realized: the real choice I was facing was not only what kind of mother I would be but, in imagining myself as the breadwinner, what kind of father. The mother part of me was confident—I could love my kid like nobody's business. But it was the father part, the provider—the clothing and feeding of my child—that was truly terrifying.

I'd always viewed fathers as people whose whole identity in life was to provide. That's the way my father always viewed himself. When I was growing up, he worked so much that he was, for many years, a stranger. He imported ladies' handbags and traveled constantly, going to the Philippines and Korea for months at a time, making sure multiple pockets zipped and pudgy, straw daisies were sewn on correctly. When he'd come home, I'd show him the books I'd written and illustrated about my life while he was away. Books with subtle titles like, *Look! Look! I'm Over Here!* I'd never understood why my father was willing to sacrifice so much time with us in order to provide. But now, as I considered having my own child, I understood his fear in a way I never had before.

I was afraid myself. For one thing, I was a writer, and not a very quick one. When I worked in television, my colleagues were stand-up comics who could come up with several jokes per minute. I, on the other hand, was the person who could come up with a fantastic joke three weeks after the show had aired. Now, writing for magazines, I found I was even slower. Fearing that I would never write another word, I turned down dinner invitations at restaurants I'd been dying to try because it wasn't in my budget. I vowed to subsist on generic yogurt and popcorn rather than invest in a new pair of jeans. Was I really going to bring a kid into this?

And then, as I wondered about how I might one day afford a teen tour of the Grand Canyon, I thought of the bond I already felt with the child I had yet to meet. The names I had chosen if she was a girl: Bebe or Gigi, names that would ensure that she would grow up to be a hooker—or with any luck, a high-class hooker. I had fantasies about watching old movies together, the way I had with my mother when she was still alive. I would tell my daughter facts like, "Mae West was the original choice to play Norma Desmond." She would roll her eyes and say, "Mom, you're so weird."

I hoped one day my child would feel lucky to have me, the way I did when my father called me one afternoon. "Sweetheart, how about we take a trip to the sperm bank together to make sure it's clean. Jet-Blue flies to California. The last thing you want is a shmutzy sperm bank."

"Well put," I said.

"And when you have this child—"

"If," I said, aware of the variable success rate.

"When," he said. "Stop with the negative. Think positive, sweetheart. You can count on me if you need any financial help. It's not easy being a single mother, but we'll manage. What the hell? I'll even babysit, because babysitters charge a fortune these days. It's such a racket."

"Thank you," I said. "That means the world to me."

I am still pursuing all my options, charting both my ovulation and the availability of children from Kazahkstan. Sometimes I picture myself carrying my biological child in a Snuggly, and sometimes I'm pushing a stroller with a toddler who looks nothing like me. But in both fantasies, I'm equally thrilled.

And this led me to thinking about how, in so many ways, all love is blind, a crapshoot, really. You love and you hope for the best. My father has long abandoned his old notions of what he hoped for me—the wedding, the son-in-law who didn't exist in a vial—opting instead to embrace each new adventure simply because I'm his daughter. You love the child you have. Or like me, the one you imagine. Whatever the price.

A Change of Fortune

LETTER TO MY OLDEST SON

Susanna Sonnenberg

Dear Ezekiel,

You ask me, are we rich?

The first time you asked, about a year ago when you were ten, I was adding green peppers to chili in the Le Creuset pot. You were eating your after-school snack, your mind no doubt churning with the information and rumor that make up your daily talk when the teacher is out of the room. I hedged. "That depends," I said. Some of the kids' families in your private school have visible, big money. Horses, for instance. Homes in Mexico. We're not like that. Only a few children appear to have less, and it's noticeable in an unspoken way—the age of their clothes, for instance. That's not us either. "We have a lot," I said. I looked at the organic ingredients waiting on the granite countertop. "Yes, we're rich."

Yes. We are warm, fed, healthy, rested. These are not givens. They are symptoms of money, luxuries made possible by having enough, more than enough. I didn't fathom the extent of the luxury until you, your brother, and I began volunteering at the food bank, where we met clients who were choosing between their power bill and their weekly food. They looked tired and sour from stress, and I felt how free our life was from such weight. I used to think of luxury in movie terms—private planes, European villas. But in our sort of luxury, we give no thought to whether or not we'll have food. We have food. We

pay our mortgage. We hire people for tasks—gardeners, house clean-
ers, babysitters. For a year we hired someone to make us dinner four
nights a week, which was an embarrassing extravagance, but we afford
it, just as we afford restaurants. We buy ourselves substantial presents,
and we travel. Last winter, returning from a week in New York, I sat
on the plane and thought, *Where next? Somewhere warm.* By the end
of the week, I'd booked the trip to Belize. In the summer we took a
month off and drove to Alaska. You are growing up to feel bounty.

B efore you were born, when your father and I had just moved to
Montana, we got basic jobs for low wages—data entry, waiting
tables—and although life was inexpensive here compared to the large
cities we'd left, we were flat broke. In a way, we wanted to be. We
wanted to feel our own fresh strengths, because it was the beginning
of our life together. We didn't need to articulate being broke because
we had no choices to make. We had enough for food and rent and
heat, enough not to feel scared, but not for new boots or new blankets.
Pulling into gas stations, we were always counting out ones and fives
on the dashboard, trying to make every little bit last a little longer.
We skipped the dentist. We had to budget, and I had never lived on a
small budget before, a careful accounting, nor had I ever considered
the impact of my money habits on someone else. I didn't even think of
them as "habits." It was hard to train myself out of instant spending on
things I wanted (like new boots or blankets). For the first time, at age
twenty-seven, I became conscious of money as a finite resource and a
privilege. Money mattered.

We live in a special world. I would like to say that your father and
I have worked hard to provide this for you, but we didn't do much. Although we lived on that careful and meager income for the first years
of your life, it was a discipline, an art, an act. Andrew and I both come
from privilege, albeit in vastly different forms, and we knew, even if
we didn't talk about it, that family wealth had conditioned us, that it
floated peripherally in the picture, available should we need it. When

we bought our first house, our families helped us, providing most of
the down payment; we made the monthly payments from our earnings. When we outfitted the nursery, our families helped. They bought
the plane tickets for your frequent journeys; they slipped us monthly
checks so we could afford some babysitting. We didn't count on this
money, but it was tacitly understood that life's transitions called for
extra, a collective family income. You were to grow up wanting for
nothing, as we had.

We were grateful for the help (and relieved). But when we started
to earn a real living—mostly your father's, as he started his therapy
practice—we tried to become financially separate, thoughtful, serious. We accepted the vast expense of our health insurance as a responsibility rather than an option. We wanted to set aside money for
your education, but we were also running up against the end of the
paycheck every two weeks. Money mattered, *our* money.

Although you were a baby, you were starting to learn about money
from us, absorbing our attitudes and habits. I used to put you in the
car and drive out to Wal-Mart for diapers. I was aware of the store's
politics and economics, so contrary to my own. And yet our situation
pushed me there. Wal-Mart's diapers were much cheaper than those
at other stores, and we needed so many. Everything there was cheap,
and I'd express my amazement at a pedal-push garbage can for $3.97
by purchasing it. I felt tricked and, trapped in the arena of the store,
a willing zombie. I hated that and bought things anyway. You watched
me and learned that stuff was bountiful, everywhere, and haveable.
If it was priced low enough, I'd buy it. But once home, I'd look at that
garbage can, knowing I'd purchased it because it was cheap and because I'd been standing in front of it. The object, which I hadn't even
wanted and certainly didn't need, made me feel I was taking care of
our money. If you could have asked then, "Are we rich?" I would have
said no, without taking into account the car, the other car, the gas,
the house, the appliances, and the vast rubric of purchasing options
I encountered every day. "We're not rich. Look at us!" I would have
said. "We're buying cheap diapers."

Gradually, we have earned more and bought more things and enjoyed more adventures. We moved into a prettier house. We purchased new furniture, had the beautiful garden planted, flew to Costa Rica. We've created the lifestyle you're going to remember, but we don't talk about money with you. We haven't called ourselves rich. When you grow up, you'll remember the "rich" people you knew—your classmate with the weekend lake house, or your friend whose father kept a Porsche in their three-car garage. But you'll also remember the regular parade of new electronics into our house, and our international trips. Will you know how they fit in? You'll remember me saying no to a hardback book you wanted, telling you it cost too much, which I know is the excuse I give when I don't want to meet your whim in a store. In other words, I know money is not the reason you didn't get the book. And if I know it, on some level you know it, without knowing how to say you know it. You hold all these competing signals about money, and you want a definition of "rich."

Your father and I have taught you to strike a match, to cross the street, to plug in a lamp. We've taught you to wash your hands, where to place a stamp. We've taught you about elections, symphonies, and public transportation. About the nervous system, the Holocaust, climate change. Our duty is to school you in the trivial and the essential so you will make your wise way in the world. But money's the thing we keep leaving out. In our discussion of organic milk—the politics of food manufacturing, for example—I've neglected to tell you that this milk costs four times the price of regular milk, and we're lucky, privileged, to be able to afford it. Complacent as I pay for it, I've forgotten this myself.

We are not yet teaching you what it means to be rich in the ways that we are. As an American, I don't even know how to teach you, especially with my family background. I take so much for granted as necessary and permanent that it's hard to keep in mind—impossible, actually—that nearby fire stations and drive-through ATMs cost money, as do running water and playgrounds. We never give a thought to such privileges, but that's what they are. Your country is rich, and its obsession with accumulating wealth means that Americans never feel they have enough, rarely understand what enough is. We're prevented from understanding, surrounded by perpetual dissatisfaction. You've already noticed from advertising that the culture wants to make sure you think about what you want, but not about spending. If you thought about money, you might not spend as much.

Now you begin to examine not just your life, but life. No longer is all your attention outward, gathering up facts and data. You've started to measure yourself against others, to question your role in a larger drama, so you want to know if we're rich, and I want to answer you, and at the same time I'm trying to know how to be responsible with our wealth, accountable. I'm glad you've asked, forcing me to put my squeamishness aside. Being your mother has always helped me refine my thoughts, and I've been answering the question "Are we rich?" ever since you asked it.

I come from spenders. When my parents married, my father's father gave them $2 million to "set them up." Your great-grandfather made an opulent fortune "inventing" the business of public relations, creating profiles for rich clients who wanted to be noticed by newspapers and Hollywood and governments. My parents were supposed to become grown-ups with this present, to buy a New York City apartment, to invest and to live on the interest. Two million dollars still sounds like a lot for a wedding gift, and my mother often explained to me that *then,* in the midsixties, it was a monumental fortune, a fountain that couldn't possibly run dry. However, she and my father were so spectacularly irresponsible, so much better at irresponsibility than anyone else, that they "blew through it." "Easy come, easy go," she liked to say. Within eighteen months, they had nothing left, having bought themselves handmade shoes and shirts, tons of fresh flowers, and restaurant meals and superb wines in far-flung European cities. My father had to go back to his parents for more money, which they weren't pleased about, even though they gave it to him (a lot less this time, and in the form of an allowance). My parents were ruled by other people's money, offered to them as luscious incentives, something to win, like favor, like love. Instead of love.

My parents almost never earned money when I was a child. They worked, off and on, at artistic, showy jobs, but they rarely had much taxable income from employment. My best friend's father was an architect, and he left their house early to go to an office. The word sounded tragic to me, an exotic bore, a place that must be dingy and cluttered. I knew nothing of offices; I never heard the term "income tax." This is what I thought a budget was: When I was fourteen at boarding school, I received a $400 check each month from my father's accountant to spend on shampoo and records and pizza and train fare. If I ran out, I got more. I remember knowing the school's tuition—$7,300—but I never knew that that was extraordinarily costly. My parents didn't pay for it anyway. My grandfather had set up a trust fund, which also provided me with summer camp and trips to Greece. When I wanted something big or extra, I'd make application to the trustees. I requested a car in high school and listed in my letter how responsible I'd be about insurance, speeding, and seat belts. The trustees said yes and gave me the money. That's what always happened, so I learned not that I had to be responsible with money, or even that I had to appreciate the value of things, but that money was always there. I just had to endure the ritual that would unlock it, as my parents had.

My stepfather had a house in the country where I took riding lessons on Saturdays. Like you, I never thought about cost. It would have made no difference to me to hear that a riding lesson cost $20 or $200, nor did I understand the connotations of country houses and stables. On Thanksgiving, we went to my father's childhood home, a mansion in New York that overlooked a private park. We ate in a room draped in red velvet and hung with a glittering chandelier, which I believed was made out of giant diamonds. My place was set with a crystal water glass and two wineglasses, one for red and one for white. I knew how to manage my arms in order to serve myself from the platter held steady by the servant. But no one said, "We're rich. You, Susanna, are rich." In my house there was always, magically, enough for party dresses and private schools, for doctors, Italian vacations, a live-in babysitter, the phone bill. I accepted that as my world, without questioning it. I didn't ask the questions you ask. Several times a year we flew to Barbados and spent weeks on my other grandmother's estate, where I took formal tea times, chauffeurs, imported upholstery, and dinner bells in stride.

My mother told me to be grateful, and she was very dramatic about money. She was always giving me mixed messages, most of them impractical, in preparing me to grow up. She had made a fuss over my opening a savings account, and I was honored to be presented with the little red book that had gold-edged pages. But then she withdrew my money when she wanted to use it. One afternoon when I was nine or ten, she pulled a $100 bill from her bag and pointed it at me. She needed a nap and wanted me and my sister to leave the apartment. She said we should go to the very posh toy store up the street, that we should split the money and buy whatever we wanted. I loved that glamorous, exciting phrase "whatever you want." We left my mother to sleep and walked the few blocks. The cash in my closed fist made me feel responsible and important. I know you'll ask me what we bought once we got to the shop with its shelves right to the ceiling, but I can't remember, because the toys were afterthoughts, overlooked by the following day, certainly lost to memory. What mattered to me, what filled me with a tight thrill, was the spending.

Your Salt Lake grandparents were frugal people who nevertheless (or therefore) amassed sturdy wealth, good with investment and savings. They bought real estate when it was cheap, and its value increased tenfold. Your grandfather was a surgeon and made a good living, and his father had started a bank, the young stock from that growing and growing. They were born just before the Depression, so they spent childhood watchful of every penny and aware of the adults' tension. As grown-ups, they tithed to the church, part of their income dedicated to helping others. Andrew grew up understanding that those who had more could and must provide graciously for those who did not, and in order to do that, you had to have more. There was a notion of service and good fortune built into his family message on money, which was secretive in its own way. Your father was confused about money all the time. Once, your grandmother said to him, "If anyone ever asks you how much we make, tell them you don't know." In fact, he didn't know; he learned he wasn't supposed to ask, wasn't *supposed* to know.

The family owned a condominium in Sun Valley, but a small one. No one discussed money, but each child received a new car at college graduation. No one talked about money, but they lived in a spacious house on a couple of acres of land. Debt was frowned upon, a bad dream from the Depression. The kids did chores, like picking thistles at the ranch, for bare-bones wages. Andrew heard about the value of land, the important role of the family ranch, but money itself was hidden, the subject fraught with tension. Unlike my family, his family didn't spend to make things easier or more fun. Grandpa Lewis did all the yard work, and Jo Jo put up peaches and milled her own wheat. Not because they had to. Your grandparents came from the generation that used any resource available with reverent economy. The kids went to public schools, because paying for school would have been wasteful. Andrew experienced the comfort, opportunity, and privilege of wealth, while also sensing the shame and fear attached to it. No one said, "Andrew, we're rich." He never heard that.

The first time I met your grandparents they took me and Andrew out to dinner at a little diner. After we ate, the waitress came and asked if we'd like dessert. At the same moment that your grandfather was saying, "Nope," I was saying, "What kind of pie do you have?" Your grandparents just stared at me. They never, ever ordered extras in restaurants, whereas I had been raised with the attitude, "Order anything you want! What the hell, let's have champagne!" So I didn't order dessert that night, and I felt like that was a moral decision, that

it made me a better person than the person I had been. I thought
Andrew, with his completely opposite history from mine, a history
of thrift and frugality, would teach me to respect money more, and
maybe he thought that I'd be able to help him relax, to make things a
little easier if we could afford it.

Like healthy eating habits and good ethics, we're supposed to teach
you to be good with money. Like many of the jobs of parenthood,
I come to this one ill prepared, winging it as I go, making snap decisions and trying to disguise that I'm almost as unsure as you are. How
can I teach you about money when I listlessly blow a few hundred on a
website purchase, or decide to have our car detailed, or eat out several
lunches a week, and then feel foolish and guilty? I beat myself up for
ill-advised spending. I don't want to pass wastefulness on to you, nor
do I want you to inherit misplaced foolishness and guilt. I want you
to feel comfortable with your money—however much you have—and
to be aware of its value in given situations. I want you to be aware of
money's power. I want you to know that money matters.

Every purchase is a choice—a political choice even. Local eggs
and insulated lunch bags from LL Bean, the fleece gloves, the ski
pass, the winter tire change on the car that takes you to the expensive
school. It never stops. Toilet paper and heat cost money, new pillows,
Motrin, the garbage pickup service, the paper on which you do your
homework, the books we read at night, the movies we rent, the water
that fills our bathtub and washing machine. Look at it all. Some of it is
special, some of it is basic and ubiquitous. I want you to feel, to think,
to consider what the choices mean, what responsibilities attend the
money we have.

Part of being an adult is being honest with yourself about money,
yet I hardly know anyone who is, anyone who can easily deal with
it. I want to encourage honesty in you, but you can see how tricky
that is when we carry this heritage. Andrew and I tend to get into
this sort of happy fog where we get excited spending and forget our

practical commitments. Or we worry and worry in a way that makes us feel threatened and afraid of money itself: Is there enough? Will it run out? Are we wasting it? A couple of years ago, we had a change in fortune. I started earning more than I had before, and we could live without other family funds. Also, we faced the novelty of having quite a bit extra. This was an unprecedented relief. When the furnace broke, we replaced it without being bothered that it cost $3,000. We put in our beautiful, elaborate garden, deciding to spend a lot on something that would bring us great pleasure (we talked it over a long time first). We realized we could pay for your orthodontia without a payment plan. But we didn't really know how to have this money, how to be people with this level of money at our disposal, in our care. What I'm saying is that it's hard, hard work, being sensible and careful and wise and aware of this. I was sick of making dinner, and a friend pointed out that we could afford to have someone else make it. We hired a chef, and it truly contributed to the general family happiness, but I felt embarrassed and wasteful, and I didn't want my friends to know about it. I want you to be proud of yourself, who you are, what you have, and the choices you make. But I have to find that in myself first. I struggle because of the mixed messages from the past, the cultural messages around me, and those early conversations your father and I could never seem to have. We've never been able to say, "We're rich."

We took our new funds and went to a financial adviser who talked about money as math, who took it out of the realm of good or bad, magic or secret, embarrassment or shame. This was a revelation to me, and to your father. For the first time we were able to talk to each other about money without getting stuck in the mud of emotion. We started to give money away, which was a wonderful feeling. To have it to give, to support the nonprofits we cared about, to invest in the life of our town, the life around you. We could use money for greater good.

When you wanted an iPod, we asked you to write a short essay about why and what you would do with it. This was different from the petitions I used to make to the trustees, because you were planning to use your own money. But I wanted you to revere its power, consider its possibilities. You listed a few scenarios in which the iPod would be useful to you, and you thought about how you'd take care of it. I wanted you to start thinking, choosing, understanding, and valuing. You wrote the essay—you even revised it—and you bought the iPod, and you've taken really good care of it, surprising me and your father. You haven't always taken care of things, or even thought to care, because you were young. But that's changing, and I'm proud of you.

It was your idea, Ezekiel, two years ago, to volunteer at the food bank. You were interested in the ethics of volunteering and in the role of the food bank in our city. I was proud of you then too, of your community involvement and curiosity. That's how I thought of it. I didn't anticipate that our work there would emphasize to me my own privilege and encourage me and your father to figure out more honest discussion. Our fortunes might reverse again; we'll earn less, have less. That's okay too. I understand richness better now, see its hidden depths, its many categories. To my surprise, contemplating food and hunger, having and worrying, I have set aside the foolishness and the guilt, the moral judgments and the social apologies. Our work at the food bank has lifted me up out of my lifetime insulation so I can start to admit what responsibilities I have. We're learning this together, which is what I love about our family, and also what hurts—that we're always figuring things out, as if for the first time. But I know what happens when we talk, what happens when you ask your questions. And I am in your debt.

Love,
Mama

PART III

Money and Self

Ignorance Is Bliss

Laurie Abraham

I'm almost afraid to admit this—afraid that I'm tempting fate, that I'll be punished for my blitheness, my avoidance of knowledge. The apple has been bitten; we all have to *know*. I'm afraid that one drizzly, gray morning, a doleful sheriff will present himself at my door, or in the middle of the night the phone will ring: "Am I speaking to the wife of Mr. Gregory Samuels?" Or that a few years from now my husband will come home to announce, tie oddly askew: "I'm leaving you for another woman." Aren't these the fates that befall women who fail to stay on top of their finances? The ones who let the menfolk handle the money, the bill paying, the investing and saving? First, their partners vanish, volitionally or otherwise—and then the women discover that they're penniless.

In *Smart Women Finish Rich* ("rich" and "smart" being the cornerstones of the monetary self-help oeuvre), financial planner David Bach, who has made gazillions writing books that tell others how to amass mere millions, recounts this conversation with a couple of women he met at one of his seminars. "We'd be in deep trouble if we left everything up to our husbands," one proclaimed. "We need to know about our finances, so we can be independent and take care of

ourselves," another chimed in. "Nobody is going to take care of me,"
said a third. "I have to take the responsibility myself." *Good girl!* you
can almost hear Mr. Bach thinking. Or, rather, *Good woman!*

For them, money is power. For me, money is a brittle skin; when
it's stripped away, I feel almost raw. I grimace slightly. For protection,
I've cultivated (subconsciously until now) a cocooning haziness about
the family finances. Our nanny is paid weekly, and I'm occasionally
the one who writes the check. Every time I have to ask her: "How
much is it?" Or I say, "I'll sign the check. Can you just fill in the
amount?" Ahhhhh. I feel so much better when I don't have to ink out
that large sum. It's like it's not happening; the outflow is staunched.
I've asked my husband at least three times how much we pay out each
month toward our mortgage, but for the life of me I can't remember
the figure. Is it $1,500 or $2,000? I think one of those is right, but I
wouldn't be shocked if I were off by $500 or more. As for the overall
size of our mortgage, I know it's a lot lower than that of our last house,
which is why we moved in the first place—to reduce our indebted-
ness. But I can't keep the number in my head.

For the record, no one would call me the ditzy sort.

Nor would anyone call my husband and me poor. I'm a busy writer
and editor, and Greg is an accomplished lawyer. While he decided to
work for himself, rather than at a more lucrative law firm, so he could
spend more time with our children, he still earns an income that—
together with my smaller contribution—puts us among the country's
economic elite. We don't *feel* extraordinarily well off, but neither of us
is craving more, more, more. Like me, Greg isn't particularly acquisitive, nor does he harbor aspirations of grandeur.

He pays all the bills; he handles the retirement accounts, the wills,
the life insurance—do we have disability insurance? I don't know,
though according to the financial self-help books, we should. I can't
bear to know the details. It's not the math. I was always pretty good at
math. It's how much being pretty good at math hurts. Just the thought
of paying for any significant expense—our two girls' education, health
insurance (because we're self-employed, the astronomical cost isn't

agreeably obscured in employee deductions)—puts me in the mind of a burn victim, the gauze being carelessly removed from her limbs.

Oddly, not thinking about money brings out my better aspects—most fundamentally, in the work I've pursued. Inspired by my parents' respective passions for their vocations—my father was an executive who rose through the ranks; my mother, who returned to work when I was ten, was a guidance counselor with a dedication to elevating the down and out—I've chosen a career that has been personally fulfilling—and has, at times, done a bit of good for the world. I chose it believing that I'd be happier stretching myself creatively and helping other people than I would be getting rich.

I've taken this to extremes, it's true. I once went a whole year without noticing that I hadn't received a promised raise. My general perception of raises had been that they're virtually unnoticeable—one's net pay barely budges—so why look at my check and be disappointed? When I mentioned the error to my boss, she offered to arrange back wages . . . and I told her to forget about it! I'd pointed out my mistake, yet was embarrassed to have to reveal my oversight. Acting nonchalant about the money puffed me up again, restored my pride—I didn't really need the raise. I know it was ridiculous to give my boss the message that raises were trivial to me—and to leave what was owed me on the table—but like I said, it was such a pittance.

What is rich, anyway? Everyone knows that no amount of money is ever enough.

At the age of forty-three, I can buy $100 shoes without feeling a bit guilty or persecuted; my mother still can't. But $300 shoes? I couldn't, I wouldn't. God, maybe I did once. In other words, if no money is ever enough, why bother being preoccupied with trying to gather more of it? Work with what you have.

I did not experience a childhood of deprivation; my suburban Cleveland family was securely middle-class. There was an aura of hardship in our household after my parents divorced when I was twelve, but that was mostly my romantic fantasy. My sister and I lived with our mother, and somehow I imagined us as characters in that seventies sitcom starring a young Valerie Bertinelli—three women on their own, making it *One Day at a Time*. But the reality was that we saw my father every Sunday, and my sister and I got everything we needed—and a bit more. We both had our Jordaches.

What I absorbed from my parents about money were two strands of thinking that have knotted together in me to produce a distasteful psychology I'll call "aggressive hoarding." My father always had an air of being slightly ripped off—not forlornly so, but cunningly, pugilistically: a person has to do what it takes to survive, even if it means cutting a few corners. (Perhaps this attitude stemmed from his childhood, where the love was as scarce as the cash.) My mother, meanwhile, clung to every last cent—or that's what it seemed like. We knew somehow never to order the most expensive item on the menu; before she went grocery shopping, my younger sister and I watched her flip through a cache of coupons and compare prices among salad dressings or peanut butter. Certain foods, like shrimp, were luxury items, and she only bought them when the price was right. At department stores, she'd track a certain sweater or skirt through the season, waiting for the big sale; if it didn't happen, she went without.

Where did my mother's tightfistedness come from? When my parents married, my father was just starting his M.B.A., and they didn't have "two nickels" between them, as my mother would say. But her thriftiness was more than a practical response to life's exigencies. Her father had turned a two-year degree from a business college into a lifelong position as a midlevel insurance executive. But I'm guessing he always felt one paycheck away from being plunged back into the truly grinding poverty of *his* parents' ugly three-chicken farm. His daughter, my mother, drank in the fear.

And me? Like my father, I rarely feel fear, I punch it. ("Hit me as hard as you can," he used to say to us, tightening his abs for my sister and me to swing away.) Thus, the "aggressive" part of my hoarder identity.

What, specifically, does the aggressive hoarder do? The most shocking manifestation is that I've been known to shoplift. I've been at a grocery store, feeling my cart growing heavier, feeling the money being torn away, and I've dropped the Camembert in my purse. *Why not take it?* I think. *The world is cheating me.* It's not that I need such luxuries for myself; I've got friends coming over, these damn, entitled New Yorkers, and they expect fancy cheeses. I'd be happy enough with store-brand Muenster.

I've never stolen from anyone I know even vaguely, including the Korean grocer down the street. My thievery, which began with a pair of hot-orange, interlocking hoop earrings at Higbee's department store, is reserved for retail behemoths, the *man*. These corporate cretins are ripping us all off, anyway. Right?

I know that such reasoning, such behavior, is, of course, as pathetic as it is amoral. (When my husband learned about it for the first time, he was appalled—and still is.) If I let myself feel the shame of being caught, my bravado slips away. A grown woman stealing barrettes! What a sad, silly nutcase! And if I imagine my daughters as teenagers following my example, I feel sick.

By not thinking about money, by keeping it in the abstract, I feel less fear—and thus less anger, and fewer larcenous urges. Perfect! Banishing thoughts of the filthy lucre keeps me on the straight and narrow, prevents me from lingering too long in that repugnantly ungrateful state where money represents everything that I "deserve" more of. Who doesn't believe that money can be a metaphor for love? Talk about something many people feel that they can never get enough of.

Blissful financial ignorance wasn't possible until I married, at thirty-five. I didn't marry for money; I married because I was besotted with my husband. But it would be ridiculous not to acknowledge that one reason I was attracted to Greg was his willingness to make my life comfortable, to provide for me and any children we might have. Unlike so many of my friends' boyfriends, he was effort-lessly generous with me from the start; what was his was mine. Even when we were not yet married, we had a joint bank account. He never criticized, not even subtly, any purchase I made. It's not that he made much money back then—he was a government lawyer—but he shared what he had, including such perks as free vacations, which come to those who have affluent parents.

Before we merged our money, however, I kept careful track of the peaks and valleys of my checking account. The only way I could have avoided it was if I'd been willing to live beyond the means of my relatively modest reporter's salary, and going into debt literally didn't occur to me. I had one credit card, which I paid off monthly—and even on my first job, I maxed out my retirement accounts. (You mean my company is going to *give* me money if I save money? Who wouldn't do that? Many young people wouldn't and didn't, I discovered. But the aggressive hoarder never misses a chance to pocket someone else's cash.)

When I was on my own, it took an act of will for me not to divide restaurant checks down to the last penny—and shame may have been the only emotion strong enough to rein in this learned penuriousness. My ritual mortification took place in my early twenties, the work of several friends whom I heard say things like: "Just split the bill equally, it doesn't matter who ordered what." *But . . . but . . . but . . . I ordered the cheapest thing on the menu,* a voice inside me howled. These days, the slippery relationship I maintain with our bank balance props up my generosity. It's much easier to play—to actually *be*—Lady Bounti-ful when you can let yourself imagine (or is it "assume"?) that the pot is full. I like being her. I also find that I'm much freer about donating to charities, though whenever possible I give through automatic de-ductions. (I want to give, I just don't want to see it go.)

Because Greg and I work from project to project, our cash flow waxes and wanes. I do occasionally inquire about our fiscal state, like when I notice that he's spending extra afternoons with the girls rather than engaging in combat on the phone. "Should I be worried about money?" I'll say. "No," he always replies. "We're okay." Though every once in a while he'll add: "You might want to hold off on big expenditures for a few months."

"*Why*?" I'll ask, a twinge of panic in my voice.

"It's no big deal. I just am having a little dry spell, but they never last long."

And usually I leave it at that.

I've thought of jumping on the computer, checking out our various balances (though Greg would have to tell me our bank password first), seeing how much we've spent on this thing and that, getting *involved*. But it would cause more marital tension than it's worth. I once floated to my husband the idea of living on a budget—the hoarder *loves* budgets, loves the (illusion of) perfect control—but he wasn't keen on that. "I only buy what I need, anyway," he said.

Really? Do you *need* double orders of organic produce every single week, when half of it goes to waste? Do you *need* every computer gadget imaginable? Do you need *seven* books from Amazon about having a dog? As much as I think all of these things are huge extravagances, I try not to say anything to my husband when yet another box arrives at our house. I try to reason relatively. Greg doesn't think we *need* a cushion for our wooden window seat, or festive napkins for Thanksgiving, or another dress for Louisa or Bess, or Botox in my forehead—but I sure do. (Well, I don't really think I *need* the Botox, and I was mortified by how much it cost when I saw the charge for it on our credit card statement—until Greg sent me this pitch-perfect husbandly e-mail: "I think you're beautiful without it, but if it makes you feel better about yourself, don't worry about the money." Does this make him my enabler?)

If I—I mean *we*—were trying to budget, I don't think I could be as benevolent. I'd want to question Greg's every purchase. Tautologically, the aggressive hoarder is not passive, and her marriage doesn't *need* a source of acrimony.

Moreover, not all is relative, and I'm pretty certain I'd be better at material sacrifice than my husband. I had thirteen years' experience living on a very modest income, with very few infusions from my parents. And beyond the practical—inside my hothouse of a head, that is—it would feel right to have to deny myself. Because, at the core, does not the person who always feels a touch gouged also feel a touch undeserving? Renunciation would give me an anorexic's rush of control, sweetened by a sense of superiority.

My husband's mental outlook, however, couldn't be more different. As a child of a moneyed family, Greg has really never had to live on a budget—and accordingly, he has a fairly loose definition of "need." Like Dr. Lydgate in *Middlemarch,* he just buys what is necessary for a man of his standing. If I were to put myself on a budget, but he were to refuse to do so himself? No anorexic's high could be strong enough to blot out my resentment: The rich boy's presumption! The injustice!

Given my baroque psychology, the high priests of personal finance undoubtedly would advise that I seek professional help. Every money book I've skimmed recommends therapy for people who, for whatever reason, avoid confronting their financial lives. I have a therapist—a bit of biographical information that would suggest to some that I share my husband's loose definition of "need"—but the subject of money arises infrequently in our sessions. (Perhaps not surprisingly, however, my therapist is quite moderately priced and lets me cancel with a few days' notice without charging for the hour or even getting testy. Could it be that my astute and kind doctor wants to signal with his actions that I really *am* deserving?)

When I say that my father felt ripped off as a boy and I inherited some of that worldview, I'm only half-right. My neediness probably also has roots in my own girlhood—my own very subjective experience of it, that is. I was loved steadily and well, and in this I know I am extremely fortunate. But what I somehow yearned for (and may still yearn for) is profligate love, unreasonable love, promiscuous, boundless, crazy love. Maybe it's not a coincidence that I started pinching earrings and mascara around the time my parents divorced. My line has always been that I was relatively unfazed by their breakup, but maybe I was "stealing" a little of my departed father's love. Maybe I didn't want to have to attack him to attract him, or see that I could affect him. Ironically, as my sensible and controlled midwestern parents have aged, as their own burdens and fears have lessened, they've loved me more effusively. (I *am* very lucky.)

It's a truism that romantic love fills whatever gaps parents unavoidably leave—and just as surely, that marriage, over time, tends to nick the vein of childhood longing. The therapist Michael Miller draws upon the language of economics—eloquently, no less—to describe the seasons of marriage. "Passion tends to cool or get complicated in the routine of domestic life—and when it does, the apprehension that love is scarce and time is passing may begin to darken the mood of a marriage," he writes in his book *Intimate Terrorism*. "[Intimate partners'] treatment of one another inevitably gets aggressive and stingy, each requiring proof of love from the other while withholding declarations of his or her own."

My marriage has experienced such a season. But, Miller believes, there are ways out of this predicament. One is for couples to let themselves experience their disappointment that things aren't what their childlike selves imagined, as opposed to striving to recapture what can't be recaptured. Disappointment contains secret hints of mutuality, he theorizes, and if couples are brave enough to deeply feel their regret, they can then move forward to try to create a "second" marriage, which—who knows?—may hold unexpected riches.

In the second marriage that Greg and I seem to be in the process of building, one thing I know is that appreciating my husband's good qualities—and what is good between us—is crucial (and so easy to neglect). Accordingly, I don't see why I need to join my husband at the helm of our financial ship when he's such an able, even daring captain. When my husband's law practice was in its infancy, I inadvertently discovered that one way he kept the cash gurgling, despite the ups and downs of our respective professions, was by taking out new credit cards when he spotted one with a 0 or 1 percent interest rate. By my estimation, we've carried massive loads of debt on these cards,

but Greg says he always paid them off—or transferred the outstand-
ing amount to another low-interest card—before we've had to start
coughing up 18 percent or more. I couldn't tolerate the uncertainty of
this strategy, but that doesn't mean I don't think it's rather brilliant.
(It would be less so, granted, if my husband weren't so relentlessly
careful.)

As traditional or unliberated or naive as it may sound, I think I
took sufficient steps to assure my financial security by choosing the
man I did. Which is not to suggest that I was a perfect rational actor
when I married. Reliability and eagerness to share are paternal traits,
of course, so it's likely when Greg presented himself to me in this way,
he fulfilled that other need, the need of the girl who wanted evidence
of big love.

To be clear, Greg is a financial genius—in fact, a major reason I
trust him is because I know he's not trying to become Donald Trump.
I trust and respect him because he's working with what we have. And
his lack of worry about money is a gift, an antidote to my angst: he
just thinks things will turn out all right, and they mostly have. Neither
the girls nor I have ever wanted for anything (though that is, in part,
because—as my husband has told me—I never want anything that is
too expensive). Another cog that makes this system hum is that Greg
trusts me as much as I do him: he knows that I'm not constitutionally
capable of spending at levels that could shock his conscience or upend
one of his artfully constructed arrangements. Because our financial
values are so in sync, my decision to stay on the monetary periphery
contributes to something that becomes ever more seductive as I age:
marital harmony, simple marital harmony.

I know that permanence is an illusion, that some tragedy could
befall Greg, or we could one day divorce. But if and when any of
that occurs, I'll deal with the knowing then; I'll figure out what I
have to figure out. Broadly speaking, I know my husband is saving for
our future, even if I'm unaware of the ins and outs. And I've never
stopped working and earning money myself. Were Greg not around,
I'd be able to support our family.

I'm confident that my husband, even if he were moved to become my ex, would not leave me with any awful financial surprises. I'm sure of this just as I'm sure he won't have an affair or endanger our children. After all, isn't that what these dire warnings to women are ultimately about? We're supposed to immerse ourselves in money matters because we can't trust the men?

Could my comeuppance be around the corner? Perhaps. But I took the measure of my husband's character when we decided to marry, and I choose not to live in anticipation of the worst. Daily life with two daughters, two careers, and one marriage is already like an emergency room. Every day, every moment my husband and I are performing triage, I'm leaving the bloody green mess to him.

The Wages of Sin

A PERSONAL HISTORY OF ECONOMICS

Kim Barnes

I.

I am ten when the older boy from our little fundamentalist church places a dime in my hand and says that I can keep it if I'll let him touch my knee. We've been playing hide-and-seek and have taken refuge in the parsonage's stairway, a steep and secret ascent to the slope-roofed bedrooms. Dusky light filters in just short of the top landing.

I'm the daughter of a gyppo logger. I live with my parents and younger brother in a shotgun shack surrounded by larch and red cedar in the Clearwater National Forest of Idaho. We pull our water from the small spring that runs outside our window. The indoor plumbing freezes in winter and runs dry in summer so that, more often than not, we trek to the outhouse to do our business. No TV but a little console hi-fi that my parents bought on time and on which we listen to the radio stations skipping in from Texas. My father hunts no matter the season. We eat the venison right down to the bones. A bag of dried brown beans gets us through the hardest winter. While my schoolmates collect baseball cards and Barbie dolls, I collect the pastel tabs of Holsum wrappers, the prices stamped in ink. With two dimes, I could buy a loaf of soft white bread.

It hasn't yet dawned on me that what this boy wants is some part of sex—a word that is never spoken from the pulpit but comes veiled in euphemisms: necking, petting, fornication. Along with such words come dire warnings of fire-and-brimstone punishment, but I have no real idea of what the words mean. Other than a book illustrated with gray diagrams of the human reproductive organs that my mother has left on my bed, I have never been instructed in sexual matters of any kind. I don't know that women have orgasms; I don't know that *men* have orgasms. What I know is that a girl who *ruins her reputation* will never have a husband, and that a woman without a husband will never have anything. We are the daughters of Eve, a danger to ourselves and those around us. Our temptation of man brought the whole world to ruin.

The boy sits beside me, waiting. My skirt is tucked, my legs together. I pull my knee socks a little higher as I consider his offer. I know that, if I take the boy's dime and allow him to touch me, it will be a sin. I know that the dime will buy me a sack of jawbreakers and bubblegum or a Coke at the confectionary—all luxuries my family can't afford. I smell the boy's peppermint breath, the fried chicken the women are cooking in the kitchen below. I feel my stomach clench and growl. I am hungry.

I hold out my hand, and the boy places the dime in my palm. I close my eyes, and a shiver of fear or expectation makes my teeth chatter. When the boy's fingers graze the band of bare skin between my long socks and the hem of my skirt, a dart of strange pleasure travels from my knee to my heart. In that moment, the dime is forgotten. Even now, I can't recall: Did I buy candy? A vanilla ice cream cone dipped in hot fudge? Or did I lose the coin in the backseat of my family's car as we traveled through the dark toward home? What I remember is this: even after the fried chicken, the mashed potatoes floated with white gravy, the thick slabs of homemade sourdough buttered and toasted, my hunger was still with me, keener now, and somehow new.

II.

1970. The year I begin seventh grade, my family moves from the small logging town to the closest small city. My father takes a job as a truck driver, and the poverty line holds steady at our feet. My mother finds an empty rental—a lovely old house on the verge of ruin. The doctor who owns it will give us one month free in exchange for upkeep, and so we move into the stucco bungalow with its dusty crystal chandelier and overgrown koi pond in back. Its empty rooms echo with our footsteps. Other than the scratchy Herculon sofa that my mother says will outlast her, we have no furniture. Our dining set is a redwood picnic table on loan from a relative, and we eat our hamburger casseroles and bread-and-gravy suppers beneath the faceted light of the chandelier. My closet is hung with a few dresses and skirts, handmade by my mother—an excellent seamstress whose fashionable impulses are overruled by the church's dictates concerning modesty: all hems two inches below the knees, no blouses that don't cover the shoulders. No adornment—jewelry, makeup—is allowed. The combination of homespun and homely in the face of miniskirts and blue eye shadow makes me slump and dodge as I walk to my new junior high school, its design blocky and modern. Even our church is different—pews that seat hundreds, central heating and air-conditioning instead of a potbellied stove and windows open to the summer breeze. When we are invited to dinner at the home of fellow parishioners, I'm fascinated by the electric dishwasher, transfixed as I watch the trash compactor grind and seal the garbage into a neat package. But it's their son, two years my elder, who mesmerizes me. He has thick blond hair, sharp blue eyes, a *component stereo system* connected to a light board, all set up in his downstairs bedroom. He shows me how the lights pulse and strobe to the music's beat. He puts on a Beatles album and plays "Strawberry Fields Forever." We sit on the edge of his bed, and when he reaches to touch my knee, I scoot a little closer. Until I'm sixteen, he will be my boyfriend. With the money he makes at his job at the supermarket, he buys me Tater Tots after Sunday church service, root beer floats after prayer meeting. A wool tartan skirt that I roll at the waist to expose my thighs and a sweater that dips suggestively at the collarbone. He teaches me how to French-kiss; his hand travels farther than my knee. When I hesitate to *go all the way,* he becomes moody, then angry. Hadn't he worked overtime to buy me the promise ring with a real diamond chip at its center?

I think I love him, of course, and maybe I do. I know that I love riding around in his car, the delicate gold cross he hangs at my throat, the first real restaurant of my life (chicken-fried steak on the menu), where he takes me to celebrate the one-year anniversary of our meeting. Who better to give my virginity to than this sixteen-year-old boy with hair like John Denver who says he will be my husband?

In a church that demands female subservience and with a father whose patriarchy is absolute, the fact that I should *belong* to a man is both encouraged and expected. And, somehow, it is with this exchange—my acquiescence for his continued affection—that my boyfriend gains ownership, as though my maidenhead were a coin he had plundered and now holds in his pocket. Sex becomes what we do instead of watching TV or listening to his extensive collection of LPs. Having offered myself once, I no longer believe I have the right to withhold. As long as I'm free with my favors, my boyfriend is happy. I begin to dream of houses with more than one level, rooms full of matching furniture, a pantry stocked with staples. Perhaps I should have heeded the words of my great aunt: "There's only one thing that women have that's worth a plug nickel, and you'd better know when to hold and when to sell." She'd kept her man home and seemingly happy for over sixty years by an iron-fisted control of the market (just because he *wanted* didn't mean he *got,* at least not until *she* got what *she* wanted), her stock gone from that of a sharecropper's daughter to the wife of an entrepreneur with certificates of deposit in every bank in town.

But I am of a different generation. The world of women is in upheaval. They are burning their bras in the streets, marching on

Washington, demanding equal rights, equal pay for equal work. My boyfriend doesn't care that I am his equal: what he cares about is that I am *his*. So that when a boy I think of as only a friend buys me a Coke after Sunday-night service, my lover is enraged. He commands me into his car, and I don't dare disobey. The other boy hesitates before driving away. My boyfriend calls me a whore, and then shoves me from his car to the pavement, where I lie for a long time in the dark, believing that I have earned this, that this is the payment for my sin.

III.

A job at Taco Time, and then at Orchard's Pharmacy. A $600 loan on a 1967 Chevrolet Impala. My boyfriend's rages grow more vengeful, and then another girl catches his eye. Even as ruined as I am, I'm relieved to see him go.

I'm a senior in high school, making enough money to buy my own clothes, my own Cokes, my own tickets to the movies that I sneak to because movie houses are *dens of iniquity* and might lead me to sin. My grades are good enough to earn me scholarship offers: I will be the first in my family to attend college. The night of graduation, my father and I have a final falling-out. He tells me that if I can't pay him absolute obedience, I must take my things and never come back.

And I do. I pack my suitcase and walk out the door, leaving behind my weeping mother, my dreams of college. Now I must find a job that will pay me a living wage. I apply for a teller's position at a local bank and am hired. The vice president is impressed by the grades I received in math.

Every day I count the money: all the bills facing the same way, all shuffled and tamped into alignment, stacked and bound with elastic bands. All the coins rolled and pinched. I'm making almost $3 an hour. I have medical coverage, disability. My life is insured. A "career girl," my grandmother calls me. I have just enough money to buy gas for my Chevy, to buy a margarita after closing on Friday night, to pay the $95-a-month rent on a studio apartment, but no money to begin work toward a degree. "You need a man," my mother tells me. "Someone to take care of you. To protect you from other men." And even though I now wear a T-shirt that reads, A WOMAN NEEDS A MAN LIKE A FISH NEEDS A BICYCLE, I don't know how to move forward down the road of my life without the ride a man might provide. All my school friends are married and having children; a few have gone off to college, where they will find men with ambition, men who are headed somewhere, who are on their way up. I don't know a single woman who lives alone *by choice* and *on purpose*.

Loneliness eats at my bones. I'm hungry all the time. I eat Top Ramen, mac-and-cheese, toast with peanut butter. At the end of each month, my money all gone, I eat white bread spread with butter, sprinkled with sugar—a sweet comfort food my mother had fed me when I needed something more. I miss my mother, miss her quiet presence, her soft assurance. It will be years before I understand how the poverty of her life was emotional as well as monetary. No high school diploma, no jobs that would offer her the minimal security my father's modest salary provided. What choice did she have but to stay in the marriage? "It could have been worse," she'll tell me. "Some husbands come home from the bars and beat their wives. It can always be worse."

That spring, when the yellow Corvette Stingray pulls up at the bank's drive-through window, I slide out the drawer and watch with mild curiosity as the man deposits his hefty paycheck. He has long dark hair, a thick beard, and a mustache, blue, blue eyes that hold me longer than is comfortable. The next week, he includes a note with his deposit: would I like to go to dinner that Friday night?

I glance at him through my pane of bulletproof glass. He isn't handsome, but unusually tall and lean, older than I am by a decade. Still, there is something about him, a kind of self-possession and worldly carriage, that attracts me. And those eyes. And that car.

And then the dozen red roses that arrive at the bank Friday afternoon and that the other tellers moon over. "Who is he?" they ask, and all I can do is give them the details that I have gleaned from his checking account: his name—David James—his address, phone, social security number. The record of his transactions. The fact that his paychecks are drawn on a long-haul trucking company. That he is a spender, not a saver. That he is picking me up at seven in the Corvette. That we will go to the most expensive restaurant in town.

I bathe and manicure, curl my long hair, add another layer of mascara. A dress from the boutique on Main Street. A pair of high heels. At the restaurant, David orders for me: filet mignon and lobster, melted butter, a baked potato with chives. A bottle of wine that the waiter opens with a corkscrew. David talks about his trips to Seattle, where I've never been. He tells me that he's a Vietnam vet, two tours. Like me, he loves to read. He's quick to laugh, easy to pay attention to. When he becomes quiet for a moment, and then asks me about boyfriends I've had, I hesitate, afraid that my past will ruin everything. He doesn't care, he says. I have to know that.

I don't pay for a thing, of course, and won't for many months to come. More flowers, midnight rides in the Corvette with the top off, cocktails in bars that have fireplaces instead of pool tables. I keep waiting for the required payback that will begin with a kiss, then a move to the couch, maybe to the bed. When no such demands are made, I am at first relieved, and then concerned. Is he married? Is he gay? I begin to fear that he doesn't find me desirable—a fearful possibility. What other value do I possess? My dress becomes more provocative, my attention more fixed. And when he finally does kiss me, I feel that remembered luscious jolt that had left me breathless in the parsonage stairway.

"Let's go slow," he says. "Take our time." I am a virgin again, shivery with anticipation. I feel doted upon and pampered, wooed and oh so won. All those roses. All that buttery, buttery lobster. I have never been more ready.

When, finally, David invites me into his bedroom, it is not the fairy-tale seduction I had imagined but a Hugh Hefner romp. No candle-light and soft music, just incandescence and rock-and-roll. Hard-core porn in one drawer, sex toys in another. He laughs at my shy naïveté. "Let's just have fun," he says. "What's wrong with that?" This thing that I have for so long thought a sin, a sure-fire road to damnation— this *sex*—he sees as nothing more than harmless entertainment. I've left the church, thrown off its injunctions against movies, dancing, drinking. Why not this?

When, on our next date, David arrives in a pickup and admits that the Corvette was not his but on loan from a friend, I say it doesn't matter. I *am* having fun, after all, spending all my free time with David. Sometimes he takes me along as a passenger in his semi-truck, most often to Seattle, where we eat cedar-smoked salmon while look-ing out over Puget Sound, then walk the wharf holding hands. When, at the end of one such day, he suggests that we stop by a sex shop, I'm curious. There's so much I want to know.

Over the next several months, David cajoles me—that's the only word for it, good-natured cajoling—into accompanying him into the sex shops, peep shows, and topless bars I hadn't known he frequented (the workers all know him by name). When, because I am missing too much work, my supervisor at the bank puts me on notice, David encourages me to quit, and I do. He moves into my apartment to save both of us money. Within weeks, my bank account is empty. When I ask David for cash to buy groceries, I am stunned: he too is broke.

"But you had thousands," I say. "I saw it."

"It's gone," he answers, and, in another few weeks, I know why: speed, cocaine, mushrooms, LSD. The many "friends" he has are people who come to party with David. They support his habit, buy whatever he is selling.

At some point, that whatever becomes me.

"You owe me," he says. "How else are you going to pay?"

No money, no job, no car. My request for unemployment denied, my car broken down, my credit in shambles. Still, I refuse. What had begun as fun has turned frankly serious. David's threats become more explicit, his posture more threatening: until I agree to do what he says, he will not talk to me, will not acknowledge my existence. He leaves the apartment, and I lie alone in our bed for days, in a paralytic state of despair, rising only to make my way to the bathroom but never to the kitchen because I will find nothing there. He's left me nothing to eat. Our cupboards are bare.

It is the economics of survival, pure and simple, that drive me to face David, to refuse his order that I have sex for money with other men while he watches, to disobey his command that I not leave the house, to borrow my cousin's car and find him where he sits in a bar with one of his other women. But economics has little to do with what comes next, which will require of me survival of another kind. The punishment for my sin is this: David returns to the apartment and rapes me. And with that violence, he leaves me with a promise—that just when I think I have forgotten him, he will return to rape me again.

As I lie on the couch where he has left me, my body aching, I feel an unexpected calm. This is the price I had expected to pay all along. I think of Jezebel, her story a cautionary tale to all women who have earned the wages of sin: her dismembered hands thrown to the streets for the dogs to gnaw.

But, still, some scrap of who I am remains.

IV.

I am twenty. My job is gone, my car. I have turned my family away from me. This time, it isn't a man I turn to for help, but a woman. I am taken in by a girlfriend, one of the few young women I know who is training for a career—she will be a nurse. She gives me a bed and feeds me until I can gather the pieces of my life and start over. I find steady employment cocktailing at one of the nicer bars, where I keep my distance from the men and their drunken offers. I sign up for classes at the local college. When I tell the financial aid counselor that I have no transportation to get to and from campus, she writes me a check for $300—just enough to buy the aging Dodge Coronet

I'd seen on the used-car lot. The salesman is good-looking and not much older than I am, but when the roses arrive at my door, along with his card thanking me for my business, I throw away the note and tell my roommate not to take his calls. The roses last until the end of the week, and then they too go into the garbage. The Dodge will last me for years.

I attend class through the day, work at the bar until 2:00 A.M., and then rise to do it all again. Even with tips, my wages aren't enough to cover my expenses. I take my portable typewriter to the food bank and trade it for cheese and peanut butter—I don't want to owe anybody anything. When I wake one frostbitten morning after Christmas with a throat so inflamed that it hurts to breathe, I go to class anyway, and then to work. Who can afford the loss of grades and money and maybe even the job itself? Over the next several days, the sore throat worsens. No insurance, no way to pay for medical care. My voice has descended to a husky alto. I stumble from table to table in a true purple haze. In one corner sits a group of businessmen, celebrating the success of an account, knocking back martinis as fast as the bartender can make them. Their leader, middle-aged but still trim and with the jaw-set of a man used to getting his way—the kind of man who might take care of me—presses a $50 bill into my palm.

"You sound just like Lauren Bacall," he says and winks. "And I've always had a hard-on for Lauren Bacall."

I stand with my tray of drinks in one hand, the fifty in the other, my throat burning with infection. I make a choice, then, one I've never regretted. I fold the fifty in my fist and walk away. The fifty buys me a trip to the health clinic and a bottle of antibiotics, and it buys me something else: a new awareness that just because men are willing to pay doesn't mean that women have to give—a lesson that my aunt once tried to teach me.

When, years later, I ask a friend twenty years my elder—no high school degree, no job experience, no retirement of her own—why she doesn't leave her domineering husband, she will reply, "Better prostitute than destitute." And how can I argue? Maybe, when it comes to love, money, and the daughters of Eve, it's always a devil's bargain.

V.

One husband, two children, three degrees in English. I take a position as an adjunct at the college where my young poet-husband, recently divorced, is already a professor, but, unlike him, I have no job security, no benefits, no tenure. Like other faculty wives, I am an anchored spouse. I teach the overflow classes, the last-minute adds. In our small community, day care is nearly nonexistent, our combined income barely enough to pay the mortgage. On the days I don't teach, I dress our small children, strap them into their car seats, and drive to parks, to beaches, to towns thirty miles away for a matinee—anything to use up the hours. Their father needs the small house quiet so that he can write. I've read Virginia Woolf a dozen times and still don't know how to ask for a room of my own.

I compose my own poems and essays while standing at the kitchen counter, a baby at my breast, a pen in my hand. I jot notes on paper towels, on receipts at McDonald's while the children sink into the brightly colored balls of Playland. Sometimes, I take my pencil and paper into the bathroom—the only room with a locking door. My son and daughter, my husband, even the dog come to the threshold to whine and inquire: when will I be out?

How can I tell them that, in that small room, still misted with the morning's showers, I am writing the story of my life? That each sentence I put to the page seems both penance and payback. I'm rebuilding the ruins, one word at a time.

Those words become books, those books a desk, a narrow office. Even so, it sometimes seems as though I'll never make back those wages lost to men. I'm fifty, closer to retirement than I ever thought I would be. After all those years of being a "trailing spouse," it's unlikely that my salary, my résumé, my retirement will ever match those of my husband, who didn't wait for anybody: his first wife, his first child, and then the family he and I made together—all fell in line behind his ambition to become a writer and teacher. In the isolated environment of the interior west, no one ever told me I might take the lead. If I'd earned truer wages through all those years of waiting for a man to take care of me, how much better could I take care of myself?

But then, even if I'd had a role model to guide me, would anything be any different? Even now, twenty-five years into my marriage, the children grown and gone, my university position finally secure, I understand the trade-off. I've given up time and money for the love of a husband and children, for the love of this place where I've chosen to live, only miles away from that backwoods parsonage with its smells of fried chicken and gravy, where the boy touched my knee and I began to fall, my sin made of nothing but a little want, a little need to know something more.

Keeping Up Appearances

J. Courtney Sullivan

I picked out my dress six months before the big day. I had been coveting it through the window of the little shop on Route 3A for almost a year—pure white lace on the bodice and a poofy princess skirt. My mother wanted me to wear the simple veil she herself had worn in 1967, but I insisted on a long, sheer number, festooned with real pink roses and ribbons running down my back. The cake was unlike anything my friends had had, with layers of buttercream made to look like a woven basket. The guest list was full of relatives guaranteed to bring great gifts. I felt so excited the night before I walked down the aisle that I couldn't sleep. My parents let me stay up late, watching *Mary Poppins,* eating cookies in my nightgown and veil. I was seven years old. The next day I would make my First Communion.

Along with a rosary and three creepy Infant of Prague statuettes, I received a little black-and-white television from my grandmother, a gold locket and a pretend office set from my parents, and a check for $100 from my uncle Richie, which thrilled me to my core, and which I never cashed. I chose instead to hide the check in a drawer and gaze at it every so often, as if it were a newborn baby or a shooting star. Even at that age, I had the tendency to imagine myself into a life—a big, glitzy writer's life in New York City. When I tried to picture how far a hundred dollars could take me in New York, the possibilities seemed endless.

The delicious extravagance of my Communion was par for the course during my childhood. (My grandfather had once hired a guy in a penguin suit to come to the front door with a handful of balloons on my birthday.) As my parents' only child, and the only grandchild on either side of the family, I was undisputedly the most spoiled kid on the block.

We lived in the suburbs of Boston, on a tree-lined street called Garden Street, where children played kickball in the road until dinnertime and mothers baked pound cakes from scratch after returning home from work. It was the 1980s, but it felt distinctly like 1952. Most of the parents on the street, including my mother, had come from blue-collar backgrounds and worked hard to improve on the circumstances of their own upbringings. They must have been proud of this, but, being Irish Catholic, none of them bragged. The very layout of the neighborhood seemed to discourage any keeping-up-with-the-Joneses-type behavior. The houses were all the same—three- or four-bedroom Colonials in shades of white or blue, with small, fenced-in yards. Talk about money usually centered on sensibility. If you complimented one of the neighborhood moms on her shoes, for instance, she might say, "Oh, God, really? I got them at Frugal Fannie's for nine ninety-nine."

The Garden Street Girls, as my friends and I were known, were an enterprising bunch. We organized businesses of all kinds—elastic conventions and bake sales and lemonade stands and string bracelet booths on the corner. We even tried having a money sale once—selling a nickel for a dime and so on, but needless to say, that never quite took off. Making money from selling things meant freedom to us, even though the things we sold usually came from our mothers' refrigerators. We shared a sense of real pride in being able to buy our own candy and troll dolls at the Five and Ten in East Milton Square.

Not that I needed the money. My parents gave me everything my heart desired and then some. They themselves were never particularly showy, but compared to my friends, I most certainly was. I had a whole room just for my Barbies. I owned every single American Girl doll, along with the accompanying tea sets and wardrobes and bunk beds and books. I never thought about what any of it cost.

"I need a new bike, and Christmas is light-years away," my friend Noreen once said after an unfortunate driveway accident in which her banana seat and handlebars were crushed by her own mother's minivan.

"Ask the Sullivans. They're rich," said Kate from next door.

I blushed a fiery red when she said it, but I also felt happy, content. I thought we were rich too.

In reality, we were like most Americans—stuck in the middle somewhere. My parents married young, in the days before Suze Orman. They had never heard of a 401(k) or thought about saving for higher education or retirement. Instead, they spent and spent and spent—on vacations, mortgage payments, presents for me, Montessori school, and all the pricey who-knows-whats that family life requires. By the time their tenth wedding anniversary rolled around, they had amassed a substantial amount of debt. That same year, my father got laid off and my sister Caroline was born. (My Barbie room became her bedroom, and my plastic empire was moved to an office the size of a walk-in closet.)

I often overheard my parents talking about money in the hushed tones that every child knows are designed to keep her from hearing. I realized with some alarm that even though they never denied me a single thing I wanted, my parents were struggling. Among the kids on Garden Street, I had always played the part of the overprivileged, and for the first time this made me feel guilty and embarrassed. In real terms, my family wasn't rich at all. Rich to me evoked a sense of eternal financial comfort and ease. We were merely playing a part and had done a good job of fooling the people around us. I had forty-seven Barbie dolls, but not a penny saved for college.

Eventually, my father got a new job and things seemed slightly less dire. But neither the tension around money in our house nor my parents' tendency to spoil us ever went away. Like everyone else's mother, ours tried to get my sister and me interested in the virtues of TJMaxx and Filene's Basement. She taught us how a few quality items of clothing could carry an entire wardrobe. But she indulged us too. My sister was fashion-conscious, even from a young age. When she turned thirteen, she declared that Kate Spade purses were "so sixth grade" and asked Santa to bring her a Dior for Christmas.

Once I hit middle school, I tried not to ask my parents for as much anymore, but I still sometimes succumbed to their generosity. If I expressed guilt over this, my mother would wave me away with her hand and say, "Don't worry, it's just money."

Even though it sometimes got them into trouble, I liked the part of my parents that thought money shouldn't own you or dictate your life choices. In high school, I dated a guy whose father said he had to go into either engineering or medicine because that's where the money was. This baffled me. I knew I wanted to be a writer, but I never thought much about how I'd make a living. It just seemed like something that would happen, because all adults eventually made a living, as sure as they got wrinkles and that unavoidable bulge around their middles. My parents never told me to follow the cash. They told me to follow my passion, and so I did.

By the grace of God and Sallie Mae, I was able to afford a Smith education. I majored in English lit without fear, even though many crotchety people told me that a degree in the liberal arts was about as useful as a Popsicle wrapper when it came to earning an actual income. I was determined to prove them all wrong and to one day write a bestselling novel so I could buy my mother a beach house in Maine and my father a recording studio where he could play his guitars in peace.

As college drew to an end, I thought a lot about my looming financial independence. I was endlessly grateful for the lifestyle my parents had given me, but I knew that as a writer I'd never be able to sustain it, at least not in my twenties. And I was terrified of debt, having seen the stress it can cause firsthand. I reasoned that it was all about figuring out what was most important: I really had no interest in clothing and makeup, but I could not live without a good haircut, the occasional dinner out, and rooms full of books. By the time I got my diploma, I had it all planned—I would simply live within my means, never pretend I could afford more than I could, pay the bills on time, and keep away from the Prada.

And then I moved to New York.

When I first got to Manhattan, I took a job at a beauty magazine that paid about as much as a paper route. I knew my parents were at home holding a long-distance safety net, and I was lucky for that, because there were some months when I couldn't make ends meet. But for the most part, I was supporting myself, and I was doing it in one of the most expensive cities in the world.

Plenty of the women at my office—some of them in their thirties and forties—had fathers who paid their rent and credit card bills. They referred to their salaries as "clothing allowances." They were my friends, but I never had the means to be like them—dress like them, spend like them—and that was fine by me. I was happy to be the only one among us who didn't enjoy recreational shopping, who would rather have $3 beers at a dive bar than wait in line to get into the hottest new club.

Even though it wasn't really a choice, I felt weirdly virtuous not taking money from my parents—being in this world of excess, but certainly not of it. I took as much pride in paying my bills from my meager paycheck as I once had in buying candy with my cut of the profits from a Garden Street hot chocolate stand.

My friends from home had always teased me about how spoiled I was. In New York, suddenly it was the opposite: friends from work noticed that I hadn't purchased a new pair of jeans since my first year of college, that I had only one pair of black heels instead of ten or twelve like everyone else. Barbie room be damned—as kids, these women had probably had their own private islands to play on. All financial problems and gains are relative, of course, and compared to the girls I worked with in New York, I was thrifty and unmaterialistic, a virtual monk.

I played the role with gusto, romanticizing myself into the league of poor but hopeful young women I had always loved in literature— Anne Shirley, Becky Sharpe, Elizabeth Bennet, hell, even the Bette Midler character from *Beaches*. I thought back to the way my mother had told us that a girl only needs a few expensive items to make her whole wardrobe look good. (Of course, when we were shopping on her dime I had never listened, but now that I was paying my own way, her advice made all the sense in the world.)

I lived on the Upper East Side with Lauren, my best friend from home. The apartment came cheap because it stood directly across from a fire station, and the moan of sirens provided a steady backdrop to every conversation. Our tiny living room offered a charming view of an airshaft, and the radiator sometimes shot torrents of boiling water up toward the ceiling for no apparent reason. We didn't have a TV stand or a dining table, so we set up our television on top of a cardboard box and ate off our laps. We had gotten quite used to living this way, and for the most part, we loved the place.

We blasted folk music late into the night, singing each other to sleep from our beds at either end of the apartment. One of our favorite bands was the Weepies, who sang about happiness and simplicity, getting up in the morning to put the kettle on and write a good song and sing it to the birds. I decided I wanted to live inside a Weepies song someday, to write novels in a big country kitchen, with the dogs at my feet and a mug of tea in my hand. I vowed to get myself there, somehow, but there was no map, and I longed to know how a person went from fixer of paper jams and filer of expense reports to contented and celebrated writer of novels.

Then, after two years in New York, something big happened. Almost by accident, I sold a book. The book was about fabulous women who can't stop dating losers, and it encouraged readers to seek out men of quality, men with a little money in the bank. It wasn't exactly the Great American Novel I'd always dreamed of writing, but it was something—an opportunity to accelerate my career and make a name for myself.

Also, I needed the cash.

The book advance was $30,000, a fortune to me. Selling a book allowed us to get rid of Lauren's pink futon and replace it with a real couch from Macy's. It let me upgrade from a Nine West bag meant to look like a Marc Jacobs to an actual Marc Jacobs. For the first time, when people asked whether I wanted to join them for cocktails after work, I didn't have to lie and say I had other plans because I only had $4.89 in my checking account. Best of all, magazine editors around town heard that I had a book coming out, which lent me some legitimacy as a writer. I started to get meatier assignments with actual paychecks attached.

But as the publication date neared, I grew wary. The term "sellout," oft-uttered in college, ran through my mind a lot. I had staked my self-sufficiency on a book that some people thought was, at its heart, about gold-digging. I had to laugh when my publisher marketed me as something like the next Carrie Bradshaw. It was clear that we weren't going to sell a lot of books by admitting that during the last week of every month I subsisted on Ramen noodles and Honey Nut Cheerios or that when I opened my Con Edison bill and saw the friendly reminder printed on the return envelope—DON'T FORGET TO INCLUDE YOUR CHECK!—I felt a wave of Catholic guilt wash over me, because I had been considering doing just that.

"I feel like a financial fraud," I told a friend over dinner one night.

"Who doesn't?" he said, though his own deception went in the opposite direction: he longed to appear down-to-earth and normal, but at twenty-four he had already made ridiculous money on Wall Street and purchased a two-bedroom apartment in the West Village, complete with a grand piano.

Another friend, who used to live in the same Manhattan apartment building as Kurt Vonnegut, insisted that everyone in New York was faking it to some extent or another. He told me how he saw the author out walking one morning in his usual tattered clothes, his hair in its customary state of disarray.

A homeless guy with an oversize backpack approached him and said, "Hey, watch my stuff while I go take a leak."

When Vonnegut declined, the guy said, "Brother, people like us gotta look out for each other."

Vonnegut looked surprised and amused. "I'm not homeless," he said.

By the time the book was released—nearly two years after I sold it—I had spent all but a couple thousand dollars of my advance money on luxuries like electricity and college loans. And okay, yes, I also bought the purse and the couch and a laptop and a ticket to Maui. ("That's the problem with women right there—they're always justifying their purchases," a friend of mine wrote to me when I told her I felt bad about buying such frivolous things instead of saving more. "A twenty-four-year-old man would say, 'I bought a car and a life-size plush horse stuffed with condoms.' Nobody would blink.")

A few months after the book hit stores, I was nearly broke. Yet I had also become the poster child for gold-diggers everywhere. I had written a book that encouraged women to admit that money matters in relationships. (And I had done it in large part because I needed money.) I thought this was a given, something that everyone already knew, not an argument that would arouse ire in some readers. It stung when I opened up a newspaper or went online and saw myself described as, among other things, a gold-digger, an idiot, and (most painful of all) a woman with a haircut straight out of *Little House on the Prairie*.

I'm twenty-six now, and I finally make enough to live alone, in an apartment I love, where I can sit by the window on a Sunday afternoon, writing my novel and watching the rain fall. I have a day job at the *New York Times* that challenges and excites me. Last year, for the very first time, I was able to declare myself a writer on my taxes—not an assistant with high hopes, but an actual *writer*, who earns her keep by writing.

I still cringe a little every time I go on a first date, knowing that the image of me as gold-digger with bad hair is just a Google search away.

Friends from home still think I'm ridiculously extravagant. They cannot believe the rent I pay. They say it's absurd that I buy shoes for more than $50 a pair and wear Victoria's Secret bras when everybody knows the cheap ones from H&M are made in the exact same factory.

And then there are those New York girls I used to work with. They bring me fancy soaps and perfume when we see each other for drinks. They eye my purse, which is now woefully out of season, and I imagine them asking their parents to adopt me and give me the life I truly deserve: *for just pennies a day, the price of a cup of coffee, you could clothe this poor victim of fashion.*

Some days I still feel like I'm faking it financially, and others I think I'm doing just fine. Maybe everyone in this city—maybe everyone, period—is faking it to some extent, going to sometimes ridiculous lengths to prove their financial success. Since none of us have the ability to peer into one another's bank accounts, we use *things*—designer shoes and trips abroad and seven-bedroom houses—to assess what others are worth. In New York, nannies carry Prada totes to the park, and famed novelists living on Madison Avenue dress like hobos. In so many fundamental ways, money shapes our lives here. But almost as important are the financial personas we project, often in an attempt to keep other people guessing. Even the language we use to talk about money is deliberately vague, almost coquettish. The oft-uttered phrase "I'm broke" always makes me wild with curiosity. *Broke as in you do not have a penny to your name and will have to take to the streets? Or broke as in you spent too much at Saks this weekend and shouldn't eat at Nobu tonight?*

I've come to realize that behind the personas and the perceptions and the parts we play is a simple fact: we all need money, and we do what we must to get it. Even the Weepies—my favorite old folk band that sang about a simple, unmaterialistic life—ended up providing the sound track to this season's JCPenney ads, street cred be damned.

Depending on who you talk to, I might seem spoiled or self-sufficient; materialistic or exceedingly humble; a savvy young career woman or a financially befuddled writer; someone determined to marry a man with money or a romantic with a long track record of dating starving artists and dreamers. Maybe all of these things are true. The whole business reminds me of one of my favorite old quotes from Walt Whitman, who once lived on the street in Brooklyn where I now reside: "Do I contradict myself? Very well then, I contradict myself. I am large. I contain multitudes."

The Perils of the
Privileged Poor

Laura Fraser

Some women wake up at forty-five and realize they forgot to have children. I realized I forgot to make money.

I've never given much thought to personal finance. Truth be told, it hasn't been a serious problem: I'm grateful I've never had to worry about having enough to eat or finding a place to sleep. Nor has money ever been a major goal, accomplishment, or dirty secret: I did not get an M.B.A. or go public with a company, and I don't worry about having to hide my wealth for fear of attracting the wrong friends. I've been annoyingly low on funds many times, but I've still always thought the whole topic of money was vaguely boring and uncool, and never much of an *issue*.

Until now.

A few months ago, at the twenty-fifth reunion of the elite East Coast college I attended, it dawned on me that I didn't have very much money, relative to my peers. That was somewhat true back when I went to the school too—there were some extremely wealthy kids there, particularly the ones who dressed in ragged old jeans—but over the years the situation had become exacerbated. Back then, I came from an upper-middle-class family—my father's a doctor—and mixed mainly with kids who were likewise from professional families. Now, I'm not sure I qualify for the middle class. If I had children, I could never afford to send them to my alma mater. I could barely buy the plane ticket to my college reunion, much less make a sizable contribution to the alumni fund. Unlike almost anyone else in my class—full of CEOs and members of boards of directors—I'd never held a full-time job. I didn't own a vacation house in the Hamptons or a pied-à-terre in Paris; I don't own my own apartment. My retirement plan came down to a big hope that I'd write a bestseller or marry a rich guy (both of which I'd tried before, to little avail).

The way I was living, I was suddenly ashamed to say out loud to any of my classmates, was the way I'd been living pretty much since college—in a rent-controlled flat in the Haight-Ashbury district of San Francisco, with the occasional roommate. How could anyone at my twenty-fifth reunion possibly comprehend that I was so unsuccessful financially, that I had to let a room in my rented apartment to strangers in order to cover my rent? Of course, I didn't let them know: I was wearing an expensive dress and stylish shoes and, despite my economic status, had a long string of accomplishments on my résumé. But I knew. I was struggling along more or less the way I'd been doing since college—and all of a sudden it had been twenty-five years, and I had no financial security to show for my efforts. Having roommates is fine after graduation, but most middle-aged people don't live the way I live unless (1) they're messed up on drugs; (2) they're artists who assume they'll be famous after they're dead, or (3) they're in serious denial about their financial situation.

I was privileged, but poor.

I'm not alone with this affliction; it seems to be rampant among my artistic friends who have always prided themselves on not selling out but are kicking themselves for not buying real estate in San Francisco in the 1980s. I have one filmmaker friend who was on the cover of the arts page of the local newspaper the same day her car was repossessed. We all came from fairly well-to-do, well-educated families, where we were encouraged to go to liberal arts colleges and then, willy-nilly, into the arts. We were also at the tail end of the baby boom generation: children of the sixties who had a certain disdain for making money as an end in itself when there was art to create and the world to save. The notion of going into business—or worse, going corporate—sounded vaguely dirty, demeaning, and Republican.

But it never occurred to us that we might end up without money. No matter how unconventional we considered ourselves, there was always an unspoken assumption that eventually we'd land in the same class as our parents, with tasteful houses, paid-for cars, and the ability to casually pick up the check with a group of friends at a restaurant. Despite our feminist studies classes, the women among us figured we'd eventually marry a doctor or lawyer or someone suitable and do our earnest writing or painting or nonprofit thing while our husband made the real money. It was the old gendered division of labor, with a new twist: he'd bring home the bacon, and I'd write witty essays about why I stopped being a vegetarian. In other words, I'd do the cultural work instead of the housework.

So I made plans to go straight from college into a freelance journalism career, without pausing to investigate how that profession might pay. Freelance writing isn't a choice most college graduates consider if they're at all practical or financially insecure; you rarely see less privileged people or ethnic minorities go into the field (which has something to do with the heterogeneity and socioeconomic slant of the media, by the way). I figured I'd eventually meet the guy with the real job—or write a bestseller, I didn't care which—and in the meantime, I'd support myself. While I never asked for money from my parents, I always knew they were there with their safety net if I ever got into serious trouble. Just knowing that net was there made all the difference between doing what I wanted to do and having to take a job that paid well. Still, I made my own living, such as it was.

I got used to living fairly frugally at college. Since my parents were footing the big bill for a private education, I cut corners—eating lentils instead of meat, pocketing apples from the cafeteria, spending little. I didn't have a car, go to clubs, or snort cocaine. When I had an internship one semester in New York City at *Rolling Stone* magazine (which basically consisted of photocopying for cokeheads for free), I shared a cheap apartment and wokked every meal; the only time I borrowed money was after I picked up a free mattress off the street and woke up the next morning to a very, very bad smell. After college, I inherited $1,500 from my grandmother and traveled around the Mediterranean on that amount for nine months. (Unlike my more practical sisters, who are now all married and own at least one home apiece, I didn't stash it for a car or house.) I stayed in cheap pensiones, slept on beaches, worked on a kibbutz, and shacked up with a boyfriend or two along the way. I always figured I would make money later on: now was the time to live.

That was my thinking when I moved to San Francisco too, in 1984, when the rents were cheap if you shared a flat and it was possible to make a living off of freelance writing with the occasional Kelly Girl or waitressing gig thrown in. The pay was very low—I recall working for two months to write a cover story for the local alternative newspaper for $300—but soon I was writing for national magazines, which seemed, at first, relatively lucrative. At twenty-five, I was living the independent, artistic life and making it work. I remember reading an estimate from the *Columbia Journalism Review* that there were only about 250 freelance *magazine* writers in the United States who made their living solely from their writing; that should've been a big red flag, but at the time I was proud to be among them. I believed I'd made it—instead of seeing the reality, which was that it was fairly impossible to make it as a freelancer.

Let me discuss the economics of freelance writing for a moment. There is an assumption among magazine editors and publishers that everyone in the world wants to be a freelance writer for the glory of having their name published in a glossy and being able to send tear sheets home to Mom. And in fact, there are vast numbers of people who think the field is glamorous and are constantly trying to get their articles into print. Since they write all the time anyway—memos, e-mails—what, they figure, could be so hard about writing for *The New Yorker*? So they mass-mail their manuscripts to every editor in New York; those editors (or at least their unpaid interns) are subsequently deluged with hopeful queries and earnest essays, which reinforces the notion that there are zillions of writers out there who could ably fill the space between the ads in magazines. There appears to be a wild oversupply for the demand.

But, having taught my share of magazine writing (taking money from just those poor souls who are flooding the market with their first-time efforts), I can reliably say that the pool of writers who are really skilled is actually rather small. There just aren't many people who can do thorough reporting, tell an engaging story, recognize a lively quote, and organize a coherent piece. Still, the myth persists that everyone can be a freelance writer and that being published is a privilege, so it's something we ought to do for love and very little money.

I have been freelancing for about twenty-five years. Twenty years ago, I broke into glossy magazines like *Glamour* and *Vogue*. They paid me $2 per word. Today most of the magazines I write for pay $2 per word. I believe that in Charles Dickens's time publications paid $2 per word.

What I dislike most about the magazine world is having to write things I don't want to write just to pay the rent. I'm not proud when a story on how to perk up your decor comes out with my name on it, or when I write another "charticle" of "how-to's" or "ten ways" or "five greats." People seem to be much more judgmental about reading an article about couch cushions with your name on it in the hair salon than if you told them you worked for Pottery Barn, pushing those same couch cushions. I became a writer to produce reported pieces, essays, and books, and if I were independently wealthy I would never write anything else. I have a friend with a trust fund who can afford to spend a year researching and writing a think piece for a national magazine. I admire that he's chosen to use his time and money that way, but I am also jealous.

To add to my freelance income, I sometimes teach. From a financial point of view, I might as well sell homemade jewelry on Haight Street.

Still, freelance writing is the career choice I made, and it's the only thing I know how to do. It's an enormous luxury to work independently in the world of words and ideas. I feel a huge sense of satisfaction when I publish something I think is worth the paper it's printed on, or when an issue I've uncovered makes a difference. I love it when a student ends up being a better writer after taking my class. I know I could trade my chosen profession for a PR job or an editing job and make more money, so it's a conscious trade-off. Occasionally, I have made a good amount of money with my writing. When a travel memoir I wrote made it to number sixteen on the *New York Times* bestseller list, I hit six figures. (Had it made it to number fifteen—the cutoff for the published list—I would have made considerably more.)

Writing does have its perks, which help maintain my illusion of living at a higher socioeconomic level than I actually inhabit. I travel more frequently than most people who have regular jobs; they save their money to go to exotic places, whereas I go there for free, on assignment. I write about food, and so I eat at great restaurants. I stay at five-star hotels (all the while fretting that I don't have enough money to cover the tips). I actually do have a fairly glamorous life as a freelancer and live well beyond my means. In the past two years, I've been to Peru, Italy, Australia, Chile, Vietnam, and Africa—more places than many well-paid executives could afford to travel to if they had the time. I'm also my own boss, and I'd estimate that not having anyone else tell me what to do on a regular basis is worth about $100,000 a year to me.

My actual living costs are fairly low, with rent control. When I'm not eating on an expense account, I cook at home. I usually take the bus to work. I manage to dodge invitations where I'll have to pony up a lot of money for dinner and accept the ones that are potluck. Occasionally I hate that I have to ponder a splurge before I go out with friends for what is, to them, a normal night out. I want the $60 bottle of Pinot Noir, and I know which one is best, but I live in fear that someone will order it and I'll have to chip in for my share.

One of the curses of being a member of the privileged poor is that I have excellent taste, if I may say so (and I always do). I have traveled throughout the world and understand the subtleties of great wine and food, which makes it hard to drink Two Buck Chuck. I like cooking for myself, but even quality ingredients—organic vegetables and meats—are costly. I've spent a lot of time in museums and art galleries and have a bad habit, when I have a little windfall, of spending it all at once on a painting I love—what's on my walls is worth more than what's in my bank account. I've worked for fashion magazines and have a passion for beautiful fabrics and well-cut clothes.

Along with my expensive tastes—which I try to indulge rarely— what fritters away my potential savings is my desire to keep up appearances, to maintain the illusion that I am successful and stylish, not downwardly mobile. Since I write for women's magazines, I have to wear the right thing when I visit editors in New York or I risk not writing for them—or at least not lunching with them—again. (In 1992, tired of showing up in the wrong thing at *Vogue*, I splurged and bought an Armani suit I figured I could wear forever. That was the last year Armani made suits with big shoulder pads.) I use excuses like the lunching-with-editors rationale to justify spending money on clothes when I ought to be saving for my future. But since I live in a rent-controlled apartment and never made a move to buy real estate, an occasional $300 cashmere sweater doesn't seem so extravagant. I am like Carrie Bradshaw: add up what I've spent on shoes, and maybe I'd have a down payment on an apartment. In Iowa, anyway.

My situation seems fine—I pay my bills and have a little left over— until I start thinking seriously about the fact that I'm in my midforties and my friends are already planning for retirement. I have an IRA, but it's about enough to afford three weeks in India when I retire, not including airfare. I have friends with money who have generously offered me their vacation places to stay when I need a free getaway— one of the perks of being a member of the privileged poor, though it generally requires an expensive hostess gift—but I don't want to couch-surf my way through old age.

Clearly, it would be convenient if a man came along and offered me some financial stability. This is an uncomfortable thought, given that I was raised in an atmosphere of feminism (though with a feminist mother who could afford to work for nonprofits because my dad was a physician). That a wealthy guy will rescue me is also a somewhat absurd hope, since I've always been more attracted to quirky, starving artist types rather than those who put on a suit and go out and make real dough. For the most part, in my relationships, I've gone Dutch.

It's not as though I've deliberately avoided men with money. It's just that they've always seemed a little too square. Plus, I'm a writer, so I usually hang out with my counterparts; I don't get a chance to meet that many investment bankers. When I do, I'm afraid I've been conditioned to believe that what they do is boring and sometimes greedy. I am getting tired, though, of splitting the tab with guys, and often wonder how they think they're making a good impression on a Match.com date when they insist on splitting the check to the nickel ("you had the second glass of wine, so I'll put in less"). It's been a huge relief when I've gone out with men who seemed both artistic and reasonably well off, such as a psychologist I once dated. He could talk about art and pay for dinner. But there's some niggling feeling in the back of my mind that I don't deserve to be treated, or that I have to always pay my share. Some of that is feminism, some of it is a poverty mentality that is too concerned about exactly what things cost, and some of it—well, I probably ought to discuss that part with a shrink.

I did once accidentally marry a man with money. He appeared to be a low-paid public defender, so I was attracted to him; had I known he had a trust fund, I might've instinctively run the other way. I quickly got used to being able to afford weekend getaways in Mendocino, nice meals with wine, and $200 shoes. But in the end I was left to my own financial devices. In California, it turns out, you only have to share whatever money you earned when you were married, and your trust fund doesn't count. Since I married a man who not only

made less money than I did but who was also a lawyer, he argued that
he didn't owe me anything—despite the fact that his house nearly
doubled in value while we lived there together and I was contributing
to the mortgage. I basically got moving expenses—and, since this was
in the midst of the dot-com boom, I was priced out of the San Francisco housing market forever. Gentle readers, take note: if you marry
a rich guy, make sure he isn't a lawyer.

All the same, a few other men with money have come along over
the years. One was a scruffy artist I met in the duty-free shop in the
Frankfurt airport. He had a long layover, so I invited him to hang out
in the airport lounge with me. (Frequent-flier miles and upgrades are
another perk of my business.) It turned out that he was an extremely
rare breed—a rich artist—and I had fun flying first-class to his opening in Spain, then meeting him at an exclusive resort in Sardinia and
imagining what life would be like on his private island in the South
Pacific. A rich artist! An interesting artist! Perfect. The only problem
was that I wasn't in love with him. Some of that may have had to do
with his friends: though he bemoaned the fact that they were all celebrity Republican money-grubbing, golf-playing bastards, they were,
in fact, his only friends. For a few minutes, I seriously considered staying with him anyway, just so I could have enough money to write
whatever I wanted to write. But the price was too high.

Then there was a very wealthy married guy who always had a shine
for me. Did I mention he was married? Broke as I might be, I'm not
cheap. It's good for men like that to have something, or someone, they
can't afford.

At forty-five, it looked unlikely that anyone was going to rescue
me from the lifestyle choices I'd made. That meant, for the first time,
I had to think about money. I had Suze Orman scolding me in my
dreams. It was a little late to change careers, and too late to buy real
estate in San Francisco twenty years ago. So I had to start husbanding
my limited resources with a little more care.

Fortunately, I've never been foolish enough to get into debt, which
was a good start. I made pie charts with my financial program on my

computer and was horrified to find that I was spending a piggish slice of my income on clothes and shoes every year. I have plenty of clothes that look good on me and aren't going to embarrass me at lunch with a fashion editor in New York. I made a resolution to stop going to boutiques, which has cut down on my spending considerably.

Then I decided I needed some security. I've rented a place in San Francisco for twenty-two years, and I may be here another twenty-two years. But I'd feel better if I had a piece of ground in the world I could call my own, where I could pitch a tent in case of an earthquake. Since San Francisco is priced way out of my league, as is most of California and the United States, I bought a tiny piece of land in Mexico, in a town I wouldn't mind living in when I retire. All the money I once spent on shoes and lattes is going into concrete and rebar. The land was cheap, and so is the construction; I'm managing it with a loan and will be happy to have a little casita to call my own.

Finally, I have stopped undervaluing my work. I don't write for free or speak without a fee; I charge a professional hourly rate for my coaching services. I sometimes write stories that aren't very interesting, simply because they pay the bills. But I am conscious that these are the kinds of choices adults who support themselves have to make.

Mostly, I have reconciled myself to the fact that I'm in charge of my financial future—not my parents, not a man who will rescue me, not the fantasy of a freak bestseller. I've also realized that while I'm not wealthy, I'm not poor either, and it isn't so bad. How much money do you really need? I'm content to live in a modest apartment, and to build a tiny house, and to live without a lot of stuff. I like knowing that all my worldly possessions don't take up a lot of space. As many shoes as I may have, my footprint here on the planet is small. I am grateful for the privileges I've had—an expensive education, the opportunities to travel, lovely places to stay with friends and family. And I hope, with some careful planning, that I'll someday be in a situation where I have more to give. That, for me, would be the real pleasure of having money.

Disco, Motherhood, and the Art of Survival

Veronica Chambers

Earn money. It's a curious phrase to someone who, like me, grew up in a house with an abusive parent. When you are, from a very young age, subject to screaming fits and the out-of-nowhere slap, you quickly learn that there is no rhyme or reason to the anger or the beatings. Certainly, you didn't earn being knocked around, from room to room and wall to wall. The supposed misdeed—up past bedtime, a dirty dish in the sink—never seems to match the wave of fury that follows it. And although you try, for a very long time—maybe from the time you are three until the time you are twelve—to figure out what you have done to earn the life you have been given, you ultimately come to the conclusion that there is no logic. There is no way that at the age of eight, or nine, or ten, you could be so overdrawn in the checkbook of life that you deserve the ass-whupping that is coming your way.

Throughout my childhood, money came into my life in the most random ways. The kind uncle who could be counted on to slip me a twenty when I saw him, although I didn't see him often. Then there was the cool boyfriend—he was a college tennis star and I was a sophomore in high school—who still wanted to date me even though it was obvious that my clothes would not even cut the mustard at Goodwill. He took me to the mall for my birthday, giving me $100 to buy anything I wanted.

Later that night, when my father came home and found those $100 worth of clothes, he beat me in the driveway of his house for being a "dirty fucking whore." He beat me from 6:00 P.M., when he got in from work, until the sun went down. All of this, despite the fact that my boyfriend and I had done no more than kiss. I could see the neighbors watching out of their windows—but nobody called the police, because nobody ever does. It was my fifteenth birthday, and I went to bed, as I had so often before, cut and bleeding.

That same year, I discovered the most powerful money of all: the scholarship kind. At the urging of a favorite high school teacher, I had applied and was accepted at two summer programs where admission was based on academic excellence. The first was a weeklong women's leadership course at Chestnut Hill College in Pennsylvania; the second was a two-week journalism workshop at Rider College in New Jersey. The days I spent on those campuses changed my life. It was like that old Gloria Gaynor disco song, "I Will Survive": I went to those summer programs, and I knew I was going to make it.

I was sixteen when I got a scholarship to attend Bard College at Simon's Rock. For the first time in my life, I had stability, safety, and three square meals a day. Moreover, there was now a governing principle in my life that I could finally understand: I got good grades, and they gave me money. Like a Wall Street banker who makes her first big trade, or a novice gambler who hits it big at slots, I fell in love with the idea of monetary exchange. Money represented real things: a roof over my head, food in my belly, an education, even non–thrift store clothes on my back. But what it represented even more was fairness. There were no random beatings in the middle of the night from the people in the financial aid office. I did not risk a slap in the face because the woman who distributed the work-study checks was having a bad day.

I spent much of my freshman year waiting for an impromptu boxing match that never came. Surely, surely, somewhere on campus—in the dorm, in the dining room, in the classroom—someone was going to accuse me of looking at them funny, and I would get my lights knocked out. It never happened.

In the years to come, many people would attribute escaping an abusive childhood and going to college at sixteen to many things: precociousness, ambition, intelligence. But in my mind, it always boiled down to one thing: money. I would have gone nowhere if it hadn't been for my scholarship. For many, the phrase itself is an abstraction: of *course* there is scholarship money at every college, of *course* talented students are afforded the funds to make their education possible. But to me, the transaction was not institutional, but personal. Someone, somewhere, wrote a check and signed a check. And that check saved my life.

Twenty years later, I am a working writer: a tenuous kind of profession that some may think ill suited for a person as obsessed with money as I am. But I have managed to do well, with a series of full-time jobs and freelance stints. Six years ago, I got married. My husband, Jason, works as an editor and makes a good living—although, like most middle-class couples, we could not survive on his income alone.

Although I am obsessed with money, I am not cheap with it. I funded a study room at my college library in my maternal grandmother's name. Together, with the help of the matching gift program at my husband's job, we've also managed to fund three named scholarships there: a Dorothy West scholarship for teen writers at the summer writing workshop; a Connie Chambers creative writing scholarship (in honor of my father's mother); and a Celia Cruz scholarship in music and voice, in honor of the late, great salsa singer. We also give, as generously as we can, to organizations that matter to us: Women in Need, Youth Communication, One by One, and Doctors Without Borders.

But I've also spent significantly on far less noble causes. A few years ago, I surprised Jason and took him to Tokyo and Kyoto on a kind of

Lost in Translation vacation for his thirtieth birthday. It was, honestly, as much a gift for me as it was for him. I am also well known among my friends as a "Prada or nada" girl; as my vast assortment of skirts, dresses, and handbags proves, I feel the way about Miuccia Prada that some people feel about their favorite movie director. (If only a pair of Miu Miu shoes cost the same as a Criterion Collection DVD!)

My life was a healthy balance of working hard and playing hard—though I always subscribed to Marian Wright Edelman's codicil that "service is the rent we pay for living." Then I got pregnant. While a lot of my mommy friends reported having anxiety dreams during this time—What if something was wrong with their baby? What if they couldn't take care of her?—all of my dreams were about money. It wasn't surprising: while I may seem like a big spender, every purchase I make has been the result of intensive planning. I paid for my grandmother's study room at Bard in monthly installments over five years. My ombre Prada bag was the result of a good six months' worth of freelance writing assignments: sending out pitch letters, landing the job, doing the writing, revising, and then waiting for the check to arrive before the bag was mine.

With my baby, I didn't have time to plan. Having waited until I was thirty-six to start a family, I assumed that it would take me months, if not years, to conceive. (This had certainly been the case for friends who had embarked on this journey in their late thirties and forties.) About a year before I stopped using birth control, I started saving for the child I thought of as "Bambino Numero Uno" by diligently depositing a couple of hundred dollars a month into a special account. The idea was to amass somewhere around $2,000 so that when the time came we could make the necessary purchases without worrying: splash out on the yuppie stroller or the Danish design crib, hire a doula if our monthly expenses were tighter than expected. I wanted to have that money in the bank.

But here's the thing: I got pregnant the very first time I had sex without birth control. I felt like a high school girl who'd decided to give it up on prom night. Now the months when I would be trying to conceive—the months when I would work extra hard, lasso in some extra assignments, and put together a nice little account for my baby— had disappeared. My child was nine months away from coming. The work that I had to do would barely cover a maternity leave—a maternity leave that I'd have to pay for myself, since I was freelance.

So I would wake up in the middle of the night, crying and scared, and stare at the walls, hung with the contemporary art my husband and I have collected over the years. How could I have been so thoughtless? I wondered. One night, in a panic, I arose and figured out that in the past ten years I'd spent more than $1,000 on hardcover cookbooks alone. And Prada—don't even get me started on Prada.

I was about six months into my pregnancy when I came to realize that my money nightmares weren't about how I would take care of my child when I was alive; they were about what I would leave him or her after my death. And I understood that I was thoroughly and completely afraid of dying in labor. Yes, I love and trust my husband. But if, God forbid, something should ever happen to him as well, I didn't want my child to live, as I had lived, at the mercy of extended family: afraid to eat too much at supper lest she be considered a burden; afraid to walk too heavily in the middle of the night lest the sound of her footsteps anger a crazy stepparent.

Money had saved me. It had given me the Virginia Woolf ideal of a room of my own, complete with a lock and a key. I wanted to make sure my child had enough—not a ton, I knew I couldn't manufacture a fortune overnight—but enough for a plane ticket if she ever needed to get to safer shores, or for a few nights in a hotel if things got violent. My husband, having never lived in dire circumstances, has a tendency to drag his feet in emergencies. When one of my extended relatives calls to say they need $100 for rent/food/a bus ticket, Jason doesn't understand why I log on to Western Union immediately, why I don't "sleep on it" and put a check in the mail. He has never spent a night on the street or stared down an empty cupboard with a growling stomach. To him, everything can wait. I didn't want my child to ever have to wait.

So I dreamed of saving money. If my unborn child was as lucky as I prayed, and her childhood was safer and more peaceful than mine, then maybe this money would just be a slush fund—something that would enable her to spend a few months studying photography in Mali, or enroll in a summer program at the London School of Economics. I was six months pregnant and I could not sleep because I did not have the time to leave my child the money, the small safety-deposit box of safety, that I so desperately wished I'd had when I was a girl.

All of this would constitute nothing more than the puerile rantings of yet another yuppie mama—except that seven months into my pregnancy, I got sick. Very sick. I went in for a routine checkup and discovered that my blood pressure was 180/110. What I assumed was a very bad headache had turned out to be the precursor for a stroke. I was diagnosed with preeclampsia, the only cure for which was to deliver the baby immediately.

My doctor hoped to keep me pregnant for forty-eight hours, since two days of taking surfectant, a drug used to increase the chances for preemie survival, would be the equivalent of an extra week in the womb. My blood pressure kept spiking, but I made it to the forty-eight-hour mark. They began to induce labor. Immediately, the baby went into fetal distress; her heart rate was dropping, and I was in danger of stroking out. And so a C-section was performed, without anesthesia. (To help me get over that, my doctors sent me to a psychologist who'd helped Gulf War soldiers recover from posttraumatic issues.)

My baby girl, Flora Victoria Clampet, was born at one pound, twelve ounces. She was immediately whisked away to the neonatal intensive-care unit. I was also rushed to the ICU; although delivery is supposed to be the cure for preeclampsia, the doctors were unable to control my blood pressure, so I required close monitoring. I'd lost a lot of blood during the delivery and later discovered that I'd suffered some damage to my pituitary gland. I also developed HELLP, another pregnancy-related complication, and my liver started shutting down. Three days after giving birth, I still hadn't seen my daughter. Delusional from the many drugs I was taking, I was convinced that the photographs they showed me weren't actually Flora.

As my doctor tells it, all of this was par for the scary labor-and-delivery course. But then, I started to experience major organ shutdown. My liver stopped performing. Then my kidneys. Then my gastrointestinal system. It was official: I might be dying. Every six hours, a new team of doctors from a different department arrived—just like on *House,* one of my favorite television shows. (I remember, at one point, saying, "Maybe it's lupus?" in a sly reference to the show. Nobody laughed.)

On day five, things started to turn around. My liver functions were up, my blood pressure had stabilized, and I was taken to see Flora. It was almost too much to bear, seeing her one-and-a-half-pound body attached to a million wires. She looked more like a little frog than a baby.

For the first time, I understood why childbirth is sometimes referred to as the miracle of life: both my daughter and I had almost died for her to be here. It is a miracle that we did not. We were lucky to be at the University of Pennsylvania hospital, which has one of the best neonatal centers in the world. We were also lucky that my husband's job had such a good health insurance plan. But during the month that I spent in the hospital and the three months that my daughter spent in the neonatal unit, I learned that a lot of bad things happen on maternity wards. Women die. Babies die. The doctors do their best. The nurses work their asses off. But bad things happen, and no amount of money can change that.

My daughter is now a year old. I spent much of the last year sitting by her bedside in the hospital—and then, once she came home, shuttling her to doctors and specialists, administering medicine, working with a physical therapist, giving her bottles, reading to her, and teaching her how to dance. I have made less money than I ever have in my adult lifetime. Since I still had to pay my half of the household bills, I lived mostly off my savings; when my savings were gone, I took money out of my IRA. Not the best financial decision in the world, but the best option I had at the time.

But when I look at my daughter, I know that not working was worth it. In her first year on this earth, Flora has cleared every medical hurdle that a micro-preemie—a baby whose birth weight is less than two pounds—can. Her doctors and therapists have said that they have never seen a baby born so early catch up so fast.

I am still hopeful that I can put aside some money for my daughter; "trust fund" seems too big a word for the small slice of freedom I long to buy her. But I no longer wake up in the middle of the night worrying that I have failed her financially. Yes, she is my dependent. Yes, she is my heir. But above all, she is my daughter. And now I understand—I finally get it—that the love I have to offer her is not a financial transaction. I spent so many nights crunching numbers that I never once considered the inheritance that my daughter spends joyfully every day: the gift of having a mother who is alive. The gift of having a mother who is here.

Rich Little Poor Girl

Bliss Broyard

I.

I'm lying in bed in my darkened dorm room, when I hear Michele, who lives across the hall, call out to no one in particular: "Anybody know if Bliss got something to eat today?" Michele, a petite blonde from New Jersey who drives a Mustang convertible (high school graduation present), is heading to the gas station mini-mart with her Exxon charge card (came with the car) and taking requests. The girls on our floor ask for cigarettes, Tic-Tacs, Diet Pepsi, microwave popcorn, black licorice (which is supposed to be dietetic). I sit up and hold my breath, to listen.

With a month to go in my freshman year at the University of Vermont, I've run through the credit in my semester meal plan, mostly by shopping at the campus convenience store for pretzels, chips, and drink mixers for impromptu parties in our dorm. When my parents send me another $200 to recharge my account, I use it to pay back all the loans I received to buy the substances ingested and inhaled during those impromptu parties.

I don't dare to ask my parents for more money. As my mother often reminds me, we are "house-poor," meaning that despite (or because of) our home in Connecticut with its field and pool and our summer place on Martha's Vineyard with its shared tennis courts and beach, we don't have any cash. Nevertheless, our veneer of wealth places me in proximity to the authentically rich, whose habits I replicate and friendships I pursue even as I struggle to afford them.

While at college, I don't consider getting a job, although I've been working during the summertime since I was eleven—first as a junior counselor at a camp, and then as a waitress at an inn where I make as much as $300 a week. When I arrive at school, I use these savings to keep up with the lavish lifestyles of my new friends—all of whom seem to come from wealthy families and have infinite sources of spending money.

But by Christmas break, my money has run out. When I don't have the funds for the spring break trip, I tell my friends that my parents are making me join them on a family vacation. When the entrance fee to some club is too steep for me, I say that I have to study. The moments when I insist on walking home rather than taking a cab or I tediously factor my portion of the bill, since I only had a side salad with my single glass of the wine, are fraught with the prospect of exposure and rejection. My new friends will realize that I'm not like them after all.

Although it's the middle of the afternoon, I'm in my dorm room trying to sleep. A sophomore I know who was in my same situation his freshman year advised me that you don't feel as hungry when you're sleeping. So I can't answer Michele's question for myself. In fact, I haven't eaten yet today, and I'm not simply craving something sweet or something salty; I'm desperate, I'm starving. If Michele doesn't bring me back some food, I'll be reduced to shoplifting my next meal from the local supermarket, again. I hate myself for squandering my parents' money so recklessly, and I hate them for raising me to want a lifestyle that they can't pay for. The shame I feel over my predicament is as self-consuming as my hunger.

When I wake up an hour or so later, I find Michele and our gang of friends in the dormitory common room, eating popcorn and watching TV. I stand in the doorway, my hand on the frame to steady myself.

Michele nods behind her. "Yours is in the freezer."

A Hungry Man frozen dinner. "Turkey!" I say, clasping my hands to my chest.

"Her favorite flavor," Michele explains to the other girls.

Twenty-five minutes later, eating my steaming turkey breast, crunchy stuffing, and mashed potatoes slicked with gravy, I see my situation as funny, ridiculous, so typical: the privileged fuckup who's blown all her food money on partying. I see it as a low point in my life, a cautionary tale whose reoccurrence I will spend the rest of my life avoiding. I see everything in this way—until the next day, when the shadow of my hunger and shame grows long once more.

Over these few weeks, I lose more than twenty pounds. Everyone, including my parents, tells me that I've never looked better. I've never felt worse about myself in my life. Rather than extracting from this experience a lesson about the perils of trying to keep up with the Joneses, I come away with a powerful appreciation for friendship's value, in all senses of the term.

II.

Growing up, I take for granted that I will one day be wealthy too. To make or marry money is the natural trajectory for young women like me—women who attend prep school and a "public Ivy," who know how to tack into the wind and volley a tennis ball and keep their skis clamped tightly against one another. No matter how mortgaged my parents' lifestyle has been, I have apprenticed as a rich person for all my young life and am prepared to move into the position. But that's not what happens.

Twenty years out of college, I'm still poorer than almost all of my friends. People say that money buys freedom, but the process of getting money has always struck me as potentially rife with confinement. As long as I can earn enough to cover the basic necessities—rent, food, and health insurance—I prefer to avoid long hours in a job that I don't like or a marriage in which my responsibilities and power will be predicated to some degree on my earnings.

Of course, I know people who make great livings in jobs they love and have relationships with partners who bring home the bacon and remember to pick up the orange juice and diapers too. But after a few years of faking my interest in a marketing job at a mutual funds company (even the required personality assessment tests recognize that I'm an impostor), I become a writer, publishing my first book when I'm thirty years old. Although this career has earned me a wage qualifying for the earned income tax credit more times than I care to remember, I am free to spend my days thinking about ideas that matter to me, trying to capture in language the peculiar texture of being alive, and experiencing the world unfettered by obligations except to my own imagination. I try my hand at dating rich guys, but when they keep proving my point about the power trade-off—one particular boyfriend's mother suggests that I unpack her son's new apartment while he is off playing tennis in Ibiza—I begin pursuing relationships with men whose humor, compassion, and intelligence can sustain me.

Ironically, jettisoning any personal ambition for a particular life-style allows me the freedom to enjoy a very comfortable standard of living. An exile from the world of nine-to-fivers, I can spend months at a time at my family's house on Martha's Vineyard, hole up for weeks on end at one of the various artist colonies that occupy the former estates of philanthropic millionaires, and enjoy the benefits of being the token impoverished bohemian among my Manolo Blahnik–heeled girlfriends.

After college, the women in my life keep getting richer and richer, and I grow more and more accustomed to accepting their generosity. My college friend Michele goes on to become a successful television producer. When she decides to get a new "power handbag," it isn't a question of affording the four-figure price tag, but stomaching it.

Diane, whom I meet shortly after college, marries a guy who races up the corporate ladder of a prominent computer software company, collecting stock options and six-figure raises along the way. They pay their housekeeper more than I earn in a typical year. And then there's Olivia, a newer friendship of about five years. After the demise of her marriage to a real estate developer, she's able to finance two houses and a horse farm, lavish vacations for her friends, several charities, and a small staff off the annual interest of her divorce settlement.

Unlike with my school friends, I don't try to hide the fact that I'm often broke. Being an impoverished writer has a lot more cachet than being the child of spendthrift parents. Also, I have begun to realize that as long as I can appreciate the finer things in life—Balenciaga handbags and Frette sheets—it doesn't matter so much whether or not I can afford them. My rich friends and I all speak the same language; we are all natives of the same country. I'm just away on an extended trip.

Once I finish the "big book," I tell myself, I will resume my rightful place in the ranks of the comfortable. In the meantime, my friends hold my spot by maintaining my standard of living. Throughout my twenties and thirties, they treat me to more mani/pedis then I can count, pass on hand-me-downs—Gucci boots, Tehen sweaters—that I can't afford to buy secondhand. They take me on shopping trips and out to expensive restaurants, loan me their beach houses and country homes, throw me parties, and send me checks for hundreds of dollars with the instruction to buy myself something nice.

My friends do this because they want to spend time together, and it doesn't cost a lot to have me join them at the nail salon or for a meal. They do it because a part of them admires my choice to live slightly off the grid in order to pursue my artistic ambitions. They do it because they believe I shouldn't be penalized for the fact that my chosen career isn't as valued monetarily as some others. They do it because it's hard to spend time with a friend who has a vastly different standard of living. They do it because they need someone like me in their lives.

III.

It's a few weeks before Christmas, and I'm at Olivia's house for her seasonal closet cleaning. If she hasn't worn something in the last few months, she gives it to me. When we start this practice, she tells me that I'm doing her a favor by taking these unworn clothes off her hands, because when her closet is overly stuffed she can never find anything to wear at all.

As we sort through the clothes piled on her bed, Olivia tells me that she is feeling depressed. I ask if she and her real estate magnate husband have hit another rough patch. No. Then I suggest that perhaps she's missing her father, who died many years before. But that's not it either. "I think the holidays just make me hate being rich," she says, slumping down on a chaise lounge. She tells me about all the people waiting with their hands out: the guys at the parking garage, the dog walkers and babysitters, the postman, the personal trainer, the nonprofits for their year-end tax-deductible contributions. The list goes on and on. It's not that she doesn't want to give them money, but she can't stand the whole ritual—how everyone grows increasingly pleasant and solicitous as Christmas approaches, all the constant wishes of "Happy Holidays," "Happy Holidays," as if she doesn't know what time of year it is, and then the feigned surprise and exaggerated gratitude when the cash or check (enclosed within the family holiday card) appears. The practice puts a price tag on the value of these relationships in her life; it translates any tenderness into legal tender.

I tell her how I think that money can make people act strangely, how it clouds their motives, even to themselves. It's like this giant invisible magnet, I continue, pulling them this way and that way, distorting their behavior, and they don't even realize it. "And nobody acknowledges that having a lot of money can be difficult too," I say, gesturing around the room. "There's so much upkeep—all this stuff to buy, the houses to take care of, the employees to manage." I shake

my head thinking of her new estate in the country, with its dozen bedrooms. "God, all those sheets and comforters to pick out!"

Olivia is listening intently, her eyebrows stuck at half-mast, as if
she's not sure whether I'm making fun of her or not.

I grin. "And the exotic trips to plan and the dinner parties to throw."

She smiles now too. "I know, I know, poor me."

"But seriously, I don't envy you," I say. "I never have to wonder
about people's motives, whether they want something from me. That
must be very crazy-making." I remind her of all the times she has contributed to her friends' charities, bought a work of their art, donated
to their kids' schools, invested in their businesses, or simply loaned
them money. "You're always very generous," I say, which I suspect is
the worry at the heart of this conversation.

Demurring, she says, "I'm just lucky that I'm in a position to be
able to help people."

She pulls out from the piles of clothes a white skirt made of a sort
of stiff waxed linen and hands it to me. "I got this at a sample sale of
this cool Japanese designer," she tells me. "It was incredibly expensive, but the salesman convinced me that it was fabulous."

I try it on and eye myself in the mirror. The lines of the fabric
swoop and curve around my body. "It's like wearing a sculpture," I say.
I imagine myself sipping champagne at an opening at a hip art gal-
lery, the skirt paired with a simple black tank, a long string of pearls,
and the black velvet, midcalf, high-heel Jimmy Choo boots that Olivia
gave me the last time we cleaned out her closet.

She stands behind me and looks over my shoulder at my reflection.
"It really *is* fabulous," she says. "You should take it. It looks great on
you."

I give my wealthy girlfriends something too. As a reminder of how
the other half lives, I help to keep them grounded amid charity
auctions, private jet rides, and spring break vacation plans that cost

more than their kids' tuition. Our friendship is safe because I neither envy them for having money nor try to compete with them—because I know that I never could. Having me in their lives is proof that their kind of people aren't only rich people. And I allow them one of the great pleasures of having money—spontaneous generosity without guilt or expectation.

Yet I often find myself keeping a running tab in my head to ensure that our accounts remain balanced. I'll factor in the gifts bestowed upon me, the favors done for the friend in question, and the monetary and psychic costs to each of us, all added up according to my own subjective currency.

When a new boyfriend and I visit Olivia for an overnight at her country house, I bring along the fixings for an elaborate seafood dinner. Olivia doesn't ask me to do this. If anything, she seems a little bemused by my offer—her housekeeper-chef could have easily prepared us a nice meal—but according to my private calculation, I'm obliged to reciprocate her graciousness with my sweat equity. I haven't, however, planned on footing the bill for all the groceries too. I spend nearly $150, which is more than I can comfortably afford at this time in my life for one evening's entertainment.

A poorer friend—on spying the multiple bags of food, the pricey halibut steaks, the bottles of Sancerre—would simply assume that we were splitting the cost. But that's not the protocol among the wealthy. (In fact, the moments of awkwardness around money between Olivia and me generally arise when she tries to decline my occasional offers to pay for something. Me, getting huffy: *I'm not that destitute. I can swing $8 for some coffees, for Christ's sake.* Her, a little defensive: *I know that, it's just that you shouldn't have to.*) I can't bring myself to ask Olivia for the $75. I want to feel like her guest, not an employee seeking reimbursement from the petty cash fund. And it might give her the feeling that she is being ungenerous, which would undermine the whole point of repaying her graciousness. I end up silent and slightly resentful.

IV.

Usually, in my friendships with wealthy women, I relish my role as bohemian artist to their benefactress, wild child to their older sister. I dine out on stories from my alternative lifestyle (skinny dipping at the artist colony with a former poet laureate) and my schemes to make money (ghostwriting a novel for Donald Trump, whom my agent convinces that I'm the perfect choice since I know his world firsthand; Trump hires me, but his publisher ends up declining the project). Being broke is just another aspect of the adventure.

I make jokes to my wealthy friends about having to look twice before crossing the street, since I can't afford my latest health insurance increase, or about how I'm going to have to roll my change for that month's electric bill. I threaten to take up the offer of the weirdo on Craigslist who buys women's used panties for $50 a pair. But occasionally my tone reveals the anxiety and weariness of those times when I can't meet even my basic needs, and I'll confess that I'm having money troubles. Surprisingly, these conversations aren't awkward. These women listen to my struggles and wish out loud that there could be something more they can do to help me.

Well, you could just give me some money.

I don't say it; I don't even really think it, which is strange because I grew up hearing my father tell stories about life in Greenwich Village in the 1940s and 1950s among his artist and writer friends. If someone didn't have his rent one month, someone else would loan him the $50 for it. Although my dad had to continually hustle to meet our family's bills, he helped to support his best friend, a reclusive, pot-smoking Blake scholar genius named Milton, for years. Milton's friends understood that he was too irascible to hold down a regular job and too talented to waste his energy on practical concerns such as the electric bill.

In my father's circle, money was a fluid commodity that could be passed among friends with the confidence that it would come back to you before long. Anyway, none of them were financing a luxurious lifestyle; they were simply trying to survive. But life today is a lot more expensive, especially if you're unwilling, as I am, to forgo middle-class comforts. I can't imagine asking someone to loan me $1,500 to cover my rent. The two occasions when I am forced to borrow money to meet my bills, I turn to friends with modest savings accounts who can't swing anything more than a onetime loan to be paid back with interest within a year. I do this so there is no risk that I'll be continually hitting them up, or that I'll "forget" to repay them with the rationale that they don't really need the money. Also, if a poorer friend turns down my request for a loan, I understand her decision as a matter of not being able to afford to help me. With my rich friends, there's no question of whether they *can* make me the loan, but simply if they will choose to. And I never want to give a friend so much power over me; I never want to appear so vulnerable before them.

Of all the relationships in our lives, friendships stand to be the most purely democratic. Friends are not obligated by blood or a civil contract to take care of each other. They don't enter into the relationship where one person holds more voting rights than the other. According to the scales of friendship, each person contains the same amount of worth. But if the roles of giver and receiver are permanently cast—if one person is continually put in the position of granting or denying the other—this illusion of equality becomes more difficult to maintain.

V.

By my midthirties, nearly all my friends are married and live in homes they own. None of them cross their fingers when taking money out of an ATM, unsure of whether they'll have the available funds or not. I'm broke, depressed, and ten pounds heavier than usual. I've been complaining to my friend Diane on the phone that I can't fit into any of my pants and I can't afford to buy new ones, when she suggests that we go shopping and she'll get me a new pair. Because I need these pants to serve all functions in my life—to be worn with boots and high heels, to be dressed up and down, to hide my thighs and my stomach—and because I'm feeling too badly about myself to think that anything I try on looks good, I drag Diane to store after store for hours.

As the day progresses, I become more and more like a petulant child determined to hold everyone hostage to her insecurities. Diane becomes more and more like a long-suffering parent, trying first to bolster my confidence with gentle reassurances and then finally throwing money at my peevishness with the suggestion that I just get the most expensive pair.

I end up with some beautifully tailored black trousers that cost $325, but I hardly ever wear them. The moment I try them on, I'm transported back to that day. And I cringe inwardly to recall my self-pitying comments about the difficulty of making a living as a writer and everything I have to do without—comments, I later realize, that aimed (albeit unconsciously) to make Diane, my good friend who was kind enough to take me shopping, feel guilty about being married to a rich guy who doesn't mind when she drops a few thousand at Barney's.

By putting myself in Diane's pants, as it were, I can more easily see the difficulty for my rich friends of spending time with someone like me. They can never make a social plan without considering the expense; if they want to go anyplace a cut above burgers or Chinese food, they will have to treat. We can't go on vacation together; we can't go shopping for shoes or light fixtures together. They can't relish recounting to me the luxurious details of a lavish trip or fabulous meal without worrying about flaunting their wealth. At the same time, they can't object to my grumblings about the ever-rising cost of living or how our culture increasingly favors material concerns over artistic ones without the risk of seeming defensive. They and their husbands work long taxing hours for their money, while I am pursuing a career that affords me my freedom and leisure time. Why should they have to pay for my choice?

VI.

After moving into my forties and starting a family of my own, I'm not as comfortable as I once was when my rich girlfriends pick up my tab. I end up marrying a college professor, a job whose dividends are similarly limited to intellectual rewards and long vacations. Having a child has made it harder for me to accept being treated like a child (even in the most benevolent, nonjudgmental way). I resist the unavoidable implication in my friends' gifts that my husband and I need help, that we can't manage entirely on our own.

The truth is that my friends' lives have grown far too grand for me to continue pretending that we all enjoy a similar standard of living. The differences between us aren't temporary. No matter how well my "big book" does, my child probably won't be attending private school, we won't be joining my friends on vacation, and it's unlikely that my husband and I are ever going to be able to afford to buy a brownstone in our Brooklyn neighborhood of New York City.

Sometimes I'll second-guess the bargain that I made for freedom over security. But then I'll consider all that this choice *has* afforded me. My husband and I are lucky enough to have our summers off. By subletting our apartment, we've been able to move to Los Angeles for a year and have financed half-year stints in Paris and Buenos Aires. When I come back home, I'll visit with my rich girlfriends. Sitting in their luxurious houses among their designer furniture and art collections, I've begun to look upon their worlds as another kind of foreign country. I might be fluent in their language and familiar with their customs, and I'm certainly enriched in many different ways by my visits there. But my pleasure in the experience depends on being able to return back home.

My So-Called
Financial Life

Rebecca Traister

SUMMER 1978

I am three years old, visiting my grandparents' potato farm in northern Maine. Nana and Pappy have retired, but the farm, with its rambling house, barn, and now-fallow fields stretching over the hill, provides me, over the thirty summers I will visit it, with everything I know about rural life. It's here that I will be taught how to can tomatoes, pickle eggs in big glass jars, fry brook trout in cornmeal, and eat green beans off the vines.

Aroostook County is remote; it is also poor in the 1970s. The farm, though big and beautiful, is caught in a time warp: life here still looks a lot like it did fifty years ago. The midday meal is "dinner," left over from the days when my grandfather would come in from the potato fields in need of enough calories to keep him picking for the rest of the afternoon. It includes a meat, a green vegetable, a yellow vegetable, and, always, a baked or mashed potato. In the evening, the spread is lighter: cold cuts or tuna sandwiches, pickled beets, maybe a bowl of soup.

It's at one of these evening meals that my grandmother asks me if I'd like some cheese. She indicates a plate of cubed yellow cheddar. I take a look, wrinkle my nose, and respond: "Could I have some Brie, please?"

Of course I don't remember this myself. It's a tale that has been hauled out at every possible moment since it happened. It's one of those early anecdotes that adults take to be predictive: like my friend Allison, at seven, pressing her face against the glass at the stock exchange and refusing to leave—that one is destined to go into finance! Or my brother exuberantly driving his walker off the top of a flight of stairs as a toddler—watch out, he'll be a handful when he gets a driver's license! Me, with my precocious desire for high-butterfat French cheeses in inappropriate contexts—well, I was going to have expensive tastes and a hunger for wealth.

Except that Allison actually became a television producer, though she admittedly has a good head for figures; my brother experienced a wild streak as a teenager, but didn't learn to drive until he was in his thirtieth year. And me? Well, I still hanker for delicious foods and aspire to beauty, comfort, and pleasure. But somewhere along the way my straight shot to wealth got hijacked. My brain got scrambled by the idea that the pursuit of happiness should *not* include a pursuit of riches—the fear that filthy lucre, should I ever make it a focus, would transform me into a person I did not want to be.

So instead of embarking on a successful quest for funds that would keep me in cheese and wine, I lived more than three decades before having enough money to open a savings account; I have demurred rather than fought for raises; I have turned down high-paying jobs. My eyes have certainly flashed green in their day, but seem always bigger than my stomach, which lurches queasily at the actual procurement, management, and investment of wealth. I am, it seems, oddly ambivalent about money.

The funny thing is, I'm not ambivalent about much. A driven woman, I am grabby about good jobs and good friends; I throw myself into the work I do and the relationships I have; I lose myself in books, gobble meals, gulp wine, wrap my brain around politics. But I have what can only be described as a push-me-pull-you relationship with money—money that I sometimes yearn for, money that I know would make the wine smoother and the food tastier, but which I seem constitutionally unable to get serious about.

Spring 1984

I'm at my best friend Elizabeth's house, where I go after school on days when my mother works. It's the height of the Cabbage Patch craze, and the news blares headlines about women beating each other up over the dolls in the aisles of K-Mart. I'm in third grade, and the mania is intense. These dolls are our earliest status symbol, and everyone in my class can reel off the stats on who owns how many kids. Elizabeth was one of the first to get her own Cabbage Patch Kid, and her sisters each have one as well. We're sitting around the kitchen table after school: the three sisters, their three dolls, and me.

This is just the beginning of what is to be an intense two or three years of material competition between girls. In those *Lord of the Flies* days preceding puberty, there will be a cold accounting run almost daily at my suburban public elementary school about whose family owns what. Not just the dolls and toys, but Guess jeans and Swatch watches and Colecovision video games and new technologies like the VCR, cordless phone, microwave, and computer.

In that earliest race for material superiority, I am a loser. I have no Cabbage Patch Kid, and my mother has told me in no uncertain terms that I will not be receiving one. Her precise reasoning falls somewhere on that delicate spectrum between "too expensive" and "too stupid"—but this deprivation is a serious social liability, and I view her refusal to bend the family finances to lubricate my social life as an act of child cruelty. One day, while food shopping along the grubby streets of Philadelphia's Italian market, I see a sidewalk table piled high with naked Cabbage Patch Kids, on sale for $5. I point, thrilled. I've found the secret Cabbage Patch Kid surplus! They're not too expensive, even if they do look just a little . . . off. I don't, in the third grade, understand the concept of a knock-off. My mother does, and simply tugs me forward, past the table and into a butcher shop.

But I don't forget that table full of dolls. And at Elizabeth's house the next week, I pipe up about them, proclaiming that I will probably get three or four of them any day now. Elizabeth and her sisters are impressed: "Whoa! Cool! I want one too!" But their mother, a slightly pinched woman who often makes me uncomfortable by asking questions like "Is that the good Christian thing to do?" quickly informs her brood of squirmy girls, "Those are probably factory rejects. The ones that aren't good enough to be sold as Cabbage Patch Kids at real stores. They're for people who can't afford the real thing."

My stomach dives; my heart beats out of my chest. My friends look at me with wide eyes, and then, even worse, remember that that's probably not the good Christian thing to do and avert their gaze back down to their Fluffernutters.

I guess this is a moment at which my fury at my cruel mother could have intensified, at which I might have made a Scarlett O'Hara–style vow to never go hungry again and also to spend the rest of my life buying up all the Cabbage Patch Kids in the world and dropping them one by one, by private helicopter, on Elizabeth's mom's house.

But what happens instead is that something in the wet cement of my pubescent identity hardens; not having a Cabbage Patch Kid suddenly becomes the single most important thing about me. Maybe it's because I feel guilt about my anger toward my mother for not getting me my toy status symbol; maybe it's that I feel bad for having betrayed my family's financial circumstances, though even then I understand that my Cabbage Patch–free existence is not reflective of impoverished circumstances so much as it is of financial practicality and distaste for overpriced fads. But whatever the trigger, at that moment I take on a superhero's cloak: I am a kid who doesn't have what her friends and their mean mom have—and who doesn't want it! I am a kid who will never again yearn for something that is wasteful and expensive and silly, and who will not grow up to be thoughtless and dismissive to other kids like me and embarrass them over marshmallow fluff snacks!

The truth was, my family was never rich—and in the early years was often on the edge of being poor. We didn't have brand-name toys and didn't own a color TV until the mid-1980s. I have memories of having to bring items in a supermarket back to the shelves when we didn't have enough money at the checkout counter. I wore hand-me-downs from my boy cousins from Brooklyn, leading to huge amounts of social embarrassment as I dressed in bell-bottoms long after they'd gone out of fashion.

But when all was said and done, I found that our family often had more *stuff* of the high-end variety than many of our neighbors. When a paycheck arrived and we were temporarily flush, money was spent on the expensive trappings of the culturally elite: trips to New York City, Broadway shows, bagels and lox. At my house, we had 20,000 books and half as many records of classical music. So while I was busy identifying as a member of a vaguely impoverished family, I was also seeing Shakespeare in Central Park, eating at Japanese restaurants, and developing an upscale palate—even as I was coming to see a focus on consumption in others as some kind of secular sin.

Fall 1993

I am moving into my dorm room in suburban Chicago. Thrilled to be starting college, but utterly traumatized by the prospect of what's ahead of me, I am nervously putting away my two suitcases of clothes and books while my parents look on. They are professors, and through their academic benefits—the same benefits that are paying my expensive college tuition—they've bought me a small computer: one of those old boxy Macs where the screen is about eight inches across and four inches high. I also have a phone made of rainbow-colored foam, new sheets and a comforter for my extra-long dorm bed, a couple of those milk crates for storage. An inveterate soap opera addict, I had pleaded—absolutely lay prostrate on the floor and begged—for a television. But the answer had been no. There would be a communal television, my parents had informed me. Much to my relief, I've discovered in my brief summertime communiqués with my roommate-to-be that she'll be bringing a set.

And she has. Next to me, my roommate and her parents are un-packing. She too has two suitcases of clothes. And the TV. And a phone, an answering machine, a VCR, a word processor, a microwave, a mini-refrigerator, a stereo, a black light, a grilled-cheese press, and a video game system that features Sonic, some kind of animated hedge-hog. I am slightly taken aback by the sheer amount of stuff. But I'm also stoked; I'll be up to my eyeballs in *General Hospital* and micro-wave popcorn.

My roommate is happy to share. Bemused by my spartan accoutre-ments, she and I become not exactly friends, but extremely functional roommates. Though we don't often venture out together, when we come home to our room at roughly the same time, lit up with keg beer and cigarettes, she dives under my bed—there is not enough space on her side of the room for all of her belongings, and so some have had to migrate to my side—and takes out a huge Tupperware box in which she keeps the stores of single-portion, microwavable Chef-Boy-R-Dee meals her mother sends her regularly. She'll select one for me, perhaps a day-glo mac-and-cheese, and pick out a beef ravioli can for herself, and nuke them both for a few minutes. Then we'll sit happily across from each other on our beds, eating processed glop to sober us up before bed.

As freshman year wears on, our schedules diverge more sharply. We rarely come home at the same time anymore. The giddiness of living with a stranger gives over to the quotidian irritations of living with someone whose habits have become far too familiar. But mostly, we're even-keeled roommates, less screamy than our constantly fight-ing next-door neighbors, less chummy than the BFF-from-the-first-day-of-college girls across the hall.

My roommate still keeps her container of junk food under my bed, and I partake of it on my own as freely as I do of the television, and the Sonic games when I'm a little stoned, and the answering machine, which is hooked up to our shared phone line. One night she comes home late and starts pawing through her drawer. She can't find any ravioli. "Did you eat my food again?" she asks me drunkenly. I stare at her blankly. "No," I respond, with knee-jerk dishonesty before I've even had time to think about it. "Don't lie," she continues. "You eat all the food. It's not yours, you know. It's mine. Why don't you buy your own food?"

Of course she's right. It's her food. By eating it, without an express invitation, I am stealing, feeding off of her excesses every time I relax to the wailing ambulance siren of *General Hospital,* every time I play a message on the answering machine, or invite my friends over and turn the black light on.

But even as I know this, I am mad at her for pointing it out. Who *cares* about the ravioli? It costs sixty-nine cents! It's not as though I couldn't run over to the Osco and buy a dozen of my own. It's true that I don't have a ton of spending money, but I have enough to eat out occasionally; I have enough to contribute when it's my turn to buy the requisite once-a-semester bottle of Absolut for pre-partying. In college, that's having enough.

But I wouldn't spend my extra sixty-nine cents on Chef-Boy-R-Dee, and the truth is, I bet my roommate wouldn't either. This stuff—the unctuous orange food under my bed—is the extra, it's the surfeit, it's the embarrassment of having too much. As I listen to her yell at me, my brain curdles with disgust—not at myself, as it probably should, for depriving her of her late-night craving that was by every conceivable right hers—but at *her,* for caring so much about all the superabundance of crap, for not understanding that it's bonus material, stupid silly superfluous stuff meant to be shared, spread around, not argued over.

I tell myself that though there are few opportunities to do so, I would share my extra stuff with my roommate in a heartbeat. In one small way, I do. During my freshman year, e-mail has arrived, and my little Mac (with help from a giant whirring modem) has the capacity to receive it. Her word processor doesn't, so I let her use my computer every day to collect whatever electronic missives come her way. It's practically an accident that I have something she doesn't—but to me, that's just the point: whatever bounty we have is all lucky accident, like my parents' academic benefits that have sent me to this school with this small computer. So why get so attached to what belongs to who, or to the idea of having more than someone else, or frankly, to the idea of having more at all?

I am back in the Cabbage Patch—distancing myself from the perceived hierarchy of ownership, trying to exempt myself from the bitter calculus of what belongs to whom as soon as I get caught out as somehow trailing behind, even as I am enjoying that most privileged of lives as a cosseted college student.

SUMMER 1997

I have just graduated. My family's finances have improved considerably since my childhood. There have been raises, promotions, tenure. No one is wealthy—far from it—but the bank accounts can now support more splurges. I'm back in my suburban Philadelphia home before heading to New York. I have a barely paying summer internship in publishing ahead of me. With a friend from college, I've just found a cheap apartment in then-déclassé Brooklyn, but I have no money to pay for it. Throughout high school and college, I worked: scooping ice cream, waiting tables, selling lotion at the mall, making sandwiches at Bruegger's Bagels, babysitting for my English professor. But that was all just to keep me in spending money. The final, nostalgic months of college have emptied my accounts.

Suddenly before me is a layout of several thousand dollars: for security, first month's rent, and last month's rent, not to mention the moving costs and the stuff I need to buy—a bed, a dresser. It's an unfathomable amount. My parents are lending it to me, no easy task, even in these more prosperous years. It has involved a trip to the credit union, some elaborate shuffling of accounts.

Newly untethered from the safety of undergraduate life, I feel a strange panic and uneasiness about how to proceed. How will I support myself? I have friends who have graduated into immediate consulting jobs, who are making an unimaginable sixty-grand right now while I begin my internship in a profession that only pays its editorial assistants, once they score jobs, a measly $18,000. My stomach slides precipitously; I remain sure that I'm not someone who is motivated by money. But is it possible that my disregard for where my rent and food is going to come from is actually irresponsible—not to mention a serious drain on my parents, who can hardly afford the start-up loan they're giving me?

I am also aware that while my sense of financial insecurity has stemmed in the past from my parents' circumstances, in this case our fortunes are divided: it's they who have more, and I who don't have anything. I tearfully, self-pityingly tell my father that I don't know when I'll be able to pay them back.

My father is calm. "My father did it for me," he says. "You'll pay me back by doing it for your children."

I can live with this financial plan—since, of course, it relieves me of responsibility—but also because it is a generous economic construction that, rather than elevating the person who has more, implicates him as someone who once had less. There is a warmth in this dynamic, one of the first instances I can remember in which I understand that while not having money may render me less powerful than my father, our imbalance is not being used to make me feel shame.

"Thank you," I say simply.

SPRING 2000

I am at dinner with a friend who is nearly ten years older than I am. The dinner is a relatively cheap one—at a reasonably priced Basque restaurant—but I am getting antsy because Lisa has just ordered more wine and I know that the $30 in my wallet is less and less likely to cut it when the check comes. As usual, the anxiety about this is keeping me from enjoying dinner. I have recently started my fourth job in New York City and have taken my third pay decrease.

My first gig after my publishing internship was as a personal assistant to a pretty famous actor, and the perks were remarkable. At twenty-two, I ate at the fanciest restaurants, traveled around Europe, and met famous people, all for a salary of close to $45,000. But I hadn't spent much of my haul, since every minute was spent in the company of my boss, a man who seemed not to even taste the $15-a-piece salmon sashimi he ate every day from the most famous Japanese restaurant in New York. On my first visit to Rome, a city I had spent years studying in high school Latin and history, I had been allowed a fifteen-minute visit to the Coliseum. The rest of the week was spent behind the glass of haute clothing stores near the Spanish Steps. I remembered looking out the window at the city that not only was I being prevented from seeing, but my boss wasn't enjoying because he was too busy deciding which leather jacket to purchase. He didn't even enjoy his wealth; he used it as evidence that he had something that other people didn't, some proof that he was worth something.

After a year, I was desperate to get out, to do something that made better use of my brain. I transitioned from celebrity gofer to media gofer, working as an editorial assistant at a glossy magazine. The job paid $30,000 plus overtime, and for my sanity's sake, the pay decrease was worth every penny. But lo and behold, life at the glossy magazine in boom-time nineties Manhattan was not exactly the life of the mind I'd imagined. Most of my duties at the start-up magazine were related to the gigantic launch party it was throwing for itself, a party where balloons alone cost more than my salary.

I barely made it a year at the magazine before I needed to escape.

Desperate to be away from wealth masquerading as intellect or literary bona fides, I took a job that paid $30,000, no overtime. It was one of the most wonderful jobs I'll ever have: reading books that a start-up company wanted to make into videos. I didn't care at all about making less money as long as I didn't have to be making anyone's dinner reservations. But the company's partners quarreled—over money—after

I had been there for six months; the one with whom I worked more closely took off, and I was fired by her adversary.

That's when I got offered the job I really wanted: as a fact-checker and reporter at a local paper. The pay was $25,000. I was twenty-five, and making $20,000 less than I had been three years earlier. I finally had a job I loved, though it was hard and scary: I was assigned the job of gossip columnist, forced to go out to movie openings and perfume launches five nights a week. Almost as annoying as anything was the fact that the newspaper I wrote for is the same one that published Candace Bushnell's original *Sex and the City* column, now a hit on HBO. I didn't watch it—because I couldn't afford cable—but the show's vision of what a single female professional life looks like has become inescapably pervasive. All of my friends from outside of New York assumed that I was knee-deep in $1,000 shoes and Cosmopolitans.

In truth, my phone was turned off, my electricity in peril. I bounced two rent checks. I rather awkwardly attended the fancy parties I was meant to cover in the single black skirt and black shirt I had owned since college. Any attempts to blend in were futile in a world and at an age where my peers were starting to converse in a patois heavy with Marc Jacobs. What my disregard for the basic rules of an aspirant professional life—for example, don't spend more than a third of your salary on rent, and never accept a pay decrease—had earned me was an antagonistic relationship with my landlord, a plummeting credit rating, and an inability to pass (as some would argue a good gossip columnist should) in the social circles that I covered.

And while I was beginning to care—about my credit rating and about my continued ability to live in a safe neighborhood—it seemed unthinkable that I would change my patterns by allowing myself to truly focus on making some more money. To do that, I thought, would change me, alchemically. I might become someone who was other than me, someone wealthy and spoiled and unappreciative. It would leach from me my comfortable identity as a girl who doesn't have a Cabbage Patch Kid and doesn't care, damn it!

In all this time, I never fantasized about a financial windfall, and I never imagined marrying rich. I knew from some of my girlfriends that the imagined possibility of an investment banker or real estate developer or, in those days, dot-com millionaire was what got them through their money worries. But it simply didn't cross my mind that a man was ever going to come along and halve my anxiety. I toyed with the idea of taking some freelance assignments, jobs that would pay me a lot of money to write something extremely stupid. But I rejected them. That would have been selling out.

When the check comes at the Basque restaurant, it does indeed exceed what I have in my wallet. Lisa tells me not to worry, she can cover me until we stop at the ATM across the street. But when we get there, I have no money in my account. I can't even take out a twenty. I am mortified, and deeply apologetic. "I'll pay you back as soon as I get paid," I tell Lisa. She smiles kindly. "You'll pay me back by one day taking a younger colleague for dinner."

Here is the generous financial and power construction of my father again. It makes me feel better about my ATM embarrassment. But it's not as powerful a salve as it was a few years ago.

Spring 2002

After two years and only a meager raise, I have managed to scrape by without eviction or starvation; I still own a phone, though the bill is past due, and I still wear the same black skirt and shirt to cover movie premieres.

But here's the punch line: what finally pushes me to take the step of doing something for money—pure, simple, dirty, avaricious money— is not any of these real-world concerns. It's a Brie cheese moment. Quite literally. My French friend, a fellow reporter, is getting married in Provence and has invited me to her wedding. I certainly don't have the money to go to France. But at around the same time, I get a call asking me to write up a chart for a glossy women's magazine in which

I review sex toys. It's the kind of assignment that I view as a bit exploitative, sort of embarrassing, not my beat. I tell them I'll do it.

Maybe it's selling out, maybe it's being practical. Maybe it's taking responsibility for having fancy tastes, or maybe it's growing up and learning that the pursuit of money doesn't turn your heart black. Maybe it's the weed of greed finally taking root in my soul and, well, blackening my heart.

In coming years, I will turn down jobs that would double my salary but that I don't think are good professional fits. And I will take jobs in which I am underpaid, but for companies I believe in. I will know that these are not the most responsible fiscal choices available to me—at thirty-three, I will still not have a retirement account. But I will also get better about asking for raises and making time for freelance work; I will finally open a savings account. The question of how to reconcile two parts of my early-formed identity—the part that rejects the trappings of wealth and the part that, like my parents, wants a house full of books and music and delicious food—will slowly become something I can wrap my brain around. I will acknowledge that there is a middle ground, an approach to my financial well-being that does not have to result in the corruption of my being. I will acknowledge that my identity does not forever have to be fused with a vision of myself as impoverished, especially when I live, and have lived for a long time, very richly.

In April 2002, I manage to pound out a review of vibrators and an assortment of warming lotions. I collect my check. I use it to travel to Provence. I eat some very delicious food. And I begin to get over myself and admit that, while I hope not to ever make it the center of my life, I kind of like money.

ABOUT THE CONTRIBUTORS

Hilary Black has spent her career as an editor in both books and magazines. She has held positions at Random House, HarperCollins, Simon & Schuster, *More* magazine (where she was a founding editor), and *Tango* magazine (where she was editor in chief). She lives in New York City.

Laurie Abraham is a freelance writer and senior editor of *Elle* magazine. Currently at work on a book about marriage and couples therapy for Simon & Schuster, she is the author of *Mama Might Be Better Off Dead: The Failure of Health Care in Urban America.* Her essays have been included in several collections, including *The Best American Essays: 2006* and *The Bitch in the House.* She lives in Brooklyn, New York, with her husband and two daughters.

Kim Barnes is the author of two novels, *Finding Caruso* and *A Country Called Home,* and two memoirs, *In the Wilderness: Coming of Age in Unknown Country,* a finalist for the 1997 Pulitzer Prize, and *Hungry for the World.* She is coeditor with Mary Clearman Blew of *Circle of Women: An Anthology of Contemporary Western Women Writers* and, with Claire Davis, of *Kiss Tomorrow Hello: Notes from the Midlife Underground by Twenty-Five Women over Forty.* Her essays, stories, and poems have appeared in a number of journals and anthologies, including *More,* the *Georgia Review, Shenandoah,* and the Pushcart Prize anthology. She teaches writing at the University of Idaho and lives with her husband, the poet Robert Wrigley, on Moscow Mountain.

Marisa Belger's work has appeared in numerous publications, including *Travel + Leisure, Natural Health,* and *Prevention.* She has also contributed to MSNBC.com, Beliefnet.com, and TODAYShow.com. She collaborated with Josh Dorfman on *The Lazy Environmentalist,* a comprehensive guide to easy, stylish green living, and with Ariane de Bonvoisin on *The First 30 Days: Your Guide to Any Change (and Loving Your Life More).* She lives in Brooklyn, New York, with her husband and son.

Veteran journalist **Leslie Bennetts** is the author of the national bestseller *The Feminine Mistake,* a groundbreaking examination of women's life choices that was named one of the best books of the year by the *Washington Post.* A contributing editor at *Vanity Fair* since 1988, Bennetts previously spent a decade as a reporter at the *New York Times,* where she covered national politics, metropolitan news, and cultural news and wrote style page features. She was the first woman ever to cover a presidential campaign for the *Times.* Her work has also been published in *Town & Country, Columbia Journalism Review, New York, Vogue, Good Housekeeping, Ladies' Home Journal, More, House and Garden, Worth, Family Life, Parents, Child, Parenting, Family PC, Condé Nast Traveler, Lear's, The Nation, Modern Bride, Glamour,* the *New York Times Sunday Magazine, Self, Women's Health, Tango,* and *Woman's Day,* among many other magazines. Bennetts lives in Manhattan with her husband and two children.

Bliss Broyard is the author of the collection of stories *My Father, Dancing,* which was a *New York Times* Notable Book, and *One Drop: My Father's Hidden Life—A Story of Race and Family Secrets,* which was named the Humanist Book of the Year by the Louisiana Endowment for the Humanities and a Best Book of the Year by the *Chicago Tribune.* Her fiction and essays have been anthologized in *Best American Short Stories,* the Pushcart Prize anthology, and *The Art of the Essay* and have appeared in *Ploughshares, O: The Oprah Magazine, Cookie,* and the *New York Times.* She is a contributing writer to *Elle* magazine.

A black Latina born in Panama, **Veronica Chambers**'s work focuses most often on the intersection of women and culture. Her memoir *Mama's Girl* was an American Library Association Best Book of the Year. Her most recent books include *Kickboxing Geishas, Miss Black America,* and a children's book, *Celia Cruz, Queen of Salsa.* Her articles have appeared in the *New York Times Magazine, Esquire, Vogue, O: The Oprah Magazine,* and *Glamour.* She also designs and produces a line of children's clothes, Florabunda Tots, available at Etsy.com. Chambers lives in Princeton, New Jersey, with her husband and daughter. Visit her online at www.veronicachambers.com.

Amy Cohen was a writer-producer on the sitcoms *Caroline in the City* and *Spin City,* a dating columnist for the *New York Observer,* and the dating correspondent for cable TV's *New York Central.* Author of *The Late Bloomer's Revolution,* she lives in New York City.

Abby Ellin is the author of *Teenage Waistland: A Former Fat Kid Weighs in on Living Large, Losing Weight, and How Parents Can (and Can't) Help.* For five years, she wrote the "Preludes" column, about young people and money, in the Sunday money and business section of the *New York Times.* She regularly writes for the *New York Times* Sunday style section and has a series on MSN.com called "How to Raise a Millionaire." Her work has appeared in numerous publications, including *Time,* the *Village Voice, Marie Claire, More, Self, Glamour,* the *Boston Phoenix,* and *Spy.* But so far her greatest claim to fame is naming "Karamel Sutra" ice cream for Ben and Jerry's.

Joni Evans is the CEO of wowOwow.com, a website for women forty and older. Her career of more than thirty-five years in publishing includes serving as president and publisher of Simon & Schuster, publisher at Random House, and senior vice president of the William Morris Agency's literary department. She has written for the *New York Times,* the *Washington Post, Vanity Fair, New York* magazine, and *O: The Oprah Magazine.* She lives in New York City and Westchester, New York.

Laura Fraser's memoir *An Italian Affair* was a *New York Times* bestseller and translated into five languages. A contributing editor at *More* magazine, she's also written for the *New York Times, Vogue, O: The Oprah Magazine, Gourmet,* and *Travel + Leisure.* Currently at work on another memoir, she lives in San Francisco.

Julia Glass is the author of the novels *Three Junes* (which won the 2002 National Book Award for Fiction), *The Whole World Over,* and *I See You Everywhere.* She has won fellowships from the National Endowment for the Arts, the New York Foundation for the Arts, and the Radcliffe Institute for Advanced Study. For her short fiction, she has received three Nelson Algren Awards, the Tobias Wolff Award, and the Pirate's Alley Medal for Best Novella; for nonfiction, she has received the Ames Memorial Essay Award. She lives with her family in Massachusetts.

Lori Gottlieb is the author of the national bestseller, *Stick Figure: A Diary of My Former Self*, an American Library Association "Best Books 2001" selection. She is a regular commentator for NPR's *All Things Considered*, and her work has also aired on public radio's *Weekend Edition*, *Marketplace*, and *This American Life*. Her articles have been published in the *New York Times*, the *Los Angeles Times*, *Atlantic Monthly*, *Time*, *People*, *Elle*, *Glamour*, *Redbook*, and *Slate*, among many others. She is the coauthor, with Kevin Bleyer of Comedy Central's *The Daily Show*, of *I Love You, Nice to Meet You: A Guy and a Girl Give the Lowdown on Coupling Up*, and her essays have appeared in numerous anthologies, including *This Side of Doctoring*, *Scoot Over, Skinny*, *The Modern Jewish Girl's Guide to Guilt*, *Mortified: The Big Book of Angst*, and *Fired: Tales of the Canned, Canceled, Downsized, and Dismissed*. She lives in Los Angeles. Visit her online at www .lorigottlieb.com.

Marnie Hanel is a reporter-researcher at *Vanity Fair*. She writes for the magazine's blog, VF Daily, and contributed to *The Filthy Rich Handbook*. Her work has appeared in *Jane*, *Tango*, and the *Seattle Times*, and on Daily Candy, TODAYshow.com, and Yahoo!. She lives in New York City.

Kathryn Harrison is the author of the memoirs *The Kiss*, *Seeking Rapture*, *The Mother Knot*, and *The Road to Santiago*; the novels *Thicker Than Water*, *Exposure*, *Poison*, *The Binding Chair*, *The Seal Wife*, and *Envy*; a biography, *Saint Therese of Lisieux*; and most recently, *While They Slept: An Inquiry into the Murder of a Family*. Her personal essays have appeared in *The New Yorker*, *Harper's*, *More*, *Vogue*, *O: The Oprah Magazine*, and many other publications. A frequent reviewer for the *New York Times Book Review*, she teaches at Hunter College. She lives in New York with her husband, the novelist Colin Harrison, and their three children.

Sheri Holman is the author of four novels, including *A Stolen Tongue*, *The Dress Lodger*, a national bestseller nominated for an IMPAC Dublin Literary Award, and *The Mammoth Cheese*, a Best Book of the

Year (*San Francisco Chronicle, Publishers Weekly*) short-listed for the Orange Prize. Holman has written for *More, Allure,* and *Self,* among others, and is a regular reviewer for the *Washington Post* and the *Barnes and Noble Review.* She lives with her family in Brooklyn, New York.

Ann Hood is the author, most recently, of the novel *The Knitting Circle;* a memoir, *Comfort: A Journey Through Grief;* and a young adult novel, *How I Saved My Father's Life (And Ruined Everything Else).* She is the author of eight other books, including a short story collection, *An Ornithologist's Guide to Life;* the novel *Somewhere Off the Coast of Maine;* and the memoir *Do Not Go Gentle: My Search for Miracles in a Cynical Time.* Her short stories and essays have appeared in publications such as the *New York Times, Paris Review,* Salon.com, *Bon Appetit, Traveler, Food & Wine, More, Good Housekeeping,* and many more. She has won two Pushcart Prizes, a Best American Spiritual Writing Award, and the Paul Bowles Prize for Short Fiction. She lives with her family in Providence, Rhode Island.

Rebecca Johnson is a writer who splits her time between Brooklyn and Pound Ridge, New York. She is the author of the novel *And Sometimes Why* as well as a longtime contributor to *Vogue.* She is married with two children and three stepchildren. Her website can be found at www .RebeccaJohnsonAuthor.com.

Karen Karbo is the author of three novels and a memoir, all named *New York Times* Notable Books. Her most recent work is *How to Hepburn: Lessons on Living from Kate the Great.* She lives and attempts to manage her money in Portland, Oregon.

Lucy Kaylin is the author of two books, *The Perfect Stranger: The Truth About Mothers and Nannies* and *For the Love of God: The Faith and Future of the American Nun.* She is currently the executive editor of *Marie Claire* magazine and has held positions at *GQ* and *Vogue.* She lives in New York City with her husband, ten-year-old daughter, and seven-year-old son.

Jennifer Wolff Perrine is an award-winning investigative journalist and essayist whose work has appeared in *Self, New York, Men's Health,* and the *New York Times.* A 2008 nominee for the National Magazine Award for service journalism, Wolff also writes "The Literate Gourmet," a literary food column in *Best Life* magazine. She and her family divide their time between New York City and Easton, Pennsylvania.

Dani Shapiro's most recent books include the novels *Black & White* and *Family History*, along with the bestselling memoir *Slow Motion*. Her fiction and essays have appeared in *The New Yorker, Granta, Elle, Vogue, Ploughshares, One Story,* and *O: The Oprah Magazine* and have been broadcast on National Public Radio. Her books have been translated into seven languages. She is on the faculty of the Graduate Writing Program at the New School, and she founded the Sirenland Writers Conference in Positano, Italy. She lives in Connecticut with her family.

Amy Sohn is the *New York Times*–bestselling author of the novels *Run Catch Kiss* and *My Old Man*, which have been translated into five languages. She is at work on her third novel for Simon & Schuster. She has written for the *New York Times, New York* magazine, *The Nation, Harper's Bazaar,* and *Playboy,* among other publications, along with television pilots for HBO, Fox, and ABC. She lives in Brooklyn, New York, with her husband and daughter. Visit her at amysohn.com.

Susanna Sonnenberg is the author of the bestselling memoir *Her Last Death,* published by Scribner in 2008. Her personal essays have appeared in a variety of magazines, as well as in the anthologies *About What Was Lost* and *Behind the Bedroom Door.* She lives in Missoula, Montana, with her husband and two sons.

J. Courtney Sullivan is a writer and researcher for the *New York Times* and the author of the novel *Commencement.* Her work has also appeared in the *Times* column "Modern Love," *New York* magazine, *Elle, Allure, Men's Vogue, Cosmopolitan,* the *New York Observer,* and *Tango* and on the website someecards.com. She is currently coediting an anthology of essays about young women and feminism. She lives in Brooklyn, New York.

Melanie Thernstrom is the author of *The Dead Girl* and *Halfway Heaven: Diary of a Harvard Murder.* She is a contributing writer to the *New York Times Magazine* and has also written for *The New Yorker, New York* magazine, the *Wall Street Journal, Vanity Fair, Food &*

Wine, Travel + Leisure, and other publications. She lives in southwest Washington State.

Rebecca Traister is a senior writer for Salon.com, where she writes about women in media, pop culture, and politics. She has written for the *New York Observer, Elle, The Nation, Vogue, New York* magazine, and the *New York Times,* among many other publications. She lives in Brooklyn, New York.

Born and raised on a steady diet of *Brady Bunch* reruns and anything written by Norman Lear, **Elizabeth Williams** is a television writer whose most recent credits include programs for the CW, CBS, and ABC. She lives in Los Angeles.

ACKNOWLEDGMENTS

This collection was a labor of love—both for me and for the extraordinary women whose stories fill this book. The courage and grace with which they approached a complicated, often private, subject was impressive, and the strength of this anthology is due to their candor, their wit, and their remarkable talent.

This project would never have come to light at all had it not been for the foresight and enthusiasm of my agent, Sally Wofford Girand. During the course of one of our many lunches, she heard the story of my recent breakup and saw in it the seeds of this book. Her business and editorial insight throughout this process has been invaluable, and I will always treasure her wisdom and her friendship.

I could not ask for a smarter, more perceptive editor than Laurie Chittenden at William Morrow. She believed in this project from the get-go—and I was particularly delighted that a friend with whom I once labored as an editorial assistant would end up publishing my first book! She and her assistant, Will Hinton, provided the perfect mix of autonomy, hand-holding, and expertise. Special thanks to the effervescent Sharyn Rosenblum, longtime friend and publicist extraordinaire, for her passion and smarts; to her conscientious assistant, Nicole Chismark; and to my publisher, Lisa Gallagher, who made this book a reality.

Many people—some contributors to this collection, some not—provided indispensable insight throughout the year that I spent trying to deconstruct love and money. I am enormously grateful to Marisa

Belger, Abby Ellin, Judith Newman, and Karen Karbo, who believed in this project from the beginning; to Sara Austin, Leslie Bennetts, Linda Carrigan, Marnie Hanel, Lauren Purcell, Steve Schneider, and Laura Shapiro, who constituted a first-rate sounding board and offered crucial feedback; and of course, to my family, whose love, understanding, and impeccable judgment I have relied on all my life.

But the most special thanks of all goes to Matthew Carrigan—for reading and analyzing every piece in this book, for understanding this project at its core, for believing in me, and for giving me the happy ending I always longed for.